PRAISE FOR
DATA-DRIVEN HR

'If you want your HR function to be relevant and drive more value to the organization, its employees and the function itself then you simply must read this book.'
David Green, Global Director, People Analytics Solutions, IBM

'*Data Driven HR* is a fantastically insightful master guide every HR professional should read. The book shows that tools like big data, artificial intelligence and the internet of things are no longer future visions of HR but actual realities today. Make sure you embrace it.'
Yanislava Hristova, Director of People Operations, Xogito Group, Inc

'Bernard Marr shows us how to put HR front and centre in strategic organization decision making. This "how to" guide gives anyone interested in revolutionizing the role of HR data a clear and logical set of steps. This isn't a prophecy – the time is now!'
Carolyn Nevitte, Marketing Director, People Insight

'*Data Driven HR* is written keeping core HR professionals in mind; professionals who are not and would not want to become data scientists or digital gurus but want to play their part in this transformational journey of making HR more intelligent. This book is well written, easy to digest and offers lots of great takeaways. I would recommend this as a mandatory read for all HR professional irrespective of their level and experience.'
Ashish Sinha, Global HR Performance Analytics Lead, Diageo

'The best thing about Bernard Marr's *Data-Driven HR* is that it offers innovative yet pragmatic solutions to some of today's most pressing HR issues. It is really well written, bang up to date and I loved the immensely useful "key takeaways" at the end of each chapter.'
Karen Lewis, Retail HR Director, Greene King

'This book provides a comprehensive guide detailing translatable tools for modern-day HR practices. Bernard Marr gives key insights into how data-driven HR should be an integral part of organizational development and design.'
Sarah Morris, Head of HR, Blenheim Palace

'A commercially focused and pragmatic guide to a topic that can influence an organization's profit margins.'
Rikesh Kotadia, People Analytics Lead, Serco

'This book is the most practical guide on how to embrace innovation through data and technologies like AI in the context of very real HR scenarios. I love that it is packed full of real-life use cases and that it is written in a friendly and conversational style. It is a great source of inspiration and practical advice I can see myself revisiting over and over again.'
Maja Luckos, Head of People Analytics, Capgemini

Data-driven HR

How to use analytics and metrics
to drive performance

Bernard Marr

First published in Great Britain and the United States in 2018 by Kogan Page Limited

2nd Floor, 45 Gee Street	c/o Martin P Hill Consulting	4737/23 Ansari Road
London	122 W 27th St, 10th Floor	Daryaganj
EC1V 3RS	New York, NY 10001	New Delhi 110002
United Kingdom	USA	India

www.koganpage.com

ISBN   978 0 7494 8246 6
E-ISBN 978 0 7494 8247 3

British Library Cataloguing-in-Publication Data

A CIP record for this book is available from the British Library.

Library of Congress Cataloging-in-Publication Data

Names: Marr, Bernard, author.
Title: Data-driven HR: how to use analytics and metrics to drive performance / Bernard Marr.
Description: 1st Edition. | New York: Kogan Page, [2018]
Identifiers: LCCN 2018004478 (print) | LCCN 2017060884 (ebook) | ISBN 9780749482473 (ebook) |
    ISBN 9780749482466 (pbk.) | ISBN 9780749482473 (eISBN)
Subjects: LCSH: Personnel management–Data processing. | Personnel management–Planning.
Classification: LCC HF5549.5.D37 (print) | LCC HF5549.5.D37 M37 2018 (ebook)
    | DDC 658.300285–dc23
LC record available at https://lccn.loc.gov/2018004478

Typeset by Integra Software Services, Pondicherry
Print production managed by Jellyfish
Printed and bound by CPI Group (UK) Ltd, Croydon, CR0 4YY

CONTENTS

What is
data-driven HR?

Companies are nothing without the right people. Those companies that are able to attract people with the right skills and talent are most likely to have the competitive edge needed to succeed now and in the future. It is therefore vital that companies put in place the intelligent systems and processes to find, recruit and retain the right people for them. Clearly, human resources (HR) is at the very centre of this need. Yet, in my experience, too many HR teams spend the majority of their time on administration tasks or legal issues. Clunky staff appraisal processes, the day-to-day minutiae of finding and managing people, and wasteful, expensive activities like annual staff satisfaction surveys (more on this in Chapter 8) take up time that could be better spent elsewhere. In addition, HR traditionally is seen as being very people oriented, and not so much about numbers and data. Even when data do play a role, they are not necessarily being used in a smart way that is most relevant to the business in question. A lot of HR data analysis comes in the form of key performance indicators (KPIs) measuring factors like absenteeism or number of training hours per full-time employee, sometimes because these metrics are easy to measure or because they are what other companies measure. These days there are far more unique and valuable metrics that can be measured, metrics that can deliver business-critical insights and have a huge impact on an organization's performance and results.

I am certainly not saying that HR should no longer be about the people who work for the organization. People will continue to be a central driver of success, even in this age of increasing automation, robotics and artificial intelligence (AI). What I am saying is the role of the HR team is changing and, as our ability to gather and analyse ever-increasing amounts of data grows, so too do the opportunities for HR teams to add more value to the organization and help to achieve its strategic goals. Step forward data-driven HR. In this chapter, I look at what is meant by intelligent or data-driven HR, explore the main ways in which HR teams can use data intelligently and set out how data are already transforming HR functions. I also take a brief look at the role of automation in our increasingly data-driven world and set out what you can expect from the rest of this book.

The rise of data-driven or intelligent HR

Things are changing fast, and our world is becoming more intelligent every day. Nowadays, almost everything we do at work can be measured, from employees' day-to-day actions, concentration, happiness and wellbeing, to wider business operations. This explosion in data means HR teams have at their fingertips more data – and the potential for more insights – than ever before.

What do we mean by data-driven HR?

Data-driven HR, or intelligent HR, is about using this data explosion in a smart way and extracting insights that not only improve the performance of people within the company (including its HR team), but also contribute to the overall success of the organization. HR teams can use data to make better HR decisions, better understand and evaluate the business impact of people, improve leadership's decision making in people-related matters, make HR processes and operations more efficient and effective, and improve the overall wellbeing and effectiveness of people, which all can have a significant impact on a company's ability to achieve its strategic aims. Right now, this idea of the data-driven HR team does not exist in many organizations, outside of perhaps the very largest or most innovative companies, but it is certainly gathering pace. HR and people management are undergoing a revolution, and starting to be taken over by this wave of data and analytics. This part of business functionality that has traditionally focused on softer elements like people, culture, learning and development, and employee engagement is becoming increasingly driven by data analysis, and with good reason. As we will see in Chapter 2, HR is one of the most data-rich functions in most organizations. Employers have been using data and analytics to some extent or other for a long time now to understand metrics like staff satisfaction. The rise of big data has accelerated this practice, as well as taking it in exciting new directions.

Adding value wherever possible

With intelligent, data-driven people management, the top priority is to add value to the organization and do this in the *smartest way possible*, using all the tools at the HR team's disposal, including data, sensors, analytics, machine learning and AI. HR teams can gain some mouth-watering benefits when they use data in a smart way and apply analytics tools to turn those data into business-critical insights. Take Google's approach to people management, for instance. Google gives staff free meals, generous paid holiday allowances, access to 'nap pods' for snoozing during the day, and space to grow their own fruit and vegetables at work.[1] Now, I am sure Google's leadership team is full of lovely, generous people, but that is not why the company has implemented these policies or, at least, it is not the only reason. These decisions were based on what the data told them would increase employee satisfaction. Google's approach to boosting staff satisfaction thoroughly disrupted the technology world, dramatically changing the way Silicon Valley employers think about employee perks, and now technology companies of all sizes, from the big players to small start-ups, seek to emulate the Google approach. And, while staff turnover is consistently high in the technology world, in the United States Google is regularly voted the number one company to work for by *Fortune* magazine.[2]

Is HR as it stands fit for purpose?

A few years ago, I wrote an article questioning whether we still need HR departments in their current form.[3] It was intended to provoke debate and perhaps a little controversy, and that is exactly what it did. My point was that HR teams as they typically stand now should be reorganized to deliver greater value, and I suggested restructuring HR into two separate teams: a people support team and a people analytics team. The people support team would, as the name suggests, be charged with supporting employees in the organization, from frontline staff to the senior leadership team. This would involve helping people with their development, monitoring and boosting staff engagement, identifying issues with company culture, and generally looking after employee wellbeing. The people analytics team, on the other hand, would step back from the softer aspects of people management and look at people in a more scientific, analytical way, supporting the company with critical insights that improve performance. The role of the people analytics team would be to find answers to key questions such as:

- What are our talent gaps?
- What makes a good employee in our company?
- How do we best recruit those people?
- How can we predict staff turnover?

Crucially, the answers to the above questions would be based on data, not gut instinct or what works at other companies. I still think there is a case for splitting HR teams in this way, as it provides a clear path to using data more consistently and essentially provides a foundation for intelligent, data-driven HR. You may agree with the two-team approach, or you may not. Either way, as the way we do business is changing rapidly, there is a clear case for HR teams to deliver more value and data provide a way to do that.

Linking to the company's objectives

With the wealth of data at the HR team's disposal, it is well placed to play a critical role in helping the company to execute its strategy and deliver its key objectives. I frequently work with companies to create a 'plan on a page': a simple one-page strategy that is concise and easy to understand. At the very top of this plan on a page is a section that sets out the company's purpose, ie its mission and vision statements. When HR teams are creating their own data strategy (more on this in Chapter 3), that company purpose should again be right at the top. The idea is for the company purpose to inform the HR team's own

Figure 1.1   Data use by businesses

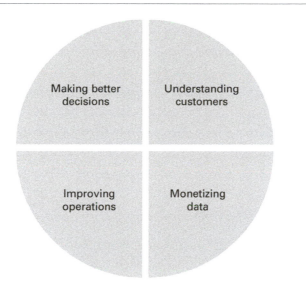

strategy, decisions and activities. In this way, the HR team is creating its own plan of how to help the organization fulfil its purpose. This is what adding value is all about.

How HR teams can use data intelligently

There are infinite ways in which businesses can make good use of data, but, in their most basic sense, they boil down to four main categories (see Figure 1.1):

- using data to make better decisions;
- using data to improve operations;
- using data to better understand your customers;
- monetizing data.

Let us look at each area in turn.

Making better decisions

The idea behind data-driven HR is all about making HR smarter in every possible way and making smarter decisions is a huge part of this. Data can help HR professionals make better decisions about their own activities (such as smarter recruitment and performance reviews), and HR data also can be used to report to elsewhere in the company and support wider company decisions. After all, leadership teams need HR- and people-related data to make their own decisions, and the intelligent HR team is well equipped to support this process. Currently, much of this data work is done in an ad hoc way or in not particularly efficient ways, such as by utilizing staff surveys that cost huge sums of money.

Improving operations

The second category, improving operations, is perhaps even more vital for HR functions. Data provide a way for HR professionals to look at their key HR functions – like employee safety, wellbeing and recruitment – and answer critical questions like 'Where do we spend most of our time and effort?' and 'How can we streamline and improve these functions?' Data analysis can help to identify areas for improvement and potentially automate certain processes to make them more efficient.

Understanding your customers

This is one of the biggest and most publicised areas of big data use today. Here, businesses use big data to better understand customers, including their behaviours, their preferences and their level of satisfaction. Using data, businesses can gain a full understanding of customers, such as what makes them tick, what they will do next and what factors lead them to recommend a company to others. Organizations can also better interact and engage with their customers by analysing customer feedback in order to improve a product or service. If you are thinking this category is only of interest to your sales and marketing colleagues, think again. As an HR professional, your company's employees are your customers. This means you can use data in much the same way as a marketing team would to better understand and interact with your customers.

Monetizing data

There is also a fourth use of data that is common in business, and that is monetizing data to create a new revenue stream for the company. One good example of this is Jawbone, the company that manufactures the UP fitness tracker band. With millions of users, Jawbone gathers an incredible amount of data, and it did not take the company long to realize that all the data it collected were more valuable than the device itself.[4] Analysing the collective data brings insights that can be fed back to users and sold to interested third parties, creating a new revenue stream over and above the original product. Jawbone still manufactures UP bands, as they are the vehicle for continuing to collect data, but the data themselves are now the company's primary focus. While monetizing HR-specific data is unlikely to happen (there would be so many ethical issues to contend with concerning selling employee data), it is worth HR professionals being aware of this data use. For instance, your company may decide to start monetizing data from other areas of the business (such as customer or product data) and this would impact on the business's overarching strategy in the future. This, in turn, may impact on HR in terms of the changing skills that the company needs to recruit for, and how HR can best add value to the organization's changing strategy.

How data are already revolutionizing HR functions

If we look at the core HR functions, there are very many real-world examples of how this idea of data-driven HR is already taking root.

Taking the guesswork out of recruitment

In recruitment, for example, taking on a new employee represents a huge investment for most companies, particularly in a professional or managerial role. So, in an age where everything can be measured, quantified and analysed, data help to take the guesswork out of recruitment (more on this in Chapter 7). Rather than relying on gut feeling or assumptions about background, education and experience, taking a data-driven approach to recruitment helps companies to find staff who are better suited to the role and the organization, who stay happy and on the job for longer. In one very simple example, one of my clients wanted to recruit self-driven people with a strong sense of initiative. By analysing different data sets from the type of people they wanted to attract and those they wanted to avoid, they found that the type of browser used to complete the job application was one of the strong predictors for the right kind of candidate. Those who used browsers like Firefox or Chrome that were not pre-installed on their computer tended to be better suited to that particular job. This simple insight helped them to dramatically streamline the recruitment process.

In another example, a bank was able to cut staff costs, and recruit a better calibre of employee, simply by analysing the performance of staff that were recruited from different universities. In the past, the bank had been recruiting on the basis that the best-performing people would be those who held top degrees from Ivy League universities. Instead, they found that candidates from non-prestigious universities outperformed the Ivy League candidates.

Understanding and boosting employee engagement

In employee engagement, some organizations are starting to use analytics tools to scan and analyse the content of e-mails sent by their staff, as well as what they post on Facebook or Twitter. Many more are using short 'pulse' surveys to measure how staff are feeling on a monthly, weekly or even daily basis.[5] This allows them to accurately gauge levels of staff engagement, without the need for traditional costly and time-consuming staff surveys. You can see examples of data-driven employee engagement in Chapter 8. Clearly, there are privacy implications concerning accessing employee communications, and the rules vary from country to country. Turn to Chapter 6 for more information on privacy implications.

Improving employee safety and wellbeing

Employee safety and wellbeing are being improved thanks to developments like Fujitsu's Ubiquitousware package, which collects and analyses data from devices such as accelerometer sensors, barometers, cameras and microphones to measure and monitor people as they go about their work.[6] Data such as temperature, humidity, movements and pulse rate can be used to identify when workers are exposed to too much heat stress, for instance. The system can even detect postures and body movements to sense a fall or estimate the physical load on a body. Find out more about data-driven employee safety and wellbeing in Chapter 9.

Transforming learning and development

In learning and development, the rise of online courses has revolutionized how companies develop their people, and allows high levels of personalized learning that is tailored to the individual. Because every move a learner makes in an online course environment can be easily tracked, it is simple to measure how they are responding to the course material; for example, is one learner taking much longer to complete a unit than they did on previous units? If so, that indicates they may need extra information on that particular topic. Others who breeze through content quickly may benefit from more advanced learning materials. These are just some of the ways in which learning can be personalized. Find out more about this and the many other ways in which data are transforming learning and development in Chapter 10.

Measuring and boosting employee performance

In performance management, data are helping companies to measure employee performance more accurately and review performance in a smarter, more agile way. One often-cited example is Xerox. The office equipment manufacturer asked an analytics firm to monitor staff performance and come up with the profile of an ideal candidate for its call centres. The surprising findings showed that previous call-centre experience was no indicator of success, and that candidates with criminal records often performed better than those without. The experiment led to a reduction in staff turnover of 20 per cent.[7] Turn to Chapter 11 to see the many other ways in which data are helping to drive people performance.

Looking to the world of sport for clues

In many ways, the world of sport provides an interesting analogy for what HR teams should be doing with data, as well as showing where HR might be going in the future. Particularly at the elite level, there is incredible pressure to be on the cutting edge of analytics. The GB Olympic rowing team – the only GB team to have won gold in every Olympics since 1984 – is just one example of a top-flight team that has been ramping up its data analytics.[8] Like HR, rowing is intrinsically analytics friendly. Most of what the athletes do can be measured, just as much of what employees do can now be measured. Two main uses for data in rowing are talent identification and talent tracking. For example, by collecting every bit of datum about every athlete who enters the training programme, new talent can be matched against profiles of former entrants, to identify the approach most likely to turn each individual into a champion. It is not hard to draw a parallel with HR activities, where data have the potential to track employees' activities and progress, and help to tailor development programmes to suit specific individuals. Data also help the rowing team to prevent injuries. Warning signs can be highlighted across all data sets – physiology, gym, medical, race performance etc – and matched with past data to show when an athlete is in danger of pushing themselves too hard and causing an injury. Likewise, as we have already seen in this chapter, organizations can use data to enhance their employees' safety and identify when individuals might be in danger of injuring themselves.

Across all sports, athletes and coaches are increasingly working with data and analytics to extract every possible insight that could lead to improved performance, and I see a similar thing happening with each function in organizations, particularly HR, which is so rich in valuable individual data.

A (brief) word on automation

There has been a lot of talk about the rise of automation and the threat this brings to jobs. From factory line jobs to professions like accounting and architecture, AI technologies like machine learning – where a computer 'learns' from what the data are telling it and adapts its decision making and actions according to what it has learned – mean that increasingly more tasks now can be automated and completed by machines or algorithms. Fields like marketing, manufacturing and even healthcare have been strong adopters of machine learning and AI – HR less so. But, as we will see in Chapter 2, a lot of HR tasks now can be automated. In many cases, machines can perform a task to a much more accurate degree than a human can. Algorithms can predict employee churn better than a human ever could, for instance.

In its annual HR survey, recruitment firm Harvey Nash concluded that AI and automation will have a major impact on HR over the next five years. The survey found that 15 per cent of HR leaders were already affected by AI and automation, while 40 per cent thought it would impact on them in the next two to five years.[9] Looking further ahead, a recent Oxford University study calculated how 720 jobs would be affected by automation over the next 20 years.[10] The study concluded that, by 2035, HR administrative jobs had a 90 per cent chance of being automated. HR officers, managers and directors, however, were much less likely to be replaced by robots.

How would automation work in practice? One good example is virtual helpdesk agents – chatbots, essentially – that could answer simple employee questions such as: 'When is the company closed over the Christmas break?' or 'How much of my annual leave have I used already this year?' AI technology is now so sophisticated that it can respond to natural, spoken language, rather than typed questions, and even detect the underlying sentiment behind the words themselves. Call centres, for example, are using this technology to analyse whether a caller is satisfied, frustrated or angry during the course of their call. So, it is clear that HR will be affected by automation over the next few years; however, in the context of intelligent, data-driven HR, this can be seen as a very positive development. Automating the simpler, administrative-type tasks frees up HR professionals to focus on more important tasks that align with the company's strategy and help to deliver performance improvements.

How to use this book

The goal of this book is to explore the key ways in which data and analytics can drive performance, both in terms of the HR team's own performance and value within the organization, and in terms of how data-driven HR can help to drive performance right across the business. I think of this book as a journey, looking at the developments that have brought us to this point and identifying a path forward for HR professionals. With this in mind, the second part of the book (Chapters 3–6) is about lining up the building blocks of intelligent, data-driven HR, including creating a data strategy, sourcing HR-relevant data and turning those data into insights. We will also look at some of the potential pitfalls and concerns surrounding using data, including privacy issues and the need for transparency. As we will see in Chapter 6, the way in which a company uses data, and how that use is communicated to staff, has a big impact on how people react. Ill-considered, poorly communicated or discriminatory uses of data erode trust, and can be extremely harmful to morale. Thankfully, there are plenty of ways in which HR teams can mitigate these potential issues and gain employee buy-in, and we will look at some of these in Chapter 6.

The third part of the book (Chapters 7–11) looks at data-driven HR in practice, and how data can drive operational improvements and better decision making across all the core HR functions: recruitment, employee engagement, employee safety and wellbeing, training and development, and performance management. I cannot stress enough how all these functions are already being transformed by data and analytics. In these chapters, I am not making wild predictions about potential future developments. The future is already here. The challenge facing HR teams today is how to keep up with developments and continually evolve to ensure maximum value to the organization. I hope that the real-world examples given throughout this book, showing how companies across all sectors are using data in incredible ways to optimize their people-related decisions and operations, inspire you to tackle this exciting new world head-on.

Key takeaways

At the end of each chapter I will be summarizing the critical learning points that have been looked at. Even if you only manage to skim over certain parts of the book, these key takeaways will give you the absolute must-have information in one simple list. The following is what has been covered in this chapter:

- Almost everything we do at work now can be measured, from employees' day-to-day actions, happiness and wellbeing, to wider business operations. This explosion in data means HR teams have at their fingertips more data than ever before.

- Data-driven HR means taking advantage of this data explosion to extract insights that not only improve the performance of people within the company (including its HR team), but also contribute to the company's overall success.

- With intelligent, data-driven people management, the top priority is to add value to the organization and do this in the *smartest way possible*, using all the tools at the HR team's disposal, including data, sensors, analytics, machine learning and AI.

- There are many ways in which businesses can make good use of data, but, in their most basic sense, they boil down to three main categories:
  - using data to make better decisions;
  - using data to improve operations;
  - using data to better understand your customers.

Now, let us start our journey into data-driven HR by exploring how we got to this point, where almost everything we do, both inside and outside the work setting, leaves a digital trace that can be mined for insights. In the next chapter I look at the evolution of data-driven HR, and how the explosion in big data and analytics technologies, including AI, machine learning and the Internet of Things (IoT), is making HR more intelligent than ever before.

Endnotes

1 Garfield, J (2017) [accessed 23 October 2017] The Most Incredible Job Perks at Top Tech Companies [Online] https://www.paysa.com/blog/2017/02/28/the-most-incredible-job-perks-at-top-tech-companies

2 Fortune [accessed 23 October 2017] Fortune 100 Best Companies to Work for [Online] http://fortune.com/best-companies/google

3 Marr, B (2013) [accessed 23 October 2017] Why We No Longer Need HR Departments [Online] https://www.linkedin.com/pulse/20131118060732-64875646-why-we-no-longer-need-hr-departments

4 Marshall, M (2013) [accessed 23 October 2017] How Jawbone Is Using Big Data to Lead the Personal Fitness-Wearable Industry [Online] https://venturebeat.com/2013/11/06/how-jawbone-is-using-big-data-to-lead-the-personal-fitness-wearable-industry

5 Morgan, J (2016) [accessed 23 October 2017] How Often Should You Measure Employee Engagement? [Online] https://www.forbes.com/sites/jacobmorgan/2016/05/30/measure-employee-engagement/#64f124ac65ea

6 Fujitsu (2015) [accessed 23 October 2017] Fujitsu Develops Ubiquitousware, an Internet-of-Things Package That Accelerates Transformation of Business, press release [Online] http://www.fujitsu.com/global/about/resources/news/press-releases/2015/0511-01.html

7 Feffer, M (2014) [accessed 23 October 2017] HR Moves toward Wider Use of Predictive Analytics [Online] https://www.shrm.org/resourcesandtools/hr-topics/technology/pages/more-hr-pros-using-predictive-analytics.aspx

8 Marr, B (2016) [accessed 23 October 2017] How Can Big Data and Analytics Help Athletes Win Olympic Gold in Rio 2016? [Online] https://www.forbes.com/sites/bernardmarr/2016/08/09/how-big-data-and-analytics-help-athletes-win-olympic-gold-in-rio-2016/#7c903b567ec9

9 Faragher, J (2017) [accessed 23 October 2017] Artificial Intelligence and HR Tech Grow in Importance, Harvey Nash Finds [Online] http://www.personneltoday.com/hr/artificial-intelligence-hr-tech-grow-importance-harvey-nash-finds

10 Shah, S (2016) [accessed 23 October 2017] Will AI Augment or Replace HR? [Online] http://www.hrmagazine.co.uk/article-details/will-ai-augment-or-replace-hr

The evolution of intelligent (and super-intelligent) HR

02

The HR function in any organization is particularly rich in data. Personal employee data, recruitment data and key performance indicators (KPIs) are just a few examples of the kinds of data a typical HR team collects in the normal course of their work. And this has been true for many years, long before the phrase 'big data' came about. Yet, a lot of the time, having all these data did not lead to a significant increase in the number of performance-related insights being gleaned from them. Hence, a lot of HR teams could be described as 'data rich' but 'insight poor'. In this chapter, I explore how the rise of big data and analytics techniques has helped to change this situation, enabling HR teams to become as rich in insights as they are in data, and giving rise to the term 'intelligent HR'. But to fully understand these developments, I will first look at the explosion of data in today's world, introduce the Internet of Things (IoT) and delve into advanced analytics capabilities like artificial intelligence (AI) and machine learning. Later in the chapter, we will take a look at the emergence of what I call 'super-intelligent HR', which refers to the dramatic increase in our ability to automate many of the HR team's day-to-day activities. Finally, I will address whether HR teams are still needed in this big data age.

The explosion of data

Eric Schmidt, executive chairman of Google's parent company Alphabet, famously claimed that every two days we create the same amount of data as we did from the beginning of time until 2003.[1] Think about that for a second: the amount of data that humans managed to generate *from the dawn of civilization* to 2003 is now being created in just two days. While some people have taken issue with Schmidt's claim, everyone agrees that the amount of data we are creating is increasing rapidly, and will continue to do so. By 2020, the amount of digital information created worldwide is estimated to hit 44 zettabytes,[2] and I have seen some estimates that say we will be creating 180 zettabytes by 2025.[3] To put that in context, in 2013, we created just over 4 zettabytes.

Nowadays, everything we do creates data

Let us think about what this means in everyday life. Almost everything we do these days creates a digital trail. Whether you are browsing online (even if you do not buy anything), searching for a local business on your phone, paying for a coffee with your credit card, touching in with your travelcard as you board a bus, taking a photograph, reading an online article or playing a video game, all this (and much more) generates data. When people talk about 'big data', they are referring to the collection of all these data, as well as our increasing ability to gather insights from these data and use those insights to our advantage, particularly in a business context.

Of course, the ability to gather data is not new in itself. Going back even before computers, we still used data to track actions and simplify processes – think of paper transaction records or personnel files. What has changed is our ability to work with these data. Computers – particularly the early spreadsheets and databases – finally gave us a way to easily store and organize data on a large scale, and make it easy to access those data, rather than poring through a load of archive files.

Working with new types of data

I mention spreadsheets and databases because, for a long time, that was the limit of what we could do with data. For data to be easy to store, access and interrogate, they had to be neat and orderly. They really had to fit into columns and rows, and this comprises what are known as 'structured data'. Anything that could not be organized into columns and rows ('unstructured data') was too difficult, or just too expensive, to work with. That all changed with the massive advances in computing power and data storage that we have seen in recent years. Today we can capture, store and interrogate very many different types of data, including all kinds of unstructured data (there is more on the different data types in Chapter 4). As a result, 'data' now can mean anything from a database or spreadsheet, to sensor data, written text (such as social-media posts), photographs, videos and sound recordings. It is these advances in computing power and analytics that allow Amazon to track how you move around its online store, what you look at and what you eventually choose to buy, and then promote other products that it thinks you will like.

Much is made of the sheer volume of data we are generating each day, week, month and year, and it certainly does make for some impressive statistics. But I prefer to focus on the *value* of data rather than volume. Data bring incredible opportunities to better understand our world and how we live in it, which is why, when I work with businesses, I always advise them to focus on the value they can get from data. When it comes down to it, it does not matter what volume of data you have, or what type of data they are, all that matters is whether you are using those data successfully to drive performance.

Introducing the IoT

Why has there been such an explosion in data? A big part of the reason for this is the IoT. The IoT refers to everyday objects – such as smartphones, smart TVs, Fitbit bands etc – that can be connected to the Internet, collect and transmit data, and be recognized by other devices. In the IoT, data are created by things, not humans. Today, there are about 13 billion devices that connect to the Internet, but, by 2020, that number is predicted to rise as high as 50 billion.[4] Whether we actually hit that huge 50 billion number remains to be seen, but no one can dispute the fact that the IoT has seen enormous growth in recent years, and that growth is very likely to continue.

Almost everything can be made 'smart' these days. Our cars are offering ever-increasing levels of connectivity and, by 2020, it is estimated that a quarter of a billion cars will be connected to the Internet. Everyday devices in the home are now routinely hooked up to the Internet, including TVs, fridges and thermostats. There are even smart versions of products you really would not expect, like yoga mats and frying pans. As for smartphones, it is projected there will be 6 billion smartphone users in the world by 2020:[5] that is 6 billion smartphones generating data every day! All these smart devices, from your phone to your TV to your Fitbit, can connect to and share information with each other. This is a crucial part of the IoT: machine-to-machine connections mean that devices can talk to each other and decide on a course of action without any human intervention. For example, in the near future, it is not unreasonable to imagine your refrigerator knowing when your milk is out of date and automatically telling your smartphone to order more in the next online shop.

Getting into machine learning, deep learning and AI

The idea of AI has been around for a long time – the Greek myths contain stories of mechanical men designed to mimic our own behaviour. Very early European computers were conceived as 'logical machines' and, by reproducing capabilities such as basic arithmetic and memory, engineers saw their job, fundamentally, as attempting to create mechanical brains. As technology and, importantly, our understanding of how our minds work have progressed, our concept of what constitutes AI has changed. Rather than performing increasingly complex calculations, work in the field of AI has concentrated on mimicking human decision-making processes and carrying out tasks in ever-more human ways. Many of the developments in AI in recent years have come about thanks to machine learning and deep learning.

Understanding the terminology

What is the difference between AI, machine learning and deep learning? Well, AI refers to the broader concept of machines being able to carry out tasks in a way that we would consider 'smart', while machine learning is one of the major applications of that concept. Machine learning is based around the idea that we should really just be able to give machines access to data and let them learn for themselves.

While machine learning is often described as a sub-discipline of AI, it is better to think of it as the current state of the art of AI work. It is the field of AI which, today, is showing the most promise. In turn, deep learning is the cutting edge of the cutting edge! Deep learning takes some of the core ideas of AI and focuses them on solving real-world problems with neural networks designed to mimic our own decision making. Deep learning focuses even more narrowly on a subset of machine learning tools and techniques, and applies them to solving just about any problem which requires 'thought' – human or artificial. IBM's Watson system is a prime example of this in action. The system 'learns' as it processes information, so the more data the system is given, the more it learns, and the more accurate it becomes.[6]

How does it work?

Essentially, machine and deep learning involve feeding a computer system a lot of data, which it can use to make decisions about other data. So, if we give the computer a picture of a dog and a picture of a stick, and show it which one is the dog, we can then ask it to decide if subsequent pictures contain dogs. The computer compares other images to its training data set (ie the original image) and comes up with an answer. Today's machine learning algorithms can do this unsupervised, meaning they do not need their decisions to be pre-programmed. The same principle applies to even more complex tasks, albeit with a much larger training set, such as Google's voice recognition algorithms. The same techniques are used by Netflix and Amazon to decide what you might want to watch or buy next.

Machine and deep learning are responsible for advances in computer vision, audio and speech recognition, and natural language processing. They are what allow computers to communicate with humans (not always 100 per cent successfully, as Microsoft's widely publicised Twitter bot proved, with its crazy and often racist tweets[7]) and make Google's self-driving cars possible. They are also the reason Facebook is able to recognize individuals in photographs to the same level as humans can, automatically suggesting tags for individuals. This technology is already being used in fields as diverse as healthcare, finance and education, as well as, of course, almost all areas of business. Whenever there is a job that requires a large amount of complex data to be processed and analysed in order to solve problems, AI, and specifically machine and deep learning, can help. As computers are more able to think like humans, we are moving into an age where computers can enhance human knowledge in entirely new ways. And, of course, because machine and deep learning technology means that computers learn from the data they have access to, this means computers' ability to learn, understand and react will increase dramatically in line with the amount of data we are generating every year.

Computers can even understand our emotions

The technology has advanced to such an extent that it is now possible for computers to recognize and respond to human emotions. Known as 'affective computing', this technology analyses facial expressions, posture, gestures, tone of voice, speech and even the rhythm and force of keystrokes to register changes in a user's emotional state. Leading organizations like Disney and Coca-Cola are already using this technology to test the effectiveness of advertisements and assess how viewers react to content.[8] The BBC uses it to measure viewers' responses to TV programmes during trials.[8] In one such experiment, a number of viewers in Australia were monitored as they watched a trailer for a season premiere of *Sherlock*. The trial showed researchers that viewers who went on to rate the show favourably showed a greater reaction to on-screen events that were tagged as 'surprising' or 'sad', as opposed to 'funny'. This led *Sherlock*'s producers to include more dark, thriller-type elements in the show, in favour of less comedy.[9]

What this means for HR

The explosion in data applies to the world of work just as much as it does to every other area of our lives. Almost everything in a business context generates data, from an employee sending an e-mail to the sensors on production-line machinery. This means businesses have more data to mine for insights than ever before, and the HR function is at the very heart of this.

More data than ever before

I said at the start of this chapter that HR is especially rich in data, and that is correct. HR teams have recruitment data, career progression data, training data, absenteeism figures, productivity data, personal development reviews, competency profiles and staff satisfaction data. In the past, these data mostly went unused or, if they were used, they were put into charts and tables for something like a corporate performance pack. Now, in the era of big data and analytics, companies are turning their data into insights, such as predicting when employees will leave, where to recruit the most suitable candidates from, how to identify those people and how to keep them happy. In addition to traditional HR data sets, companies now can collect so many more data – data that were not available before – including things like capturing employees on CCTV, taking screenshots when staff are using company computers, scanning social-media data, analysing the content of e-mails and even monitoring where they are using the data from geo-positioning sensors in corporate smartphones. We have seen mind-boggling improvements in our ability to store and analyse all sorts of data. What is more, we now have big data analytics tools that allow us to compute huge volumes of data, which enable us to combine the analysis of traditional structured data with the analysis of unstructured data, such as written text and images.

All this means that the data and analytics revolution has some significant implications for HR teams. In the last couple of years, according to a 2015 report from the Economist Intelligence Unit, 82 per cent of organizations planned to either begin or increase their use of big data in HR between 2015 and 2018.[10] This has given rise to 'intelligent HR' as a bit of a buzz phrase. In theory, intelligent HR boils down to this: the more information we have, the better decisions we can make. Despite this, HR data are not always used in the most intelligent way. Research has shown that only 23 per cent of companies have HR systems that can always provide sufficient data to measure the execution of their business strategy.[11] The application of HR analytics is still too often ad hoc, and not always used with driving performance in mind. Truly intelligent HR focuses HR data and analytics on the goal of adding value and driving performance across the organization all the time, not just every now and then or on specific projects.

Crunching the wrong HR data

With all these data, the challenge is to establish which HR data are really going to make an impact on the company's performance. One big problem I have seen is that most HR departments simply start crunching the masses of quantitative data they have in the hopes of finding something. This is like looking for the proverbial needle in a haystack. As with any big data or analytics project, the key is not in the quantity of data points, but in the quality of the questions being asked about the data. What HR departments should be doing much more is embracing qualitative data and analysis. Instead of analysing the masses of structured numeric data, like accounting and finance departments might do, HR departments need to build on their strengths and capture more qualitative data. The less quantitative and more qualitative side is what HR departments have traditionally been good at and it is where big data offer huge opportunities. For example, instead of counting training hours per employee and crunching the data to death, one of my clients is now using ethnography-type data collection to gain powerful insights about training effectiveness using qualitative methods. The company is now collecting and analysing data using written training journal logs, video analytics and performance impact assessments. The company realized it needed to look beyond the simple existing metrics to answer the real business questions.

Learning from Google

Unlike most HR departments, Google's HR team states the objective: 'All people decisions at Google are based on data and analytics'.[12]

Initially, Google's founders believed that middle management roles were not important, so they did away with these positions.[13] When it became obvious that this belief was false, they brought the managers back, but the *perception* that the managers were not valuable persisted. So, Google turned to data to quantify the value of managers. Through data, the company was able to go from the opinion 'Managers don't impact performance' to proving that great managers had a statistically significant impact on team performance, employee engagement, employee churn and productivity. For this analysis, Google looked at data from performance reviews as well as qualitative interviews and the submissions for a 'best manager' award programme. By extracting the insights from that analysis using qualitative methods such as text analytics, Google was then able to identify and articulate what made a great Google manager and what caused less-proficient managers to struggle. These insights were then embedded into Google's culture through twice-yearly performance evaluations of these factors, which act as an early warning system to detect both great and struggling managers. For those that are struggling, there is access to improved training and support as well as plenty of role models to learn from. And for those who are doing well, there is the Great Manager Award. All this was possible because the company started with the right question, refining that question until it got to practical, verifiable analytics. In order to ask the right questions, you need to be clear about what it is you want to achieve, both in terms of HR objectives and in supporting the business's wider goals. This is where having a clear data strategy for the HR team comes in, and there is more on this in Chapter 3.

Super-intelligent HR is already here

Chances are you have already heard of the 'intelligent HR' buzz phrase. But, just as HR teams are getting to grips with what this means for them, I would argue that we are already moving in to the age of 'super-intelligent HR', brought about by the dramatic rise in automation. If you think automation does not apply to HR, think again. In fact, as we will see, it is increasingly possible to automate many HR tasks. Therefore, super-intelligent HR means making use of AI techniques like machine learning and deep learning not only to automate various HR activities, but also to carry them out better, faster and more accurately than a human. It is about HR teams working alongside intelligent machines and systems to make better decisions and make operations more efficient.

Pretty much all administrative tasks potentially can be automated, but super-intelligent HR goes way beyond this into critical functions like recruitment or employee engagement. Machine learning in particular is having a major impact on HR. For example, in application tracking and assessment, machine learning tools help HR teams to track applicants' journeys and speed up the process of giving feedback to candidates. The Peoplise digital recruitment platform, for instance, calculates a fit score for candidates based on digital screening and online interview results, helping HR professionals and hiring managers to decide on who is the best candidate for them.[14] Machine learning also can help to identify the risk of someone leaving the company, for example, by identifying specific risk factors based on responses to an employee survey or analysis of e-mails or social-media posts.

Chatbots facilitate greater automation

A recent survey by the IBM Institute for Business Value found that half of chief HR officers surveyed recognized the power of AI technologies to transform key dimensions of HR.[15] One often-cited example is chatbots, which are computer algorithms that mimic human conversation. Chatbots can be used across a number of HR activities, including providing real-time answers to HR questions and personalizing learning experiences; companies like IBM are already targeting so-called 'intelligent assistants' (or chatbots) that do exactly this. Chatbots are becoming increasingly common in our everyday lives, and their popularity was cemented when, in 2016, Facebook announced it was incorporating chatbot capabilities into its popular Messenger app.[16,17] Many large brands are already using chatbots to interact with customers, mainly by answering questions and giving advice. eBay's ShopBot, for example, helps shoppers to find and buy eBay items from within the Messenger app. You can even hail an Uber or order a pizza through Messenger using chatbots. So, as we become increasingly more used to interacting with chatbots in everyday life, we can expect to interact with them more in the workplace too. Plus, as our workplaces become more geographically dispersed, and the number of remote workers continues to rise, chatbots can fulfil a vital need for employees who do not have easy access to HR colleagues.

Intelligent assistants also can play a role in talent acquisition, from scheduling interviews to supporting (or even making) decisions about applicants. Talla is one example of a chatbot that is designed to serve as a real-time advisor to HR professionals as they source new hires.[18] Talla can provide a set of interview questions based upon the role being recruited for and even conduct a Net Promoter Score survey following the recruitment process.

In learning and development, chatbots are already being piloted by those who teach massive open online courses (MOOCs) as a way to support students while they learn by answering questions, reminding them of deadlines and providing feedback on work. As the popularity of online learning grows, intelligent assistants increasingly will be used to enhance the role of human teaching assistants. Increasing automation like this makes it easy to provide adaptive, personalized learning that is tailored to each individual learner's needs, which, in a business setting, can dramatically help to improve the employee experience.

AI and super-intelligent HR

Looking beyond chatbots, AI techniques like machine learning are beginning to make an impact on HR functions in many other ways. Machines being able to 'think' and make decisions like humans can benefit every aspect of HR, including recruitment. Software already exists to help identify potential candidates for jobs, or narrow hundreds of candidates down to a select few, but AI means this process can be done a lot more accurately. Some people have concerns that this strips away a lot of the 'human' side of HR – after all, HR is all about people. But there are many positives that come from incorporating AI into HR processes. For example, with a faster, more streamlined feedback system in place, handled by AI technology, potential candidates are likely to feel greater engagement with the company, not less. Even if they are unsuccessful in their application, this positive experience is likely to encourage them to try again for future positions. And, when it comes to sifting through applicants, machines can make decisions without any of the potential biases that humans bring to the table. Clearly, much of this recruitment work would be done in conjunction with human HR professionals, rather than just handing the entire process over to a machine, but there is no denying that the technology exists to automate and augment a lot of recruitment processes.

Another example comes from employee retention, where AI techniques can give unprecedented insights into a company's talent, specifically, how they are really feeling and performing. For example, sentiment analysis of e-mails or social-media posts, which involves mining text for insights into the sentiment behind the words being written, can be used in place of staff satisfaction surveys. Machine learning algorithms make it possible to analyse an employee's e-mails and social-media posts to assess their level of engagement with the company, how they react in certain situations and how well they fit with the company culture (whether this is ethical or even legal is another matter – turn to Chapter 6 for more on this). This process can help to predict, with far more accuracy than humans alone, whether someone is fed up and about to leave the company, or whether someone is ripe for promotion, for instance.

So, will we still need HR teams?

With all this automation, I am seeing increasingly more articles theorizing that soon we will no longer need HR teams at all. I have even written on the subject myself.[19] So, do I think machines will replace HR professionals, managers and directors? No, I do not. I believe it is inevitable that machines and algorithms will take certain tasks away from HR teams, just as they will across all areas of business over the coming years, but I do not believe HR teams will cease to exist altogether. They will simply adapt and refocus.

Embracing new technologies and greater automation

Personally, I strongly believe the increase in automation and advances like chatbots/intelligent assistants are great things for the HR profession as a whole. We all understand that a lot of HR time and resources, at present, are swallowed up by day-to-day administrative tasks. When such everyday, mundane or administrative tasks can be automated, it frees up HR to focus on more strategic things that are critical to the business's success. HR can then shift its focus to adding greater value to the organization. To me, that is a very positive transition, and it is the idea at the very heart of intelligent HR. Therefore, HR teams need not only to be aware of and prepared for the rise in automation, I would argue, they should even embrace it. The HR profession as a whole needs to get on board with AI, rather than fearing the impact it will have on jobs. HR leaders and professionals should feel encouraged to learn as much about these new technologies as they can. Business is changing dramatically, and many are calling this the fourth industrial revolution.

The fourth industrial revolution, or Industry 4.0

First, steam and the early machines mechanized industry. Then the second industrial revolution came with the invention of electricity. Computers and early automation brought us the third industrial revolution. And now we are entering the fourth industrial revolution, Industry 4.0, in which computers and automation come together in an entirely new way, with robotics and AI systems that can learn, control functions and make decisions with very little input from human operators. If we look beyond the HR team for a moment, as a result of this fourth industrial revolution, automation is already having or will soon have an impact on many people's jobs, across many different industries. As automation increases, computers and machines will replace workers across a vast spectrum of industries, from drivers and accountants to estate and insurance agents. One estimate based on a study by Oxford University claims that as many as 47 per cent of US jobs are at risk from automation.[20]

HR professionals therefore need to have the knowledge and resources to deal with the impact of this revolution on their industry and their organization, and the people who work for that organization. HR needs to be very much involved in the company's discussions concerning preparing for the increase in automation. HR professionals need to become technologically fluent, in order to have these conversations with their organization's leadership team. Automation is going to impact on many different areas of how we work in the future. And some of these changes will be huge, especially in industries like manufacturing. HR professionals therefore need to keep up to date with the rise of automation and develop an understanding of what it may mean for their business, as well as the HR team itself; because, as the nature of business continues to change, HR teams will be central to answering business-critical questions that the leadership team will have, such as: 'What types of skills and capabilities do we need to attract in order to work with these automated systems?' The HR team's expertise, and the wealth of data HR teams have, can help to answer such questions and prepare the organization for changes that may come about. For me, this is a critical part of intelligent and super-intelligent HR: supporting the business as its needs change and evolve.

Challenges and opportunities

It is clear that data, analytics and even automation bring both major changes and major opportunities for HR teams. The way in which HR teams deliver their service will certainly change over the next few years, as the more repetitive tasks can be fulfilled by computers. From sourcing and hiring talent to supporting employees as they learn and develop, automation will help to save time, increase efficiency and improve the decision-making process. As HR moves away from the more mundane and time-consuming tasks associated with day-to-day people management to focus on wider strategic issues, the HR team itself becomes arguably more valuable to the organization, and more critical to its success. So, while I understand that discussions regarding automation do make HR professionals (and employees and often leadership etc) nervous, I think these developments should be viewed within the wider scope of HR becoming increasingly more intelligent and providing greater value to the organization. Just as almost every other area of life is becoming smarter, from our phones and TVs to the way we shop, so too is the way we work. No one can predict with absolute certainty how the technology will evolve, on what scale and on what timelines, but it is absolutely clear that all this technology is only going to go in one direction: forwards. It is not going to go backwards or become less popular. We are only going to have more data, more intelligent algorithms, better machine learning programs, more sensors, greater automation etc; not less, more. HR teams need to be ready for this transformation. Despite the challenges involved, data, analytics and automation present massive opportunities to improve the way we do business, making employees' working lives better and increasing HR's contribution to the organization. For me, that is what is so exciting about intelligent (and super-intelligent) HR.

Key takeaways

It is clear that data and analytics have come a long way since the early computers and humble databases, and the explosion in data is going to dramatically change how HR operates – just like every other area of business. Below is a rundown of what has been covered in this chapter:

- Almost everything we do these days creates a digital trail and we can now capture, store and interrogate many different types of data. The IoT, with its smart, connected devices, has played a key role in this data explosion.

- With all these data, the challenge is to establish which HR data are really going to make an impact on the company's performance. The key is not in the quantity of data points, but in the quality of the questions being asked about those data.

- Companies are now turning their HR data into value-adding insights, such as predicting when employees will leave or where to recruit the most suitable candidates from.

- Whenever there is a job that requires a large amount of complex data to be processed and analysed in order to solve problems, AI (specifically machine and deep learning) can help.

- We are already moving in the age of 'super-intelligent HR', brought about by the dramatic rise in automation taking place across all industries.

- HR needs to embrace new technologies and increasing automation. When everyday, mundane or administrative tasks can be automated, it frees up HR to focus on more strategic things that add greater value to the organization.

In the next chapter we will look at how HR departments should be preparing for this transition by laying the foundations for data-driven HR, starting with creating a robust and smart data strategy that links to wider organizational objectives and creates a clear business case for data.

Endnotes

1 Siegler, M G (2010) [accessed 23 October 2017] Eric Schmidt: Every 2 Days We Create as Much Information as We Did up to 2003 [Online] https://techcrunch.com/2010/08/04/schmidt-data

2 Turner, V (2014) [accessed 23 October 2017] The Digital Universe of Opportunities [Online] https://www.emc.com/leadership/digital-universe/2014iview/executive-summary.htm

3 Kanellos, M (2016) [accessed 23 October 2017] 152,000 Smart Devices Every Minute in 2025: IDC Outlines the Future of Smart Things [Online] https://www.forbes.com/sites/michaelkanellos/2016/03/03/152000-smart-devices-every-minute-in-2025-idc-outlines-the-future-of-smart-things/#77d1b5ed4b63

4 Ericsson (2010) [accessed 23 October 2017] CEO to Shareholders: 50 Billion Connections 2020, press release [Online] https://www.ericsson.com/en/press-releases/2010/4/ceo-to-shareholders-50-billion-connections-2020

5 Lunden, I (2015) [accessed 23 October 2017] 6.1b Smartphone Users Globally by 2020, Overtaking Basic Fixed Phone Subscriptions [Online] https://techcrunch.com/2015/06/02/6-1b-smartphone-users-globally-by-2020-overtaking-basic-fixed-phone-subscriptions

6 IBM [accessed 23 October 2017] Watson [Online] https://www.ibm. com/watson

7 Price, R (2016) [accessed 23 October 2017] Microsoft Is Deleting Its AI Chatbot's Incredibly Racist Tweets [Online] http://uk.businessinsider.com/ microsoft-deletes-racist-genocidal-tweets-from-ai-chatbot-tay-2016-3

8 Murgia, M (2016) [accessed 23 October 2017] Affective Computing: How 'Emotional Machines' Are About to Take Over Our Lives, *Telegraph* [Online] http://www.telegraph.co.uk/technology/ news/12100629/Affective-computing-how-emotional-machines-are- about-to-take-over-our-lives.html

9 Marr, B [accessed 23 October 2017] How the BBC Uses Big Data in Practice [Online] https://www.bernardmarr.com/default. asp?contentID=710

10 The Economist Intelligence Unit (2015) [accessed 23 October 2017] What's Next: Future Global Trends Affecting Your Organization [Online] http://futurehrtrends.eiu.com

11 SAP SuccessFactors [accessed 23 October 2017] Global HR Survey Shows Why Employees Want a Single Source of Analytics [Online] https://www.successfactors.com/en_us/lp/global-hr-survey.html? Campaign_ID=21487&TAG=Q413_Global_HR_Survey_EC_ LinkedIn&CmpLeadSource=Public%20Relations

12 Sullivan, J (2013) [accessed 23 October 2017] How Google Is Using People Analytics to Completely Reinvent HR [Online] https://www.eremedia.com/ tlnt/how-google-is-using-people-analytics-to-completely-reinvent-hr

13 Garvin, D A (2013) [accessed 23 October 2017] How Google Sold Its Engineers on Management [Online] https://hbr.org/2013/12/ how-google-sold-its-engineers-on-management

14 Peoplise [accessed 23 October 2017] Superior Talent Experience. Mobile. Faster [Online] http://www.peoplise.com

15 IBM [accessed 23 October 2017] Extending Expertise: How Cognitive Computing Will Transform HR and the Employee Experience [Online] http://www-935.ibm.com/services/us/gbs/thoughtleadership/ cognitivehrstudy

16 Constine, J (2016) [accessed 23 October 2017] Facebook Launches Messenger Platform with Chatbots [Online] https://techcrunch.com/ 2016/04/12/agents-on-messenger

17 Messenger [accessed 23 October 2017] Messenger Bots for Business and Developers [Online] https://messenger.fb.com

18 Talla [accessed 23 October 2017] Never Answer the Same Question Twice [Online] https://talla.com

19 Marr, B (2013) [accessed 31 January 2018] Why We No Longer Need HR Departments [Online] https://www.linkedin.com/pulse/20131118060732-64875646-why-we-no-longer-need-hr-departments/

20 Frey, C B and Osborne, M A (2013) [accessed 23 October 2017] The Future of Employment: How Susceptible Are Jobs to Computerisation? [Online] http://www.oxfordmartin.ox.ac.uk/downloads/academic/The_Future_of_Employment.pdf

Data-driven strategy: making a business case for more intelligent HR

03

In order to crystallize your goals, get the most out of data and get buy-in for your activities, you need to make a clear business case for data-driven HR. In practice, this means mapping out a clear HR data strategy that links to wider operational objectives and demonstrates how HR will contribute to those objectives; as well as identifying HR-specific objectives and how those objectives can be achieved through data and analytics. In this chapter I explore why it is so important to have a data strategy and why it needs to be linked to wider organizational objectives. I then set out the process of creating a 'smart strategy board' or 'plan on a page' to help you crystallize your objectives, and work out how you want to use your data. After that, I delve into the process of creating a strategy for intelligent or data-driven HR, including understanding the four layers of data and the six critical questions that form the basis of any good data strategy.

Everything starts with strategy

As we saw in Chapter 2, the explosion in data is affecting almost every area of our lives, including work. We now live in a world in which the amount of data being generated every day – even every second – is, frankly, astonishing. And when it comes to what we should do with all these data, I have found that many companies, or functions within organizations, fall into one of two camps: some are so eager to ride the data train, they dive in and start collecting all kinds of data simply *because they can*, with no thought as to how those data benefit the business, while others prefer to bury their heads in the sand, often because they are so overwhelmed they do not know where to start. This is where a data strategy comes in.

Understanding the data you really need

It is never a good idea to start collecting huge amounts of data that you do not really need; and this is especially true with a lot of HR data, because it is so personal in nature. Collecting people-related data just because you can may lead to mistrust or morale problems, as people feel that Big Brother is monitoring what they do with no clear sense of *why* or how it benefits them and the company as a whole. (As we see in Chapter 6, trust and transparency are vital when it comes to utilizing data successfully.)

I always say that the power of data is not in the impressive amount that can be collected, or the super-cool analytics that can break down the data in a myriad of ways. The power of data lies in how you use them. It is about how you use the insights that you glean from the data to improve decisions, better understand your employees, optimize operations and add value to the company. Therefore, you need to be very clear about what it is you want to achieve and, specifically, what kind of data will help you to achieve that aim.

Why 'big' is not always better with data

Ideally, you should collect, store and analyse the smallest amount of data possible to achieve your goals. I once did some consultancy work with one of the world's largest retailers and, after my session with the leadership group, the CEO went to see his data team and told them to stop building the biggest database in the world and instead create the smallest database that could help the company to answer its most important questions. This is a great way of looking at data. Despite the hype concerning 'big' data, small is something to aim for. Keeping your data as small as possible means you are keeping a tight focus on where you want to go and which data will help you to get there.

Of course, big data giants like Google and Facebook collect everything they possibly can and never throw data away because potentially it could be valuable in the future. Google even captures misspelled words in Internet searches, using those data to create the world's best spellchecker. While Google has the manpower, expertise and budget to cope with enormous amounts of data, most companies do not, which is why it is better to collect only the data that are absolutely necessary for you to reach your goals. Creating a robust data strategy helps you to develop and maintain a laser-like focus on which data are best for your department. Plus, having a strong data strategy in place will help to ensure the whole process runs more smoothly, as well as preparing the HR team and others in the organization for the journey ahead.

Where to start: linking your HR strategy to wider organizational objectives

Which data you gather and how you analyse them will depend entirely on what you are looking to achieve, so you need to consider this as the very first step in creating your data strategy. The best kind of HR data strategy is directly linked to the organization's wider objectives and, in effect, should cascade down from those corporate objectives to create HR-specific objectives that will help to fulfil the corporate goals. Therefore, a good place to start is not with HR at all, but the company-wide strategic plan. In an ideal world, the organization's strategic plan would be a concise, simple document that anyone in the organization can read and understand – something like a plan on a page that clearly sets out where the organization needs to go – however, this is not always the case and I recognize that some organizational strategic plans are overly long and complex, making it difficult to determine what actions need to be taken. Whatever your company's strategy looks like, it should set out intended outcomes for the company, including financial and non-financial objectives, and (hopefully) the core activities and enablers that will lead to those outcomes being achieved. If you struggle to understand this from the company's strategic plan, have a discussion with your leadership team before going any further, as it is vital you understand exactly where the business wants to go.

With the company's strategic objectives in mind, you can begin to create your own HR plan that links to those objectives and identifies what you need to achieve in order to contribute to the company's success. Say, for example, one of the corporate objectives is to reduce operating costs over the next three years, this will clearly influence your HR-specific objectives and, in turn, the kind of data you will want to work with.

Creating a plan on a page or smart strategy board to inform your data strategy

I cannot recommend strongly enough that you keep this objectives phase simple. Do not be tempted to create a list of 100 HR objectives that cover everything you could possibly want to achieve. Instead, focus only on core objectives. After all, you cannot create a robust data strategy if you are not crystal clear on what exactly you need to achieve and, in turn, what areas or activities you need to focus on to achieve those aims. A list of 100 nice-to-have objectives will lead to a very muddled (probably very expensive) data strategy that delivers little real value. To clarify your objectives and activities, it is a good idea to create an HR plan on a page, or what I call a 'smart strategy board'. This is divided into six simple sections, as outlined below, and each section should be developed with the overall organizational objectives firmly in mind.

The HR purpose

Here you set the scene and provide an overarching context for your strategy by laying out, in simple terms, exactly what the HR department is aiming to achieve. A good way to do this is to include your purpose and vision statements. Your purpose (or mission) statement should be a brief, simple statement that neatly encapsulates why your team exists. As the name suggests, it answers the question: 'What is our purpose?' Your vision (or ambition) statement defines your purpose, but with the focus on what you want the HR function to look like in the future. It should set out your ambitions in an inspiring way, including your values and what behaviours the HR team adheres to.

Your customers

For any HR team, its primary customers are the organization's employees. Therefore, this section is about understanding the company's people:

- what you already know about them;
- what you do not yet know;
- what you need to find out if you are going to meet your goals successfully.

As with each section, remember to tie this into the larger organizational objectives and how they relate to the organization's employees.

The finances

In this section you need to clearly set out any financial goals and ambitions as they relate to the organization's strategy. Yes, part of this may be about cutting costs, but it should also be about creating additional value for the company, such as by boosting your brand as an employer and attracting the best talent. We know that finding, training and keeping hold of good talent costs organizations a lot of money, so many of your financial goals and ambitions may centre around this area. For example, one of your goals might be to streamline training and onboarding by moving to online training modules, while, at the same time, demonstrating greater value from that online training (ie using data and analysis to demonstrate a clear link between training, performance and even retention).

HR operations

Here you need to carefully consider your operations and any changes you need in order to deliver your goals. For example, do you need to partner with external providers and, if so, do you already have a relationship with those partners or do you need to build that relationship? Also, look at internal competencies and whether there are any gaps you need to fill in the team (and, if so, how will you fill them?). Your HR systems and processes also will come under this section.

HR resources

The aim here is to define exactly what resources you need in order to achieve your objectives. This covers IT systems, infrastructure, people, talent and cultures, and value and leadership. Clearly, there is a lot to consider concerning data and how they impact on IT resources, but you do not need to go into lots of detail at this stage. Remember, this plan on a page is about clarifying what you want to achieve and what you might need in order to do that. There is more on the systems needed to turn data into insights in Chapter 6.

Your competition and risks

In this section, you should consider what competition you will be facing as you work to deliver your strategy and what risks you may face along the way. Ask yourself: 'Who is the main competition (such as external HR services) and why?' Also consider what external factors may threaten your success, such as market, regulatory or people-related risks. And what are the internal financial, operational or talent risks you face? Being aware of these threats before you move forward is the best way to mitigate them.

Working out how best to use data

Having created your plan on a page, you should have a firm idea of where the HR team needs to go in the future, how you can add value to the organization and what areas you may need to develop.

Next, before we delve into the data strategy itself, it is worth thinking about how best to use data. As we saw in Chapter 1, there are many ways in which data are used in business, but, in their broadest sense, these uses boil down to four categories:

- improving decisions;
- optimizing operations;
- understanding customers (or, in the case of HR, employees) better;
- monetizing data.

In this section we look at each usage again in relation to your HR strategy. I recognize that every organization is different, and you may feel some of these options do not apply to you. For example, some HR teams may face greater operational challenges, while other companies are suffering significant morale problems and need to develop a better understanding of their people, fast. When it comes to monetizing data, this is particularly problematic for people-related data; however, I still recommend you look at all four areas in turn before deciding how best you can use data. It is likely your core focus will lie in one or two of these categories, but it is best to consider all four before you start to get your data strategy down on paper.

Using data to improve your decision making

Making better business decisions is the goal for the majority of clients that I work with, and data increasingly are fuelling decision making at all levels in organizations, from multinational corporations to small start-ups. So much of a company's success comes down to making better, more informed business decisions, and data are providing the insights needed to make those decisions. There are two key strands when it comes to making better HR-related decisions. The first is the HR team itself making better decisions that address the organization's and HR team's objectives, as well as critical people-related challenges. The second is about the HR team helping others, ranging from the leadership to other functions right across the business, to make better decisions using people-related data. There has been a strong move towards democratizing data, and giving wide (often real-time) access to data in order to aid decision making across businesses. Therefore, every HR team should be thinking about how it can make relevant HR data available to those who need it, in real time where necessary. Increasingly more companies are building cultures of data-based decision making, as opposed to basing decisions on gut feeling or how things have always been done. We have already seen examples of this in Chapter 2 (Google's data-based decisions on managers) and Chapter 1 (Xerox creating a data-based profile of the ideal call-centre worker). The HR function potentially provides a wealth of data that can make a valuable contribution to this data-based culture.

Using data to optimize your operations

This use of data is about optimizing HR processes and everyday operations in order to make improvements, generate efficiencies and deliver a better service. As we saw in Chapter 2, increasingly this is about automating as much as possible, putting internal systems in place that allow you to automatically make use of people-related data. Automation is something HR teams can no longer afford to ignore. But this category is not all about automating processes and replacing HR professionals with, say, chatbots. In its broadest sense, it is simply about looking at key processes and activities, understanding what the HR team spends its money and time on and looking at how to make those processes better. I delve into specific HR functions and activities in Chapters 7–11.

Using data to better understand your customers

This is one of the most common uses of data in business, with examples ranging from Amazon and Netflix using data to make helpful recommendations on what to buy or watch next, to high street stores tracking how customers move around a shop and which displays catch their eye. This category is all about understanding your customers – where they come from, what matters to them, what they like and do not like etc – as well as wider trends in the market.

Clearly, as an HR professional, your customers are the organization's employees (and, to some extent of course, the leadership team). The more you can understand about your customers, the better you can serve them. There is both an internal and an external side to this category. Internally, the HR team can use data to better understand employees and the organization's culture, including how happy they are, how engaged they are, how safely they are working etc. With the many different analytical techniques available today, such as text analytics and video analytics, not to mention the boom in wearable technology, it has never been easier to gain critical insights into how your people are feeling and performing. Social media also has made it easier than ever to build up a rich picture of customers. Externally, data can help the HR team look beyond the organization and understand your employer brand (using platforms like LinkedIn and Glassdoor). Data can give valuable insights into your company's perception from the outside, and how to attract the kind of talent you need to succeed. This category has a lot of crossover with making better decisions. Armed with a better understanding of your customers, you can make much smarter decisions on how best to serve them – decisions rooted in data, rather than hunches or assumptions – which is why this category and the first often go hand in hand.

Monetizing data

Data are valuable, and companies are increasingly being bought on the basis of the data they have. Microsoft's purchase of LinkedIn for US $26.2 billion, for example, gave Microsoft access to the professional network's more than 400 million users, and the data they generate.[1] These data will be integrated with Microsoft's collaboration and productivity tools, potentially allowing greater personalization within Microsoft's products, which could help the company become more competitive in the enterprise market.

The ability to sell data to third parties is a growing area for many businesses; take Facebook, for example. The social network is free to users, but it has created a revenue stream from that user data by making certain data available to other businesses, for a fee.[2] Amazon, too, has commercialized its data on an impressive scale (and, unlike Facebook, Amazon's data relate to how we spend our hard-earned money, which makes them especially valuable to businesses). This makes the company now a head-on competitor with Google, with both online giants fighting for a chunk of marketers' budgets.[3] And, with the launch of Amazon's home voice assistant Alexa, and Google's Google Home, both companies will continue to fight it out for the best, most valuable, user data.

Naturally, this category of data usage presents significant challenges for HR because so many HR data are personal and sensitive. It is therefore unlikely you will be able to create a new revenue stream from employee data (and even if you could, would you want to?). In the United States there have been stories of agencies collecting pay-related data from companies, including Fortune 500 companies, and providing access to those data to interested parties like collection agencies.[4] On the whole, this practice is largely unheard of; however, in terms of adding value to the company, HR data certainly do have a monetary value. When HR data are used to improve decisions, make employees happier and optimize processes, of course they add value to the company. For me, this usage is about seeing HR data as comprising a key business asset that can deliver significant value for the business. But, as your HR data become a core asset, the need for careful data governance becomes even more pressing. One of the biggest concerns regarding data, particularly personal data, is privacy and governance, and with good reason. I talk more about data security, privacy and governance in Chapter 6.

Which usage is best for you?

Having looked at all four areas, and with your HR objectives in mind, you can now begin to figure out where the biggest opportunities lie for data-driven HR in your organization. For example, say your company has a corporate objective to become a top-three provider of specific consultancy services within the next three years. That will translate into various HR-related actions such as assessing and optimizing your employer brand in order to attract the best talent. This will mean the biggest opportunities for data-driven HR are likely to lie in better understanding your customers and making better decisions. Then, once you have a sense of where the biggest opportunities lie and how you might want to use data, you can begin to pull everything together into your HR data strategy.

Figure 3.1 The four layers of data

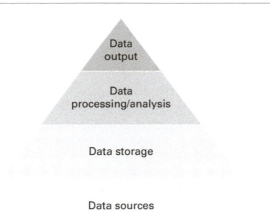

Understanding the four layers of data

Now we are ready to start delving into the data strategy itself. But, when starting to pull together your data strategy, it is important to understand the four layers of data, because a good data strategy should clearly map across these four layers (see Figure 3.1).

1 Data sources layer

This is where the data arrive with the HR team. This layer includes everything from your sales records (for key performance indicator (KPI) purposes), customer feedback, employee surveys and feedback, e-mail archives, personnel files and any data gleaned from monitoring or measuring aspects of your operations. Data could also arrive from outside the organization, through data collection tools like Google Analytics, or social-media networks. One of the first steps in setting up a data strategy is assessing what you already have and measuring this information against what you need in order to answer the critical questions you want help with. You might have everything you need already, or you might need to establish new data sources.

2 Data storage layer

This is where your data live once they have been gathered from your sources. In line with the general explosion in big data, sophisticated but accessible systems and tools have been developed to help with this task, such as the Apache Hadoop computing software. As well as a system for storing data that your computer system will understand (the file system), you will need a system for organizing and categorizing these data in a way that people will understand (the database).

3 Data processing/analysis layer

When you want to use the data, you need to be able to process and analyse them. One common method is by using a MapReduce tool, which selects the elements of the data that you want to analyse, and puts them into a format from which insights can be gleaned. These days, there are many proprietary tools and systems you can use to query data and many of them are designed to be used by non-data scientists.

4 Data output layer

This is how the insights gleaned through the analysis are passed on to the people who need them, whether that is inside the HR team, the company's leadership team, or other functions in the company which can use the data. This output can take the form of reports, charts, figures and key recommendations. Whatever format it is presented in, the information needs to be clear and concise, making it as easy as possible to identify critical actions.

Creating your data strategy: asking the right questions

With the four data layers in mind, an HR data strategy can be easily broken down into clear sections or questions. Keep in mind that there is more on how to implement each section later in the book. Here

Figure 3.2   Creating your data strategy: asking the right questions

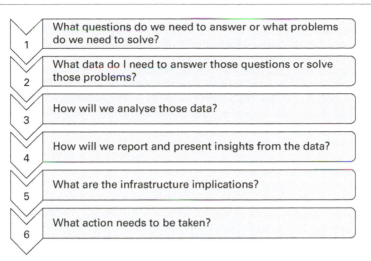

1	What questions do we need to answer or what problems do we need to solve?
2	What data do I need to answer those questions or solve those problems?
3	How will we analyse those data?
4	How will we report and present insights from the data?
5	What are the infrastructure implications?
6	What action needs to be taken?

your focus should be on understanding what you want to do. You may need some expert help to pull your strategy together and put it into practice. Depending on the size of your company and the expertise within it, it is clearly a good idea to involve your IT team in this process. For those smaller companies which lack the data knowledge and expertise in-house, there are many data consultants who will be able to help you determine the best course of action for your needs. As illustrated in Figure 3.2, the following six questions will help you to understand and really clarify what you want to do, and they form the basis of any good data strategy. Answer all six questions in the order set out below, rather than skipping over various sections.

Question 1: what questions do we need to answer or what problems do we need to solve?

Many of the organizations and functions I work with tend to ask for as many data as possible, not because they plan to do very clever analytics, but because they do not know which data they really need; however, it is far better to start by returning to your strategic objectives, rather than thinking about the data themselves. After all, why bother collecting data that will not help you to achieve your goals?

Remember the plan on a page we talked about earlier in the chapter? Here you start by identifying the key questions that relate to that plan. So, having set out what it is you want to achieve, you now need to pin down the big unanswered questions you need to answer if you are going to deliver that strategy. Some of the questions will have been identified already as you worked on the plan on a page, while others will need careful thought at this stage. Defining these questions helps you to identify exactly what you need to know. And by making sure your questions are linked to your company's priorities, you can ensure they are the most strategically important questions, rather than asking every little 'nice to know but not essential' question.

Question 2: what data do I need to answer those questions or solve those problems?

I have mentioned it a couple of times now, but it is something I see time and time again: too many companies or departments get caught up in collecting data on everything that walks and moves, simply because they can, rather than collecting the data that really matter. When creating your data strategy, it is vital you stay focused and do not get caught up in exciting data possibilities that are not relevant to your goals.

Look at each question you identified in question 1 and then think about which data you need to be able to answer those questions. Many of those data will come from within the company itself, but you also may need to make use of external data providers, particularly when it comes to recruitment. Establish which data you already have access to, and which you do not yet have access to. For the data you do not have access to, do you need to partner with an external provider or can you set up new data collection methods to gather the data internally? You can read more about key sources of HR data in Chapter 4.

Question 3: how will we analyse those data?

Having pinned down your information needs and the data you require, next you need to look at your analytics requirements, ie how you will analyse those data and turn them into valuable insights to help you answer your questions and achieve your goals. When it comes to analytics, much of the promise of data lies in unstructured data, like e-mail conversations, social-media posts, video content, voice recordings etc. Combining these messy and complex data with other more traditional data, like KPIs or sales data, is where a lot of the value lies. There is more on this in Chapter 5.

Question 4: how will we report and present insights from the data?

Data and analytics, and all the interesting insights gleaned from data, are absolutely useless if they are not presented to the right people in the right way at the right time, so that the right actions can be taken. Options for reporting and presenting insights vary from fancy dashboards with real-time access to data through to simple reports with key insights presented as visuals. Keeping your target audience in mind is perhaps the most important thing to remember at this stage. Therefore, you need to define who the audience is for your data and work out how best to get that information to them. The HR team itself may be the largest audience, but no doubt you will also need to present insights to others elsewhere in the organization. Indeed, this is a critical part of HR teams adding greater value to the organization. So consider now who exactly might need access to the information, and how you intend to provide it. Why do you need to think about this now? Because your method(s) for presenting data may have critical implications on your data infrastructure requirements. Which leads us to the fifth question.

Question 5: what are the infrastructure implications?

Having defined which data are needed, how they will be turned into value and how they will be communicated, the logical next step is working out the infrastructure implications of these decisions. Essentially this comes down to what software and hardware will be needed to be able to capture, store, analyse and communicate insights from the data you have identified. For example, if you are looking at gathering significantly more performance data, is your current data storage technology up to the task of storing all those new data, or do you need to supplement them with other solutions? What current analytical and reporting capabilities do you have and what else do you need to get?

Question 6: what action needs to be taken?

Having answered the five questions above, you are now ready to define an action plan that turns your HR data strategy into reality. Like any action plan, this will include key milestones, actions and owners of those actions. As part of this step, you will also need to identify training and development requirements to help you put this plan into action, and pinpoint where you might need external help.

Making the business case for data-driven HR

There is no doubt that getting the leadership team and key decision makers involved will help you to create a more robust data strategy. Not only that, but getting leadership's buy-in at this crucial early stage means they are more likely to put your people-related data to good use in their own decision making. Thus, an important part of creating a robust data strategy is making a strong business case for a data-driven HR approach, to help get people (both inside and outside the team) on board with the idea of data-driven HR. The more people are aware of and excited by the possibilities of data, the more likely they are to buy into the idea.

'Selling' data-driven HR across the company

This extends across all levels of the company and all functions, not just the company leadership. After all, data-driven HR is about people, and their data. When the people in an organization understand what data-driven HR is all about, and how it benefits the company as a whole and them as employees, they are more likely to be on board with, for example, capturing new kinds of employee data. When the business case for data-driven HR is not communicated properly at every level, it can breed mistrust and have serious negative consequences for the organization's culture. Making a business case for data-driven HR is a bit like an entrepreneur making a business case (or business plan) for their new venture. So, naturally, you will want to do the same sorts of things as an entrepreneur would in their business plan, including giving a good outline of the data strategy and its goals, ie what you are hoping to achieve with data, as well as the tangible benefits to the business and its employees. It is also vital you are open and realistic about the time frame, likely disruption to the business and costs, especially in discussions with the leadership team. You need to make the best case for data-driven HR, which means it is important not to gloss over these issues.

'Selling' data-driven HR is a crucial consideration on the way to intelligent HR. It instils confidence in data, inspires feelings of trust and transparency, and emphasizes the HR team's value to the company as it works to achieve its goals. Plus, when you want your HR data to be used by other functions across the company, ensuring everyone understands the value of your people-related data means they are much more likely to incorporate those data into their decision making further down the line. By making a business case now, you are sowing the seeds for data-driven decision making and adding value through data in the future.

How to go about this in your company

How you communicate your plan for data-driven HR depends on a number of factors, like how big your company is and the usual process for kicking off new initiatives. One good way to go about it is by distilling your data strategy into key points that can be communicated in a short presentation. Keep it simple and brief (there is no need to go into masses of detail on analytical possibilities or data storage options, for instance) and remember that your enthusiasm for this new age of data-driven HR will be infectious. Use examples to demonstrate how other companies are leading the way in data-driven HR and what this means in practice (it is even better if you can find examples that relate to your specific industry). Hopefully, the examples given throughout this book will help you to do this, and remember to focus on the benefits that data-driven HR will bring, both to the organization as a whole and to the people who work there.

Returning to your strategy in the future

No strategy is ever set in stone. Things change, markets shift, organizational priorities evolve etc. It is therefore very likely that you will need to revisit your data strategy on a regular basis to check it is still in line with the company's overall priorities. Even if nothing has changed, revisiting the strategy helps you to stay lean and remain focused on the outcomes. Also keep in mind that, as you get further down the road of data-driven HR, significant new opportunities or questions may present themselves. For example, when answering one of your strategic questions, the data may throw up other, more pressing questions that also need to be answered, and this may lead to a slight tweak in your strategy. The technology concerning data and analytics is evolving fast and what will be possible in one or two years' time may be completely different from what is possible now. While you want to follow through on the actions in your strategy, remember that the point of data-driven HR is to add greater value to the organization and do things in a more intelligent, streamlined way; it therefore makes sense to stay alert to new ways of working.

Key takeaways

I cannot stress enough how important strategy is in making good use of data. And, as we continue to create unprecedented volumes of data, having a clear strategy will become more important than ever. Below is a list of what has been discussed about data strategy in this chapter:

- In this world of ever-expanding data, you need to be very clear about what it is you want to achieve and, specifically, what kind of data will help you to achieve that aim. This is where your data strategy comes in.

- Big is not always better. Keeping your data as small as possible means you are keeping a tight focus on where you want to go and which data will help you to get there.

- The best kind of HR data strategy is directly linked to the organization's wider objectives. Once you are clear on where the organization is trying to go, you can map out HR-specific objectives to help the company achieve its goals.

- To clarify your objectives and activities, it is a good idea to create an HR plan on a page, or what I call a smart strategy board.

- Having created your plan on a page, you should have a firm idea of where the HR team needs to go in the future, how you can add value to the organization and what areas you may need to develop. This will help you to work out your priorities for using data.

- When starting to pull together your data strategy, it is important to understand the four layers of data: data source, data storage, data processing and data output. A good data strategy should clearly map across these four layers.

- To create your data strategy, answer the six key questions set out in this chapter.

- Finally, an important part of creating a robust data strategy is making a strong business case for a data-driven HR approach, to help get people on board with the idea of data-driven HR.

As we have seen in the first three chapters of this book, there is a huge variety and volume of data available today. Having a strong data strategy will help you to filter out the noise and identify the best types of data for your goals. In the next chapter I explore in much more detail some of the main sources of HR-relevant data.

Endnotes

1 Feller, G (2016) [accessed 23 October 2017] This is the Real Reason Microsoft Bought LinkedIn [Online] https://www.forbes.com/sites/grantfeller/2016/06/14/this-is-the-real-reason-microsoft-bought-linkedin/#695b191cf04a

2 Facebook [accessed 23 October 2017] Advertising and Our Third-Party Partners [Online] https://www.facebook.com/notes/facebook-and-privacy/advertising-and-our-third-party-partners/532721576777729

3 Maverick, J B (2015) [accessed 23 October 2017] How Amazon Competes with Google [Online] http://www.investopedia.com/articles/investing/060215/how-amazon-competes-google.asp

4 Carrns, A (2013) [accessed 23 October 2017] Checking the Data Collected on Your Work and Pay [Online] http://www.nytimes.com/2013/08/31/your-money/exploring-companies-that-collect-more-than-the-standard-credit-data.html

Capitalizing on the data explosion: identifying key sources of HR-relevant data

04

We know that pretty much everything we do nowadays leaves a digital trace, and this means it is now possible to get data on almost any aspect of people management. After all, data are by-products of computing and, these days, everything is essentially a computer, from the smartphones we carry everywhere with us and the vehicles we drive to modern manufacturing equipment. Even basic office equipment can be made 'smart'. For example, the humble office chair has been given a 'big data' facelift: BMA Ergonomics' Axia Smart Chair has sensors fitted in the seat, and the data gathered from these sensors are used to give feedback on the employee's posture, helping them to sit properly and avoid the health problems associated with bad posture.[1] It is clear then that HR teams have exciting data options that go way beyond data that must be collected for statutory reasons or data from the normal annual performance review cycle. But even traditional HR data can be optimized and used more intelligently. Instead of using just a simple scoring mechanism on performance review data, for instance, you could use text analytics to reveal more detailed insights about your employees' performance and level of satisfaction (there is more on text analytics in the next chapter).

To help you determine which data work best for you, this chapter sets out the different categories of data and explores specific types of HR-relevant data, namely activity data, conversation data, photo and video data, and sensor data. I will also look at options for sourcing and collecting the data you need, and address the question of whether any one type of datum is better or more effective than another.

Distinguishing between different types of data

Before we get into the various different sources of HR-relevant data, it is important to understand the key overarching ways in which data are categorized. As illustrated in Figure 4.1, data are either internal or external, and either structured, unstructured or semi-structured. Let us look at each category in turn.

Internal data

Internal data comprise any proprietary data that are owned by your business, including all the data you currently have and all the data you have the potential to collect in the future. This includes employees' personal data, performance review data, employee surveys, sales and financial data, customer feedback etc. Internal data can be structured, unstructured or semi-structured (more on this later). The obvious big advantage of internal data is that they are usually

Figure 4.1 Types of data

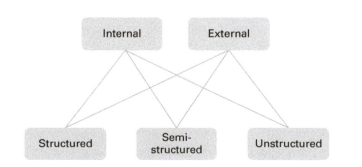

cheaper and easier to work with than buying in or paying to access external data. They are also uniquely tailored to your business and industry (as opposed to external data, which may not be), which makes internal data incredibly useful and valuable. This points to a disadvantage, however: because your internal data are so uniquely tied to your business, they may not provide a rich enough picture to meet all your strategic goals and may need to be supplemented with some external data (particularly when it comes to recruitment) to get all the information you need. Another important point to note about internal data is that you are responsible for looking after and properly securing those data, particularly sensitive personal data (more on this in Chapter 6).

There is a lot of hype and excitement concerning data but, often, internal data are not viewed as terribly exciting or cutting edge – after all, they might well be the same old data you have been collecting for years; however, the value of internal data should never be overlooked. US-based recruitment and training firm Kenexa was acquired by IBM in 2012 for US \$1.3 billion,[2] partly on the basis of its valuable internal data, gained from assessing millions of employees, managers and applicants each year. IBM was able to analyse these precious data to gather insights on the key characteristics of successful sales people. After comparing employee tests and surveys with assessments by managers, IBM found that, rather than the obvious 'outgoing personality' characteristic typically associated with sales positions, 'emotional courage' was actually the most important trait for a successful sales person to have. This insight allows IBM to test for emotional courage in future sales applicants and hire only those that score highly for this trait.

External data

External data comprise all the data that exist outside of your company, be it public data that are freely available or data that are privately held by another organization. These data include social-media profiles and posts, recruitment data from sites such as LinkedIn and Glassdoor, economic data, data on social trends and much more. Like internal data, external data also can be structured, unstructured or semi-structured. While some external data can be accessed for free, you may have to pay to use certain data, particularly data owned by private, for-profit companies. Therein lies an obvious downside: these data may not be cheap. Access rights also can be an issue in that there is always a risk that an external provider could cut off access or jack up prices. Therefore, if you are reliant on certain external data for absolutely critical insights, it is worth exploring whether you can possibly generate or gather those data yourselves in-house.

Despite these considerations, external data offer some huge advantages. They are often richer and more detailed than the average company's internal data, giving HR teams access to vast and complex data sets that they could never hope to build internally. Complications concerning storing and managing data are reduced by working with external data providers, as they will look after and secure their own data. Silicon Valley-based networking solutions company Juniper Networks provides a great example of a company using external data intelligently. Juniper uses the vast amount of data available through LinkedIn to analyse where its most successful and best-performing employees come from – and where people move on to when they leave Juniper.[3] This gives the HR team a useful picture of career paths in the networking solutions industry, information that they can use to help attract and keep the industry's best talent.

Structured data

As we saw in Chapter 2, the term structured data essentially means any data that can be organized neatly in rows and columns, usually in a database or spreadsheet. This may include employee personal data, sales data, test scores, performance review scores, absence data, salary information, data points from sensors etc. Clearly, the average HR team has the potential to tap into vast amounts of structured data, particularly internal structured data. In fact, for most businesses, until very recently, the majority of data analysis was based on structured data because, by their very nature, they are much easier (not to mention cheaper) to organize, structure, store and interrogate.

And they often can be interrogated by non-analysts (most employees can find their way around a database, for instance), which is another big advantage. Despite their fixed nature, structured data still can be incredibly powerful. One such example of the power of structured data was seen in Chapter 1, where a bank analysed the colleges their employees came from and determined their best-performing people came not from the top-tier schools, as expected, but from less-prestigious universities.

Another example can be found in the book *Work Rules!* written by Laszlo Bock, former Senior Vice President of People Operations at Google.[4] Bock describes how structured data help Google to optimize the hiring process. Interview questions are all computer-generated and completely automated to make sure the company hires the best talent, without human bias getting in the way. But one big downside to structured data is that they account for only approximately 20 per cent of all the data in the world – the rest are unstructured or semi-structured data.[5] This means, if you focus on structured data alone, you could be seriously limiting the number of insights available to you. And those insights are likely to present a less detailed and rich picture than if you combined structured data with unstructured data. Take employee turnover rate, for instance. Using structured data, you can determine that your employee churn rate is 20 per cent. But that is all the structured data can tell you. You will need to make use of unstructured data, such as the detailed answers given in an employee exit interview, to understand *why* employee churn is 20 per cent.

Unstructured and semi-structured data

Unstructured data are essentially all the data that do not fit neatly into a spreadsheet or database, whether they are internal or external data. Unstructured data are often text-heavy, but the term could also refer to audio or visual data. Examples include social-media posts, employee e-mails, employee and customer feedback, photos, videos (eg CCTV footage) and audio recordings (eg customer-service calls). These messy data types used to be too difficult or expensive for the average company to work with, but that has all changed in recent years. Now, thanks to massive advances in storage and computing power, increasingly more companies are benefitting from unstructured data.

As you can probably guess, semi-structured data sit somewhere between unstructured and structured data. They have some sort of structure (like descriptor tags, for instance), but lack the strict structure found in databases or spreadsheets. For example, a tweet can be categorized by author, date, time, length and even the sentiment behind the tweet, but the text itself in the tweet is generally unstructured and therefore would be a little more complex to analyse. This is the main disadvantage of unstructured or semi-structured data: they are more complex to work with. They tend to be bigger, which means they require more storage, and they are more difficult to organize and analyse, requiring specialist analytics tools. Obviously, all this has an impact on costs; however, that should not put anyone off using unstructured or semi-structured data as there are some serious benefits. Clearly one big benefit is that you are broadening your view much more than you would if you stuck only with structured data (which, as we know, excludes around 80 per cent of the data available). You should also be able to gain a much more detailed, rich picture by combining these messy data with structured data.

Facebook has long been able to make some scarily accurate predictions about us based on the unstructured and semi-structured data found in our profiles, our likes and the content of our posts. Recently, it has been working to use this predictive power to help save lives. In March 2017, the company announced AI-driven tools and algorithms that can spot users who may be at risk of self-harm or suicide.[6] These algorithms mine data from users' posts and comments added by concerned friends looking for words and phrases that are linked to suicide or self-harm. The idea is to flag posts that raise concern more quickly and easily, and connect those at risk with mental health services. Similarly, a few years ago, Microsoft announced that it had developed a method for identifying Twitter users at risk of developing depression.[7] It is easy to see how developments like these can potentially benefit HR teams charged with looking after the wellbeing of their employees.

Identifying HR-relevant data

Now let us look at the main types of data that are relevant to HR. Essentially, HR-relevant data can be categorized as follows:

- activity data;
- conversation data;
- photo and video data;
- sensor data.

It is important to understand that all of the above are still either structured or unstructured/semi-structured data, and they can include both internal and external data. For example, sensor data are structured data and they can be internal or external, depending on which sensor data you are using; conversation data are likely to be unstructured or semi-structured and can be internal or external etc. Over the following sections I will look at each data type in turn.

Activity data

Activity data, which provide a record of human activities or actions (whether online or offline), can be incredibly valuable from an HR perspective. Think about all the things you do in the course of a normal day – they all generate activity data. If you wear a fitness band with a sleep tracker, like I do, even your sleep and the time you wake up generate activity data. Then you travel to work, perhaps paying for a ticket with a bank card or touching in with a travelcard. Assuming your phone is a smartphone, it will generate records of your location while you are on the move. If you make or receive a phone call on your way to work, or post a photo on Twitter, that generates data. Then you get to work and send countless e-mails, type hundreds or maybe thousands of words a day and look at numerous webpages. Maybe you buy something online or head to the supermarket in your lunchbreak. Even browsing online for ideas for your partner's birthday next month generates data.

Understanding what your people really do

The sheer volume of activity data available to HR teams can be overwhelming, so it is important to always refer back to your strategic objectives and focus only on the data that help you to achieve your goals. But the real advantage of activity data is that they allow you to assess what your employees *actually* do, as opposed to what they are supposed to do or what you assume they do. Some companies take this to the extreme. Bloomberg, for example, reportedly gathers data on every single keystroke made by its employees.[8] Others focus more on specific activity data. The Container Store, for example, uses wearable technology to track employee activity, how they communicate with customers and other staff, and where they spend most of their time.[9] Performance-related data are particularly valuable for HR teams. By tracking such activity data, companies can accurately monitor individual performance and use this information to identify top performers and those who may need help.

Activity data in action: recruitment and retention

Of course, when you know who performs well and what characteristics top performers share, you can focus on hiring more people who match those characteristics. San Francisco software provider Evolv has created pioneering online tests to help refine the recruitment process. Evolv's tools help businesses gather data on everyone who applies for a job at the company and everyone who gets hired. With a data set of over 300,000 candidates who have now taken their online assessments, Evolv has some incredibly valuable performance-related data. The company can pinpoint, with an extremely high level of accuracy, which characteristics make for a more successful retail sales person, for example.[10]

We briefly looked at Xerox in Chapter 1 and saw how the company had gathered valuable insights on what makes a successful call-centre worker. Xerox is just one of the big companies that has used Evolv's tests to refine its hiring practices. And with roughly 45,000 employees working in Xerox's 150 US customer care centres, finding those workers who will perform well and stay in the job is critical. Xerox switched to online assessment of candidates back in 2010.[10] An algorithm analyses the applicant's test scores, alongside factual information provided by them on their application, and allocates a traffic light rating to each application: green means they are good to hire, red means they should be avoided and orange means they are in the middle of the pile. It was these tests that showed Xerox that previous call-centre experience had no impact on retention or productivity – a major assumption on which hiring managers had been basing their decisions. The tests also showed that how close candidates lived to the office was a strong marker of retention and employee engagement. In the initial pilot period alone, employee attrition fell by 20 per cent.[10] And the longer-term benefits of the improved quality of hires included an increase in the number of promotions.

Activity data in action: fostering innovation

Another example comes from video game start-up Knack's collaboration with Royal Dutch Shell. Knack's video games, which were designed by a team of data scientists, psychologists and neuroscientists, are not just about having fun – they are about measuring human potential. All sorts of factors are logged as a player participates in the games: every move they make, how they solve problems, how long they pause before taking action etc. This builds a thorough picture of the player's level of persistence, creativity and even intelligence, as well as their ability to prioritize tasks and how quickly they learn from mistakes.

Royal Dutch Shell's GameChanger unit, which is charged with identifying the best business ideas from inside and outside the company, was extremely interested in the potential of these games to improve and speed up the process of identifying the best ideas. So the unit devised an experiment: 1,400 Shell employees who had previously proposed ideas to the GameChanger team were asked to play a couple of Knack's games. The GameChanger team then shared with Knack information on how well three-quarters of the players had fared as idea generators (whether their ideas made it all the way, for instance). Knack used this information to develop game-play profiles of the best idea generators in comparison to the weaker ones. Using information based on these top innovators' game profiles, Knack was then asked to guess from the remaining quarter of the players who had had the best ideas. This was done with startling accuracy, clearly identifying those who had previously generated winning ideas based only on the way they played the games.[10] Based on this experiment, Knack and Shell were able to identify the key characteristics of top idea generators, such as social intelligence and task-switching ability. This has allowed the GameChanger unit to devote more time to those employees whose ideas are likely to have more merit.

Conversation data

Conversation does not just mean two employees having a conversation around the coffee machine. It covers any conversation people may have in any format, whether it is a call with a customer, an instant message sent via phone or computer, company e-mails or written survey responses, social-media posts etc. These are all examples of conversation data. These types of data are incredibly valuable to HR teams because they can give in-depth insights into how happy and engaged your employees really are, as well as how positive your employer brand is (eg by analysing data on Glassdoor). Thanks to advances in analytics, conversations now can be mined for the content itself (what is said) as well as context (how it is said). In other words, you can understand what is going on from the words used and the mood of the person engaged in the conversation. This means companies can tell how happy, irritated or stressed an employee is, or even if they are telling the truth, just by analysing the tone of their voice. For example, the US Department of Homeland Security is using voice analytics to detect when those entering the country are lying. Using its Avatar system, a computerized 'agent' with a virtual, human face and voice asks several questions.[11] The person's responses are monitored to detect fluctuations in tone of voice, as well as the content of what exactly was said. These data are compared against a database, and matched against factors that indicate someone may be lying, based on previous experience. While this may seem a little hard core for most HR teams, it shows how far the technology has progressed.

Conversation data in action

Let us look at a more viable example for the average HR team. Very few people enjoy filling in employee surveys. In fact, staff surveys are notorious for either not being completed at all or not being completed truthfully (because employees feel they should say what the company wants to hear or worry that their responses could be individually tied to them). Conversation data allow you to assess how people are actually feeling, as opposed to them saying what they think you want to hear. These data are particularly useful in understanding what makes an employee want to leave (or, for that matter, stay with) the company. By analysing text from open-ended questions in surveys and exit interviews, as well as social-media posts, e-mails and team assessments, HR teams now can accurately predict what makes an employee more likely to leave or stay with the company.

Hiring is another area that can benefit from conversation data, and it is not uncommon for employers to scour social-media profiles for glimpses into what potential hires are really like. This potentially could be done on a larger scale to identify the types of content and the sentiment behind things that successful employees post on Twitter and Facebook, and then use that knowledge to assess potential candidates in the future.

You could also assess conversations employees are having with each other and customers to assess their satisfaction (both the employee and the customer) and pinpoint behaviours of successful team members. Wearable technology potentially has a big role to play in this area in the future. Wearable technology company Sociometric Solutions (now part of Humanyze) has created electronic employee badges that capture information from conversations as employees go about their day, including the length of the conversation, the tone of voice involved, how often people interrupt, how well they show empathy etc.[12] Sandy Pentland, the brains behind the badges and head of the Human Dynamics Lab at MIT, says data from the badges can be used to predict which teams are likely to be more successful, which employees are more productive and creative, and which show signs of being great leaders.[13]

Mining e-mails for insights

For many companies, e-mail is an especially rich source of conversation data, giving insights into employees' productivity, treatment of colleagues etc. Text analytics software is getting better and cheaper all the time, making it possible for companies to search through employees' e-mail traffic, hunting for words, phrases or patterns of communication that are linked to certain success (or failure or attrition) metrics.

It goes without saying that there are implications to gathering and analysing conversation data. When it comes to phone calls, for instance, generally speaking, you cannot record customers or employees just because you feel like it; what you are recording must be relevant to the business. You may also need to inform the parties that they are being recorded. Use of e-mail data also can be restricted depending on where you are in the world. In the United States, any e-mail sent in the course of work can be used for analysis. In Europe, employers should be more cautious about reading communications, especially if the conversation is of a private nature. There is more on such pitfalls in Chapter 6.

Photo and video data

Photo and video data refer to any kind of photo or video image (such as CCTV footage). The amount of photo and video data has exploded in recent years, largely thanks to the advent of smartphones and the increasing use of CCTV (especially in the United Kingdom). Photo and video data can be big, which can make them trickier (and potentially more expensive) to store and manage; however, your company may be collecting these data as a matter of routine already (perhaps through security footage), so it may not be very difficult or expensive to find new ways to use these data more intelligently. If your company is not collecting photo or video data already and you are interested in doing so, make sure you have a clear business case for working with these data (purely because it can be expensive) and that the benefits clearly link to your objectives.

Photo and video data in action

So, how could you use photo and video data? One example comes from the brightly lit world of Las Vegas. The analytics team at Harrah's worked out that card dealers and waiters smiling had an impact on customer satisfaction. The hotel and casino now reportedly tracks the smiles of card dealers and waiting staff, presumably to monitor who could be performing better in the smile department.[10] Facial recognition software means that individuals now can be easily identified in photos and videos. Facebook has been at the forefront of this movement and its own facial recognition software can now accurately identify an individual 98 per cent of the time, which makes it more accurate than the FBI's facial recognition technology.[14]

Connecting photo and video data to AI

Microsoft also gave some interesting examples of how photo and video data could be used in the workplace at its 2017 Build developer conference.[15] Its vision of the workplace of the future includes, among other things, cameras connected to artificial intelligence (AI) programmes. One example given for the use of video data involved a camera detecting that an employee was not wearing the appropriate safety gear, prompting a notification to be sent to the employee's supervisor. In another example, an employee was captured on video taking a selfie while in charge of a dangerous piece of machinery. The cloud-based computer support system recognized the activity and the potentially hazardous setting, concluded that the individual was acting recklessly and notified a supervisor.

Sensor data

Sensors are being built into an increasing number of products, ranging from factory machinery to office chairs and yoga mats. And these sensors generate a wealth of data that can help HR departments improve their functions, including employee performance, employee safety etc.

Combining sensor data with other data sources

Because sensor data tend to lack context (they are just telling you what the sensor recorded at any given time, not what might have caused the event), keep in mind that they may need to be combined with another data set to get the best results, depending on what you are trying to achieve. But sensor data are self-generating, meaning they are very easy to capture, once the data capture tools have been put in place. Some devices, such as smartphones, contain ready-to-use sensors that can be used to the company's advantage (eg a delivery company using their drivers' phones to track driver behaviour).

Sensor data in action

Clearly, wearable technology has a huge role to play in utilizing sensor data, and the workplace wearables market is booming. One survey by Forrester Research of over 2,000 technology decision makers found that one-third of respondents said workplace wearables were a 'critical' or 'high' priority.[16] Honeywell's 'Connected Worker' solution is one example of this.[17] Using a series of connected wearables sensors, the solution measures an employee's heart rate, breathing, motion and posture to assess whether they are under physical stress or in potential danger (it can detect toxic gas, for instance). This kind of technology will become increasingly more common in the future, especially for workers in physically demanding jobs, or those who work in dangerous or isolated locations.

Some of the most innovative uses of sensor data come from the world of sport, and it gives us a glimpse of how companies might be using these sorts of data in the future. In American football, for example, injury levels have been reduced due to wearable sensors that monitor the intensity of activity and impact of collisions and compare this information with historical data to determine when a player might be in danger of overexerting or injuring themselves. One Olympic sports team I worked with used wearable devices to track how well athletes slept at night, and then correlated those data with track performance. This enabled coaches to assemble their teams based not only on past performance, but also on how well individual team members had slept the night before.

Sourcing and collecting the data you need

Having identified what you want to achieve with data (Chapter 3), it is a good idea to start by seeing whether the data you need already exist internally. If they do not, you will need to look at whether you can generate those data in-house.

Sourcing data internally

As we have already seen in this chapter, nowadays, you can gather activity data from almost any activity undertaken by the company's employees. From test scores, to interview answers, to performance reviews, there is the potential to gather valuable performance-related data from any sort of activity. And wherever the HR team and your company's employees are currently having conversations, there is an opportunity to collect conversation data. For example, if you operate a telephone sales department or customer-service department, you can record those conversations and analyse the content and sentiment for useful insights into how staff are performing. Surveys, e-mails, customer feedback comments, social-media platforms etc all provide useful sources of conversation data.

Video and photo data can be obtained by simply starting to collect them using digital cameras. For example, retailers can use their network of CCTV cameras to analyse how the presence of staff members in certain sections of the shop floor impacts on how likely a customer is to buy something. And with modern sensors being smaller and cheaper than ever (small enough to fit into an employee's badge, for instance), they can be incorporated into almost anything, from manufacturing equipment to office equipment.

It is clear that internal data comprise a vital part of any data-driven HR strategy. But you may also need to combine those data with some external data to get a fuller picture that truly answers your strategic questions.

Sourcing external data

There is a wealth of external data already out there. As increasingly more companies view data as a business commodity, a market is emerging where practically any organization can buy, sell and trade data. (Indeed, many companies exist purely to supply other companies with data.) LinkedIn and Glassdoor are perhaps two of the biggest sources of HR-related data. In addition, there are lots of smaller, more industry-focused, data providers. So, even if you are looking for quite specialized data, there is a good chance someone out there has them.

Social-media platforms are obviously key sources of useful data, and they provide a wealth of information on current, past and potential employees. After LinkedIn, Facebook and Twitter are likely to be your first stop for social-network data. You can, for example, use sentiment analysis (more on this in Chapter 5) to find out what past employees are saying about your company culture online or how happy current employees are with their working environment. Or, say if there was a change in company policy or working conditions, you could assess employees' tweets to find out how people are reacting to the changes. Sentiment analysis can tell us a lot about users' feelings, opinions and experiences, without having to trawl through individual tweets one at a time – just like the example given earlier in the chapter where it was possible to identify people at risk of developing depression based on the content of their tweets.

Other sources of HR-relevant external data may include census data, which provide a very useful source of population data, geographic data and education data. This could be useful, for example, if you were looking to set up a new office in a new location and wanted to assess the potential workforce in that area using local demographics. In addition, weather data are often used by companies to help plan staffing levels according to the number of visitors expected on a sunny weekend, for example.

The importance of automating data collection

I keep coming back to the automation point, but with good reason. Wherever possible, you should put in place systems to collect or generate the data you need *automatically*. Whether you want to collect activity data related to employee productivity, or sensor data in a hazardous working environment, or whatever, the data collection should ideally take care of itself. The whole point of data-driven, intelligent HR is to free up HR time and resources to focus on adding greater value to the company. If HR professionals are engaged in lengthy data collection exercises, this completely defeats that purpose. Of course, with any new data project, time is needed to set up, fine-tune, maintain and assess those processes, but once that time has passed, you should be looking to collect data with the minimum effort possible, which leaves the HR team to focus on turning those data into insights, and then acting on those insights.

Identifying the most effective data type

Ultimately, no one data type is better than another. It all comes down to knowing what it is you want to achieve and finding the data that best help you to do that. A lot of the more exciting big data case studies focus on innovative uses of unstructured data, and it is easy to see why. But if it is possible to achieve your goals by working with structured data only, then why would you not do that? Unstructured data are not inherently more valuable than structured data. External data are not 'better' than internal data, just because there are more of them. And remember, what is best for one business may not be best for yours. With so many data available these days, the trick is to focus on finding the exact, specific pieces of data that will best benefit your organization, which is why it is vital you have a robust data strategy as your starting point (see Chapter 3). By working out what it is you need to know in order to achieve your objectives, you can go from there and identify the best data to give you those answers. Some data obviously will be more viable than others, and you can assess data options based on the ease and cost of sourcing those data versus how close they get you to your goals. But, ultimately, it does not matter whether the data are structured, unstructured, internal or external, or a combination of all these, the main thing is that they do the job you need them to do.

It is most likely that you will actually need a combination of data sets across different types of data, which is a good thing. If you rely on just one data set (employee responses to a survey, for example) to make critical decisions, you may be getting a very limited picture indeed. By combining those survey data with other data (such as activity data or conversation data), you can create a much richer picture of what is really going on. You can also verify insights rather than continuing down a road based on false assumptions from a limited data set. Say, for example, you are working to improve the company culture. To do this, you might well need a combination of internal structured data (like yes/no answers or 1–10 scores on an employee survey) with some external structured data (like your Glassdoor score), as well as internal unstructured data (like conversation data from employee interactions or open-ended survey questions) and external unstructured data (like social-media posts). The most intelligent HR teams will combine data to get at the most useful insights in relation to their goals. In my experience, it is often the combination of internal and external data and structured and unstructured data that provides the most valuable insights.

Key takeaways

The wealth of data options available can be overwhelming, but generally speaking, data boil down to a handful of key categories, as follows:

- Data are either internal or external, and either structured, unstructured or semi-structured. HR-relevant data generally can be categorized as activity data, conversation data, photo and video data, and sensor data.

- Activity data, which provide a record of human activities or actions (whether online or offline), can be incredibly valuable for understanding what your people really do.

- Conversation data cover any conversation people may have in any format. They are particularly useful for understanding what people really think and feel.

- Photo and video data cover photos, CCTV footage and any other kind of photo or video image. They can be particularly helpful in improving employee safety and security.

- Sensors generate a wealth of data that can help HR departments to improve their functions, including employee performance, employee safety etc.

- Options available for collecting data are:
  - making use of existing internal data;
  - generating new internal data (eg through sensors or surveys);
  - sourcing external data (eg through sites like Glassdoor).

- Ultimately, no one data type is better than another. What matters is knowing what you want to achieve and finding the data that best help you to do that.

Once you have identified the data you need, the next step in intelligent HR is turning those data into insights through data analysis. In the next chapter I look at the various types of data analytics and how they can provide critical insights for HR teams.

Endnotes

1 BMA Ergonomics [accessed 23 October 2017] Axia Smart Chair [Online] https://www.bma-ergonomics.com/en/product/axia-smart-chair/#ad-image-0

2 Bersin, J (2012) [accessed 23 October 2017] Why IBM Acquired Kenexa [Online] https://www.forbes.com/sites/joshbersin/2012/08/27/why-ibm-acquired-kenexa/#d6aa4f71372f

3 Roberts, B (2013) [accessed 23 October 2017] The Benefits of Big Data [Online] https://www.shrm.org/hr-today/news/hr-magazine/pages/1013-big-data.aspx

4 Bock, L (2015) [accessed 23 October 2017] *Work Rules!* [Online] https://www.workrules.net

5 Schneider, C (2016) [accessed 23 October 2017] The Biggest Data Challenges That You Might Not Even Know You Have [Online] https://www.ibm.com/blogs/watson/2016/05/biggest-data-challenges-might-not-even-know

6   Callison-Burch, V, Guadagno, J and Davis, A (2017) [accessed 23 October 2017] Building a Safer Community with New Suicide Prevention Tools [Online] https://newsroom.fb.com/news/2017/03/building-a-safer-community-with-new-suicide-prevention-tools

7   De Choudhury, M *et al* (2013) [accessed 23 October 2017] Predicting Depression via Social Media [Online] https://www.microsoft.com/en-us/research/publication/predicting-depression-via-social-media

8   Seward, Z M (2013) [accessed 23 October 2017] Bloomberg's Culture Is All About Omniscience, down to the Last Keystroke [Online] https://qz.com/83862/bloomberg-culture-is-all-about-omniscience-down-to-the-last-keystroke

9   Sacco, A (2014) [accessed 23 October 2017] How the Container Store Uses Wearable Tech to Think outside the Box [Online] http://www.cio.com/article/2378126/infrastructure/how-the-container-store-uses-wearable-tech-to-think-outside-the-box.html

10   Peck, D (2013) [accessed 23 October 2017] They're Watching You at Work [Online] https://www.theatlantic.com/magazine/archive/2013/12/theyre-watching-you-at-work/354681

11   US Department of Homeland Security (2014) [accessed 23 October 2017] Rapid Screening Tool: the Avatar [Online] https://www.dhs.gov/sites/default/files/publications/Rapid%20Screening%20Tool-NCBSI-AVATAR-Jan2014.pdf

12   Humanyze [accessed 23 October 2017] People Analytics. Better Performance [Online] https://www.humanyze.com

13   Berman, A E (2016) [accessed 23 October 2017] MIT's Sandy Pentland: Big Data Can Be a Profoundly Humanizing Force in Industry [Online] https://singularityhub.com/2016/05/16/mits-sandy-pentland-big-data-can-be-a-profoundly-humanizing-force-in-industry

14   Lachance, N (2016) [accessed 23 October 2017] Facebook's Facial Recognition Software Is Different from the FBI's. Here's Why [Online] http://www.npr.org/sections/alltechconsidered/2016/05/18/477819617/facebooks-facial-recognition-software-is-different-from-the-fbis-heres-why

15   Sullivan, M (2017) [accessed 23 October 2017] At Build, Microsoft's Vision of the Future Workplace Looks Both Helpful and Intrusive [Online] https://www.fastcompany.com/40419938/at-build-microsofts-vision-of-the-future-workplace-looks-both-helpful-and-intrusive

16 Gownder, J P (2014) [accessed 23 October 2017] How's Your Enterprise Wearables Strategy? [Online] http://www.informationweek.com/mobile/mobile-business/hows-your-enterprise-wearables-strategy/a/d-id/1316342

17 Galman, D (2017) [accessed 23 October 2017] Honeywell Launches New Connected Worker Software Aimed at Boosting Safety, Productivity, press release [Online] https://www.honeywell.com/newsroom/pressreleases/2017/05/honeywell-launches-new-connected-worker-software-aimed-at-boosting-safety-productivity

Data-driven HR tools: turning data into insights with HR analytics 05

These days, most HR teams are already data rich, but that is not the same as being *insight* rich. To be insight rich, you need to be able to turn the data you collect into valuable insights that answer your strategic questions and help you to deliver your strategic goals. In this chapter I look at some of the more advanced data analytics methods available today, and explore some of the most valuable and useful people-related analytics. I also discuss why it is important to combine analytics to get a complete picture. Finally, I look at how to turn data and analytics into insights, and communicate those insights to the people that need them. As you read this chapter, keep in mind that it is very easy to get caught up in the exciting opportunities that analytics bring. It is therefore important to keep the focus on insights to avoid getting side-tracked by new and exciting analytics approaches that do not actually have an impact on performance. Organizations are doing very cool things with analytics, but what works for one business may not work for yours. Your challenge is to identify the best, most accessible, most achievable analytics approaches for you. In recent years, many companies have sprung up offering all sorts of analytics services, tools and platforms. So, for most of the options outlined in this chapter, there are numerous commercially available tools on the market that simplify these analytics processes.

Figure 5.1 Analytics techniques

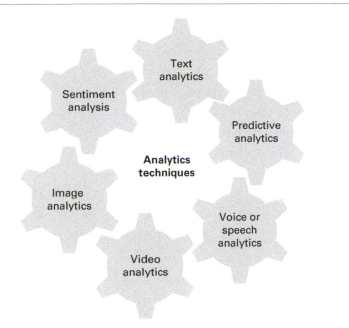

Looking at the latest analytics techniques

As illustrated in Figure 5.1, some of the key techniques for analysing data include text analytics, sentiment analysis, image analytics, video analytics, voice analytics and predictive analytics. Let us look at each area in turn.

Text analytics

Text analytics is the process of extracting value from large quantities of unstructured text data. Most HR teams have either ownership of or potential access to large volumes of text-based data, including e-mails, survey responses, job applications, performance review files, social-media posts etc. Until recently, however, these data were not always that useful from an analytics perspective. Access to huge text data sets and improved technical capability means text now can be analysed to extract high-quality insights over and above what the text actually says. In this way, text analytics helps us to get more out of text, so that we can understand more than just the words on the page or screen and identify larger patterns. This makes text analytics especially helpful for understanding more about your employees. For example, text can be mined for patterns such as an increase or decrease in positive feedback from customers, and this may help to identify customer-service representatives who are performing well and those who may need extra support to improve in their role. I know of one organization that uses text analytics tools to scan and analyse the content of e-mails sent by its staff as well as their social-media posts. This practice allows that organization to accurately understand the levels of staff engagement, meaning it no longer needs to carry out traditional (and expensive) staff surveys and it no longer has to wait to assess staff engagement on an annual basis.

Sentiment analysis

Sentiment analysis is closely related to text analytics, since it helps to extract subjective opinion or sentiment from text (it can also be used on video or audio data to assess the sentiment behind spoken words). The basic aim is to understand the attitude of an individual or group regarding a particular topic (such as proposed changes to the company's incentive scheme) or overall context (eg wider company culture) and whether that attitude is positive, negative or neutral. In this way, sentiment analysis helps us to get at the real truth behind communication. And, in this age of constant digital connectivity and our increasing desire to share our thoughts and feelings about all sorts of things – including companies – on social media, sentiment analysis has become mainstream.

You would use sentiment analysis when you want to understand stakeholder opinion, with stakeholders primarily being your employees, but also your leadership team and the company's customers. Advanced sentiment analysis also can go further by making a classification as to the emotional state involved. For example, in Chapter 4 we looked at the Avatar system used in US immigration. Not only does the system analyse what a passenger is saying, it can also analyse the tone of their voice, facial expressions, body language etc to determine whether the person is calm or under stress (indicating that they might not be telling the truth).[1] The vast majority of our communication is picked up non-verbally through body language and tonality, and this now can be analysed on a large scale.

Image analytics

Image analytics – the process of extracting information, meaning and insights from images such as photographs, medical images or graphics – relies heavily on pattern recognition. In the past, the only analysis that was possible on images was via the human eye (such as a doctor looking at a patient's scan). If computers were used, they could only categorize images using descriptor keywords (tags) that were manually added by a human being to each image. Advances in image analytics mean computers now can understand and recognize the content of an image (eg an individual's face), as well as analysing the digital information associated with the image (date taken, location etc). Image analytics can be used in a number of ways, such as facial recognition for security purposes or recognizing your brand or product in photographs shared by your employees on social-media platforms.

Video analytics

Video analytics is the process of extracting information, meaning and insights from video footage. It includes everything that image analytics can do, but additionally it can measure and track behaviour. A good example of this is the use of CCTV cameras that can detect when an employee is not wearing the appropriate safety gear, such as a hard hat.[2] You could use video analytics if you wanted to increase security or understand more about how your employees behave when they are on site. You could also use video analytics to reduce costs and risk and assist in decision making. For example, a number of providers now offer software that allows you to automatically monitor a location 24/7. That video footage is then analysed using a video and behavioural analytics solution which alerts you in real time to any abnormal or suspicious activity. Once installed and provided with the initial video feed, the software observes its environment and learns to distinguish normal behaviour from abnormal behaviour. The system is also self-correcting, which means that it continuously refines its own assumptions about behaviour and no human effort is required to define its parameters.

Voice or speech analytics

This is the process of extracting information from audio recordings of conversations. Voice analytics can be used to analyse the topics or actual words and phrases being used (content), as well as the emotions behind that conversation (sentiment). You could, for example, use voice analytics to help to identify recurring themes regarding employee satisfaction, or, in the case of a customer call centre, employee performance. Voice analytics also can help you to identify when your employees are getting frustrated or angry. By analysing the pitch and intonations of conversations taking place in your call centre, you can gauge the emotional state and performance of customer-service representatives and identify those who are top performers, as well as those who may need additional training or coaching.

Predictive analytics

Predictive analytics uses data, statistical modelling and machine learning (see Chapter 2) to predict the likelihood of future outcomes based on historical data. By understanding as much as we possibly can about what has happened in the past, it is possible to identify patterns and build models for working out what will happen in the future. This is an incredibly useful tool for working out how likely something is to happen and the level of risk, particularly when it comes to identifying when key personnel may be likely to leave. Google, for example, used this technique to work out that new sales people who do not get a promotion within four years are much more likely to leave the company.[3] As the volume of data we have and the computing power available are increasing all the time, our ability to predict future outcomes is improving too. Predictive analytics and tools like IBM Watson are therefore becoming increasingly popular with businesses of all sizes.

Looking at critical HR analytics

Having just looked at the general categories of data analytics being used today, it is worth us spending some time on the specific types of people analytics available to HR teams. Usually, these people analytics options make use of the techniques already outlined in this chapter, eg capability analytics (the first option we look at below) might make use of text analytics to analyse questionnaire or interview answers. It should be said that there are very many different types of people analytics, but some add more value than others. Based on my experience of working with HR teams, the following are the most important and useful people-related analytics being used by HR teams and managers to better understand their people (see Figure 5.2).

Capability analytics

The success of any business depends on the level of expertise and skill of its workforce. Capability analytics is a talent management process that allows you to identify the capabilities or core competencies you want and need in your business. Once you know what those capabilities are you can then analyse your current staff members to see if you have any capabilities gaps. Capabilities, of course, do not just mean qualifications and skills – they also include capabilities that may not be formally recognized, such as the ability to develop and maintain relationships.

Figure 5.2   Critical HR analytics

Capability analytics	Corporate culture analytics
Competency acquisition analytics	Recruitment channel analytics
Capacity analytics	Leadership analytics
Employee churn analytics	Employee performance analytics

Why use capability analytics?

Knowing what skills you need and what you already have in your business can alert you to issues you may not have been aware of, allowing you to retrain or support individuals to close those gaps more effectively. Too often we hire new employees without really knowing exactly what skills we already have and what additional skills we need. As a result, we hire based on gut instinct, what is written on a CV or how well or otherwise someone comes across in an interview. There may be a laundry list of 'ideal candidate characteristics' but they are often generic personality issues such as 'honesty' and 'integrity' rather than 'capability in X software' etc. When these new recruits join the business, you may hope that they will fit in and work well with the existing team, but if you are unsure exactly what capability you expect them to bring to the table beyond being another pair of hands, then you end up being disappointed with the appointment. Capability analytics helps to avoid this scenario so that you know exactly what you need, what you have and what additional capabilities you may need to recruit (or what additional training you need to provide for those that are already in the business) to close that gap. I would say capability analytics is especially important if your business, industry or market is changing quickly.

It is always wise to conduct capability analytics at least once a year and certainly before every significant or important appointment. For existing employees, capability analytics can slot into the performance review process to inform ongoing training and improvement initiatives. It is also sensible to run capability analytics if your business is changing and moving into a new area or slightly different direction that will require additional or different capabilities. Knowing who can do what will also help you to move people around the business as appropriate, and provide additional training or support to those who could adapt to a new role or position. Just because someone is doing one job now does not mean they do not have the capability to do another. But you will not know what someone is fully capable of unless you conduct capability analytics.

How to use capability analytics

Capability analytics can be conducted via questionnaires, as well as by interviewing the individual being assessed and the people who work with them closely. Say, for example, you are an IT manufacturer. The speed of change in the IT industry, in terms of both the technological capabilities of the machines we use and buying behaviour, means that it is a highly volatile industry. Just a decade ago the industry was riding high, manufacturing large mainframe computers as well as smaller machines for the personal-use market. But the advent of cloud computing has massively changed the market. By conducting detailed capability analytics, you realize the capabilities that made you a dominant force in the last decade will render you obsolete in the next. To stem this potentially disastrous outcome, you create a competency framework for your business outlining specific and generic capabilities. For example, you might appreciate that everyone in the business needs to improve their 'customer focus' competency. In addition, you might appreciate that, within your specialist IT centres, you need to focus on big data competencies, including Hadoop skills and cloud computing skills that do not currently exist in the business. This competency framework helps the HR team to source appropriate training and/or recruit new employees to kick-start the skill shift.

While skills and capabilities are critical to success, remember that team fit, cultural fit and existing relationships are also very important. It is therefore often much easier to keep all that and retrain personnel to create the capability needed, rather than find the capability and hope that individual then fits into the culture or team.

Competency acquisition analytics

Competency acquisition analytics is the process of assessing how well or otherwise your business acquires talent. This is done by identifying key competencies that are vital to your organization's success and then measuring how effective you are at attracting those competencies. Competencies may refer to specific skills or knowledge (like data analytics skills) or certain attributes or behaviours (such as leadership qualities or the ability to work well with others).

Why use competency acquisition analytics?

Talent recruitment and management are critically important for the growth of most businesses. The competition for talent is fierce and talented people can be very expensive to recruit and keep. Competency acquisition analytics helps you to assess how successful your talent strategy is and how well (or otherwise) your business acquires talent. Competency acquisition analytics should be something you assess at least every year to see how well your business is doing at: 1) identifying the competencies you need and want; and 2) finding those competencies cost-effectively.

It can be relatively easy to identify key players in any industry and, if your business has deep pockets, those individuals often can be attracted to your business. But individuals who only take a role because of the money will probably not stay that long or fully engage in the vision of the business. Finding ways to identify talent before it is fully fledged is key and competency acquisition analytics allows you to do that. It is therefore important to know how well your business is performing in the task of identifying talent early before stepping in to secure it at a reasonable price.

How to use competency acquisition analytics

A good starting point is to identify the key competencies your business requires now and in the future in order to stay competitive. This identification can be achieved using a number of tools and techniques such as text analytics, focus groups, interviews and surveys. Remember, as well as job-specific skills and knowledge, behaviours and attributes are just as important (if not more so). Depending on specific jobs and the organization's goals, these attributes may include:

- communication skills;
- teamwork;
- coping with change;
- analytical thinking;
- conceptual thinking;
- managerial qualities like the ability to motivate and support others.

The next step is to assess the current levels of these competencies within your business and the gap between what you would like to have in terms of competencies and what you actually have at present. Then it is a good idea to create regular assessments so that you can track your progress in acquiring these key competencies over time, such as how effective you are at spotting and recruiting candidates with those competencies, how well you are able to close the competency gaps and which competencies are proving most difficult to acquire.

A great example of this in action comes from the world of baseball. You are probably familiar with the story from the book and film *Moneyball*. As in many sports, historically new baseball talent was 'spotted' by experts and talent scouts who would travel around the country watching baseball games in the hope they would be able to identify an up-and-coming star. The process was very subjective and, for the most part, it came down to experience and luck. Baseball advisor Bill James changed all that. He developed a scientific evidence-based approach to 'spotting' new baseball talent that broke a player's behaviour and actions down into multiple measurable elements.[4] Billy Beane, the general manager of the Oakland Athletics (aka Oakland A's) baseball team heard about James's theory and decided to work with him to acquire competency or talent. James's hypothesis worked. Despite having the third-lowest payroll in the league, the Oakland A's team was able to buy under-valued talent that took the club all the way to the playoffs in 2002 and 2003.[5] Prior to this data-driven approach, the club simply was unable to successfully compete with deep-pocketed baseball clubs like the New York Yankees. Competency acquisition analytics changed all that, and changed the club's fortune.

A final word of warning: competency acquisition analytics is only going to be successful if you are able to effectively identify and track competencies in your organization. Many companies do not concentrate on the vital (or difficult to get) competencies and instead produce generic competency frameworks that make the process of tracking and assessing competencies very complex and cumbersome. Key to effective competency acquisition analytics is focusing on a *small* set of *absolutely key* competencies.

Capacity analytics

Capacity affects revenue, which should make it a key focal point of intelligent HR. Capacity analytics seeks to establish how operationally efficient individual employees are in a business, eg are people spending too much time on administration and not enough on more profitable work, or are individuals stretched far too thinly? It also allows businesses to establish how much capacity they have to grow, allowing HR teams to identify patterns and trends in employee performance that then can be used to improve recruitment or training and development.

Why use capacity analytics?

If you do not know what your people are doing, you cannot manage those employees' capacity appropriately. A consultant operating at full capacity, who is asked to pick up the slack with a new client, may end up stressed, unhappy and potentially look to leave the company. Meanwhile, another consultant who is spending too much time on administration tasks is not being as productive or profitable as you need them to be. Obviously, people are people, not machines, so an individual's capacity will fluctuate throughout the year based on a variety of factors. These peaks and troughs of productivity are normal; however, capacity analytics can help to alert you to negative or worrying productivity trends. This analysis allows you to then step in with additional training or support to help the individual get back on track before they become too demoralized or negative.

How to use capacity analytics

As long as you have a system that tracks data on how people spend their time, you can use these data to establish capacity levels. The data can come from time-tracking systems (where people clock in and out) or from sensors (such as sensors in name badges, as mentioned in Chapter 4). Say you are a software engineering company and you have 20 software engineers working in your business. Capacity analytics allows you to track how much time they actually spend coding and how much time they do other work. This ratio then can be tracked over time to ensure the actual time spent (obviously relative to the billable output) on programming is not going down. It also allows the company to understand how much capacity it has to take on new projects. If everyone is at 100 per cent capacity then taking on any more work is not advisable unless capacity can be increased by recruiting new staff.

Fortune cited one real-life example of a manufacturing company that discovered some of its junior managers were spending upwards of 30 hours a week 'managing up', ie attending status meetings or giving reports to senior executives.[6] Clearly, that left them only around 10 hours a week for getting on with revenue-generating work. Using this knowledge, the company has now implemented a strict policy of fewer meetings. The tricky part is establishing these systems without creating huge administrative burdens and without alienating employees with a 'Big Brother' approach. Capacity analytics can make people very nervous, so be careful how you represent capacity analytics to your people. The idea is not to find out who needs to be whipped into doing more work but rather to identify gaps in capacity that then can be closed to increase profit.

Employee churn analytics

Your employees are your most important and often most expensive asset. Using analytics to assess capability and hiring the people with the right capabilities is just part of the process. You also have got to keep them. Hiring employees, training them and then integrating them into the business costs time and money. When that investment is lost because too many employees are leaving, this can have a detrimental impact on the business. Plus, high staff turnover levels can be extremely disruptive to the remaining team members and lead to a decrease in morale and staff productivity.

Why use employee churn analytics?

Employee churn analytics is the process of assessing your historic staff turnover rates in an attempt to predict the future, so that you can intervene earlier and reduce churn. While some employee churn can be desirable to prevent stagnation, it is important to identify a healthy level of churn and develop a system to pinpoint the 'regrettable' churn. Some businesses have higher staff turnover than others. Call centres, for example, have notoriously high staff turnover, especially compared to a more traditional industry like manufacturing. In fact, some estimates put call-centre turnover as high as 30–45 per cent.[7] Depending on the volatility of your business, you should track employee churn analytics every six months or annually. Essentially, you need to know the trend, ie is there more, less or stable employee churn in your business? If the trend is heading up then this can provide a red flag for further investigation to stabilize turnover or even reduce it further.

How to use employee churn analytics

Historical employee churn can be identified through traditional key performance indicators (KPIs) such as the employee satisfaction index (ESI), employee engagement level and staff advocacy score. In addition, surveys, exit interviews, performance reviews and social-media data can help to gather further information that then can be mined (perhaps using text analytics) for greater insights. Historical employee churn rates can be useful as a benchmark but the real value lies in comparing your business against industry averages, seeking to identify patterns in employee churn in your business and, most useful of all, applying different analytics techniques to understand *why* people are leaving. Once you know why, you can predict employee churn in the future and, most importantly, take any necessary internal action that could solve the problem and keep employees engaged.

One example of this in action can be seen on the Watson Analytics blog.[8] The use case describes how a simple analysis by IBM's Watson platform of data on past and current employees can be used to identify factors that are related to employee attrition and predict how job role and performance evaluation relate to employee churn, based on the data from employees who have left the company. Overtime, job level, number of years with the current manager and employee age were all significant drivers of employee churn. It also broke the data down by job role, showing that people in an HR role or management position were more likely to stay with the company than people who worked in sales or quality control. And, in this case, employees who worked more than 15 hours of overtime a week were most likely to leave the company. This may seem like a reasonable assumption for any HR professional to make: people who feel overworked are more likely to leave. But one of the critical things about data-driven HR is basing decisions on data rather than gut reactions. In this case, the data proved beyond doubt that the number of overtime hours was a significant driver of employee churn, allowing the HR team to make intelligent, evidence-based decisions to tackle this and prevent future employee churn.

You may have guessed by now that I am not the biggest fan of annual employee surveys. If you are using annual surveys to measure your employees, I believe you are almost certainly missing valuable data. A better way to use employee surveys, instead of getting all your employees to complete a survey once a year, is to invite one-tenth of the workforce to complete the survey every month for 10 months. In this way, everyone still only completes the survey once a year but you have 10 data points not one, giving you a picture of an employee churn trend, which can allow you to make in-time corrections to minimize employee churn.

Corporate culture analytics

Culture is notoriously difficult to pinpoint and even harder to change. Culture is not something that can be hung on the wall like a values statement, it shows up as the collective actions of the people in the business. Corporate culture analytics helps you to assess and understand more about your corporate culture, or the different cultures that exist across your organization, which then allows you to:

- track changes in culture that you would like to make;
- understand how the culture is changing;
- create early warning systems to detect toxic cultures in their development;
- ensure you are recruiting people who do not clash with the corporate culture.

Why use corporate culture analytics?

Essentially, corporate culture analytics can allow you to uncover the genuine culture of the business in order to amplify the good bits and help change the unhelpful parts. Part of the reason why culture is so difficult to change is that the people in the business do not fully appreciate what it is to start with. This type of analytics can lift the lid on culture, which, in turn, can influence strategy. Corporate culture is usually fairly stable. Once you have assessed it initially, you can then put systems in place to track key elements of that culture in an ongoing fashion, using data collections to create early warning systems of a mismatch between the culture you would like to have and what the data are showing you.

How to use corporate culture analytics

Perhaps the most common tools for culture analytics are surveys, focus-group research and employee interviews. The challenge with these approaches is that people can tell you what they think you want to hear; plus they can be expensive. There are now many more analytics tools that can be used to give a better and more accurate insight into corporate culture. You can, for example, collect data from internal intranet sites, social media and internal written communication, and analyse them using text analytics and sentiment analysis. Customer-service conversations also can provide a rich vein of data for assessing corporate culture. If you record customer-service conversations, or interactions between employees, these data can give some very useful insights into corporate culture. You can apply voice analytics to these data or text analytics and sentiment analysis tools. Say, for example, you believe that your corporate culture is efficient but fun. You may think that your business operates like a family, with a strong focus on excellent customer service, and those are values that have been driven home to employees. Your orientation for new recruits draws their attention to these values and the corporate culture that you believe exists. But what happens after six months, are those employees embodying these values or is something else calling the shots? You could ask your new employee or you could conduct annual surveys, but the quickest way to get to the truth is to assess what your employees are saying and doing as part of their day-to-day life, perhaps through activity data or conversation data: this is your culture. If you believe you are driven by high-quality customer service and yet no one answers the phone after 4.45 pm, chances are that culture is not quite as real as you would like it to be.

Recruitment channel analytics

As an HR professional, you will know that employees represent both the greatest cost and the greatest opportunity in most businesses. Plus, getting recruitment wrong can be really problematic for a business. A poor employee can disrupt a team and cause upset as others need to cover for their poor performance, which of course can increase employee churn. And, sadly, it is usually not the person you want to get rid of that leaves. Recruitment channel analytics is the process of working out where your best employees come from and what recruitment channels are most effective. It can help to ensure you recruit the right people from the start.

Why use recruitment channel analytics?

There are many ways to recruit employees, such as print advertising, advertisements in specialist journals or magazines, online recruitment websites and recruitment consultants. Their costs vary widely and the time required to recruit through these various channels also varies significantly. Knowing which ones are working and which channels are most cost-effective is therefore important for ongoing recruitment. The purpose of recruitment channel analytics is to allow you to use only those channels that yield high-value candidates. Traditionally, recruitment success has been measured by simply counting the number of applications delivered or the number of positions filled. Modern recruitment, however, is full of data and allows us to track reach, engagement, costs per appropriate candidate etc. But the ultimate measure is how many people are successfully recruited and actually stay with your organization.

How to use recruitment channel analytics

Recruitment analytics will involve some historical assessment of employee value using standard KPIs such as return per employee

(RPE). These KPIs will help you to identify who your most productive and valuable employees are. Surveys, entry interviews, aggregator sites like Glassdoor and social-media sites also can be used to gather more data. You can then use these data to identify patterns or connections between high-value recruits and recruitment channels. The best results tend to come from mixing qualitative and quantitative insights, eg mixing referral rates, quality of candidate, quality of hire, and candidate and manager satisfaction with measures like cost to hire and time to hire. Say, for example, you use a recruitment consultant to help you hire for more senior positions. While they do help you to find suitable candidates and they pre-screen those candidates, saving you valuable time, the costs can really add up. Using recruitment channel analytics, you may identify that online recruitment overall is more effective. Further analysis also may show that your most high-value candidates always held positions prior to starting with you for three years or longer. These insights then can be used to fine-tune the assessment process and discount candidates who do not meet that criterion.

Leadership analytics

Poor leadership, whether of the whole organization or a specific team, costs money and holds the company back from fulfilling its potential. If a leader is not great at empowering and engaging their employees then this will impact on results, productivity and profit.

Why use leadership analytics?

Leadership analytics seeks to uncover how good leadership is in your business. So much of leadership is subjective. We are told that great leaders are born not made but is that really true? Leadership analytics unpacks the various dimensions of leadership performance via data to uncover the good, the bad and the ugly. Leadership is best assessed on an ongoing basis but, if that is not possible, then you can assess it at regular intervals, eg every six months or so. If someone is new to a leadership role, then it is probably wise to perform leadership analytics more frequently to track their early progress, which will allow you to pick up any failings early so as to get the individual back on track.

How to use leadership analytics

Data about leadership performance can be gained through the use of surveys, focus groups, employee interviews and possibly employee conversation data. Where you are directly asking employees for input, it is advisable to make the data collection anonymous so that employees can really open up. Few employees would feel confident or safe talking about their leader or manager if they knew that person may have access to their opinion. It is also possible to conduct behaviour profiling of leaders. Really good leaders tend to demonstrate certain personality traits or characteristics. These can be generic attributes or you can analyse your existing leadership to identify what the really good ones have that the less successful ones do not. These insights can be used to direct training and support programmes, as well as the recruitment process. Text analytics is a very powerful way of extracting key leadership characteristics, both of good and not so good leaders. You also can use financial metrics (ie turnover and profit demonstrate how the company is performing financially under the leadership), as well as data such as employee satisfaction or churn in assessing leadership.

In Chapter 2 we briefly looked at how Google used data and analytics to assess and increase the value of managers in its organization. Here we revisit that example by looking in detail at how it worked in practice. In an effort to raise leadership performance, Google set out to answer two questions: 1) What is it that makes a great manager? and 2) What are the behaviours that make managers struggle?[9] Based on some extensive leadership performance analytics, including interviews with its managers, 360-degree feedback surveys of its employees and regression analysis of things such as job performance and employee satisfaction, Google was able to identify eight behaviours that make a great manager:

1 is a good coach;

2 empowers the team and does not micromanage;

3 expresses interest/concern for team members' success and personal wellbeing;

4 is productive and results-oriented;

5 is a good communicator: listens and shares information;

6 helps with career development;

7 has a clear vision/strategy for the team;

8 has important technical skills that help them to advise the team.

In addition, the research alerted Google to the top three reasons why managers were struggling in their role:

1 having a tough transition (eg suddenly promoted or hired from outside with little training);

2 lacking a consistent philosophy/approach to performance management and career development;

3 spending too little time on managing and communicating.

Acting on these valuable insights, Google now gears the 360-degree feedback surveys for managers around these aspects and conducts them twice a year, thereby instigating an early warning system to detect both great and struggling managers. In addition, Google has revised its management training and recruitment in light of its findings.

While there are some generic leadership assessment models that you could use in your business, it is always better to create your own model based on which leadership characteristics you value in your particular corporate culture. Draw on data and insights from other analytics tools, such as employee performance analytics (which I will look at next) and corporate culture analytics, to help you establish what makes a great leader in *your* business. This was why Google was so successful in its quest to identify leadership excellence: it took the time to figure out what leadership excellence looked like in its unique culture first.

Employee performance analytics

Your business needs capable, high-performing employees in order to survive and thrive. Unless you measure performance, it easily can get lost in the day-to-day operations of the business. A poor employee can effectively be carried by a productive one, which will eventually irritate the productive employee. Your job is to know who is doing what and who needs support so that you can provide that support and lift performance across the board, which is where employee performance analytics can help you.

Why use employee performance analytics?

Employee performance analytics seeks to assess individual employee performance. The resulting insights can identify who is performing well and who may need some additional training or support in order to raise their game. An understanding of employee performance also can feed into the recruitment process so more of the right types of employees are recruited and costly mistakes are avoided. Most companies assess employee performance annually, but, in this world of big data, just once a year is not enough. In order to be effective, performance should be assessed on a regular and less formal basis, and modern data collection methods allow us to collect data from many different sources to aid in the assessment.

How to use employee performance analytics

Today, we have many innovative ways of collecting and analysing performance, ranging from crowdsourced performance assessments to sensors in employee badges, like the Sociometric Solutions badges we saw in Chapter 4. These data can be analysed in a number of ways, including text analytics, sentiment analysis and voice analytics. Such analyses may help to identify any patterns that you may not have been conscious of, which can be used to improve ongoing performance. For example, one of Sociometric Solutions' clients, a major bank, noticed that its top-performing employees at call centres were those who took breaks together. Based on this knowledge, the bank instituted group break policies and performance improved by 23 per cent.[10]

Employee performance analytics can be particularly useful in businesses that traditionally have a high staff turnover, such as call centres. It is important to understand the different call lengths for each operative, how many calls they get through per hour, how many of their calls escalate into issues and how many end in resolution and a happy customer. These and countless other data points also allow you to detect patterns, and identify your star performers so that what they do can be replicated by others. These insights also can be used to fine-tune customer processes, recruitment, and training and develop-ment initiatives, so that you get more great employees and fewer poor ones. Not only does this improve results, but it also can significantly reduce staff turnover and recruitment costs.

If done well, performance analytics provides a positive experience that contributes to the overall employment and career development experience and helps to strengthen the relationship between line managers and their staff; however, be aware that, whenever you moni-tor the performance of employees, the monitoring itself will affect performance. Usually when people know that specific elements of their job are monitored, they make sure they perform particularly well at them. This can skew their attention away from simply doing a good job to simply focusing on the things that are being monitored and analysed, which is why modern data capture techniques such as video and sensor data are so helpful. Using these techniques, it is possible to analyse performance more holistically, being less focused on specific parts of a job that might cause the employee to skew their behaviour.

Combining analytics to get the best results

Often, to get the most out of data-driven HR, you will not be able to rely on one analytics tool alone. Just as we saw in Chapter 4, while it is usually a good idea to combine different data sets to get a fuller picture, the value of HR analytics lies in the insights that can be gained from combining different types of analytics. For example, corporate culture analytics may tell you that your culture is moving away from the values you have prioritized, but you may need text and sentiment analysis to tell you why that is. The idea behind combining analytics is to base your decision making and HR operations not just on what one set of analysis is telling you. Combining information from more than one source and using different analytics approaches allow you to verify insights from more than one angle.

All the approaches I have outlined in this chapter show only some of the analytics possibilities available to HR teams today. Just a few years ago, much of this was not possible; we could not do sentiment analysis on text, for example. Analytics in particular has made such huge leaps that no one knows for sure what is going to be possible in 10 or even 5 years' time. Therefore, an important part of data-driven or intelligent HR is staying open to new opportunities that data and analytics may provide further down the road.

Turning data and analytics into insights

Data are only really valuable if you can turn them into insights and actionable knowledge. By analysing your people-related data using some of the analytics methods outlined in this chapter, you should arrive at various insights. Presenting these insights in a helpful way to the people that need them is a key step in turning insights into actionable knowledge. After all, businesses gain competitive advantage when the *right information* is delivered to the *right people* at the *right time*.

Who needs access to the insights you uncover?

For each objective outlined in your strategic plan and each data set related to those objectives, you will need to ask yourself: who are the decision makers who require access to the insights from those data? In some cases, it will be just those within the HR team, while in others it will be the leadership team or managers across the business. It is important to involve all the key players that relate to the business's goals and strategic questions. What is the best way to disseminate insights to the people that need them? It depends on what you are measuring, who needs to know about it and how you usually communicate across the company. You could, for instance, have an indicator (such as employee performance) included in a monthly report that is distributed to the people who need it. Or, you may need more sophisticated, real-time information in the form of a dashboard that allows decision makers to access information whenever and wherever they want; indeed, this kind of democratized approach to data is becoming increasingly more common. According to a survey of 2,000 employees in the United Kingdom and United States,[11] more than half of respondents said that knowing company performance data contributed significantly to their own positive performance. In other words, employees want to be included in discussions about overall business performance and that means, in an ideal world, key data would be communicated across every level of the business.

How best to disseminate insights

But even when people have widespread access to data and the insights generated from them, they do not always interpret those data in the same way, and this means they may need help extracting key messages. A blended approach therefore may work best for your company, combining widespread access to data across the company, where people are encouraged to use data as the basis of future business decisions, *as well as* a strong overarching narrative that sets out key insights and trends, just to be sure that the most critical messages are understood by everyone. However you decide to disseminate the information, keep in mind that the format in which it is presented plays a big role in how useful that information will be. People are less likely to act if they have to work hard to understand what the information is telling them. It is therefore vital that insights are presented in a clear, concise and interesting way.

Communicating and visualizing insights from data

Data-driven HR is about turning people-relevant data into insights and actions that add value to the business. In order to do this successfully, you need to ensure it is easy for the various decision makers, whoever they may be, to extract insights from the data. The easier it is to understand the data and pull out key insights, the easier it is for people both within the HR team and beyond to make decisions and act on those data. This is why data communication and specifically data visualization have become such big topics in recent years.

There are many different options for communicating data, from simple graphics and written reports, through commercial data visualization platforms that make the data attractive and easy to understand, to management dashboards that provide your people with the information they need whenever they need it. Different audiences have different needs, in terms of both the types of data they need and how they will use them. Therefore, when thinking about disseminating and communicating data, it is important to define who will have access to those data (or the insights from those data) and what their needs are. For example, what format works best for your data consumers? How will they access the information (web interface, reports, dashboards etc) and how often? Knowing the answers to these questions will help you to decide on the right visualization/communication tools for your needs. Data visualization tools are particularly helpful because they can very clearly highlight the most important data or results and help to identify trends in the data. There are now many excellent and inexpensive data visualization tools, like Tableau, Qlik or Google's Analytics 360 suite. In addition, many commercial analytics platforms come with their own built-in visualization tools.

Visuals are great for conveying information because they are quick and direct, and they are far more interesting to look at than a page of text. But, unless we know how to decode its message, a picture also can be difficult to read. Words, on the other hand, usually have a very direct meaning and are simple to understand. With a short narrative you can ensure everyone understands the data in the same way. This is why using visuals and narratives together is much more powerful than using either on their own. For instance, a graph may be a good way of showing employee churn trends over time, but a simple narrative alongside it can pull out the key messages and put that information into context, explaining what might be behind those trends and why there was a spike in churn in late 2016, for example.

Key takeaways

I am aware that this has been a pretty chunky chapter, with lots of new information to process. The following is a quick rundown of the key points on data analytics:

- The key analytics techniques can be broadly categorized as:
  - text analytics;
  - sentiment analysis;
  - image analytics;

- video analytics;
- voice or speech analytics;
- predictive analytics.

- In my experience, some of the most useful and valuable HR-specific analytics are:
  - capability analytics;
  - competency acquisition analytics;
  - capacity analytics;
  - employee churn analytics;
  - corporate culture analytics;
  - recruitment channel analytics;
  - leadership analytics;
  - employee performance analytics.

- To get the most out of data-driven HR, you probably will not be able to rely on one analytics tool alone. Often, the value of HR analytics lies in the insights that can be gained from *combining* different types of analytics.

- Data are only really valuable if you can turn them into insights and actionable knowledge. Businesses gain competitive advantage when the *right information* is delivered to the *right people* at the *right time*.

- The easier it is to understand the data and pull out key insights, the easier it is for people both within the HR team and beyond to make decisions and act on those data.

- Data visualization tools are particularly helpful because they can very clearly highlight the most important data or results and help to identify trends in the data.

Clearly, there are many new and exciting ways to use data and analytics across HR functions. But with these new and exciting methods comes increased risks. Part of using data intelligently is ensuring that they are properly protected and that employees' privacy is not violated. Transparency, data governance and data protection are therefore vital things every HR team needs to consider. In the next chapter I explore the various pitfalls and risks concerning data usage, and set out good practice for avoiding those pitfalls.

Endnotes

1 US Department of Homeland Security (2014) [accessed 23 October 2017] Rapid Screening Tool: the Avatar [Online] https://www.dhs.gov/sites/default/files/publications/Rapid%20Screening%20Tool-NCBSI-AVATAR-Jan2014.pdf

2 Shrestha, K (2015) [accessed 01 February 2018] Hard hat detection for construction safety visualization, *Journal of Construction Engineering*, [Online] http://dx.doi.org/10.1155/2015/721380

3 Van Vulpen, E [accessed 23 October 2017] Predictive Analytics in Human Resources [Online] https://www.analyticsinhr.com/blog/predictive-analytics-human-resources

4 Adams, M (2015) [accessed 23 October 2017] The Man behind Moneyball: the Billy Beane Story [Online] https://www.domo.com/blog/the-man-behind-moneyball-the-billy-beane-story

5 Lewis, M (2004) [accessed 23 October 2017] *Moneyball* [Online] http://michaellewiswrites.com/index.html#moneyball

6 Clancy, H (2015) [accessed 23 October 2017] What Can Big Data Reveal about Corporate Culture? Get Ready for 'People Analytics' [Online] http://fortune.com/2015/03/20/analytics-corporate-culture

7 Reynolds, P (2015) [accessed 23 October 2017] Exploring Call Center Turnover Numbers [Online] http://www.qatc.org/winter-2015-connection/exploring-call-center-turnover-numbers

8 Alexander, F (2015) [accessed 23 October 2017] Watson Analytics Use Case for HR: Retaining Valuable Employees [Online] https://www.ibm.com/communities/analytics/watson-analytics-blog/watson-analytics-use-case-for-hr-retaining-valuable-employees

9 Blodget, H (2011) [accessed 23 October 2017] 8 Habits of Highly Effective Google Managers [Online] http://www.businessinsider.com/8-habits-of-highly-effective-google-managers-2011-3

10 Kuchler, H (2014) [accessed 23 October 2017] Data Pioneers Watching Us Work [Online] https://www.ft.com/content/d56004b0-9581-11e3-9fd6-00144feab7de?mhq5j=e6

11 Whittick, S (2015) [accessed 23 October 2017] Research Report: One in Four Employees Leave due to Mushroom Management [Online] https://www.geckoboard.com/blog/research-report-one-in-four-employees-leave-due-to-mushroom-management/#.V2GV1sdcJ6A

Potential pitfalls: 06
looking at data
privacy, transparency
and security

Today's HR departments are collecting, or have the potential to collect, huge amounts of data, and this can bring great rewards for those who use those data intelligently. But, data also bring their own unique challenges. Therefore, before implementing any intelligent HR approach, it is important to consider the potential pitfalls and legal issues that surround employee-related data, particularly when it comes to employees' personal data. In this chapter I look at data privacy requirements, ethical issues and the need for transparency, and data security considerations. Collectively, all these factors come under what is known as 'data governance', and I finish the chapter with some practical steps for good data governance. This is absolutely vital because practising good data governance will help to ensure that your HR data remain a valuable asset, and do not turn into a liability. Before we get started, please do keep in mind that these are all huge topics in their own right and the regulatory landscape is changing. Specialist legal advice is therefore recommended.

Understanding which data you have

You cannot properly protect data or practise good data governance if you are not entirely sure which data you have. This can be a challenge for HR teams in particular because employee-related data can be housed in all sorts of departments and systems outside of the HR team itself. Think of payroll data, for instance, or data related to performance, targets and incentives. Therefore, an important first step in data governance is being aware of all the people-related data owned by your organization, including where those data reside, exactly which data are involved (critically, do they include personally identifiable information?), who those data are divulged to, how those data are processed or analysed and how they are then used within the organization. Do not forget to consider any data that may be used or processed by third parties (a payroll company, for instance) or anything stored with off-site data providers or in the cloud.

The thorny issue of data privacy

I am not a lawyer and, at the time of writing, European legislation on personal data and individuals' right to privacy is changing significantly. On top of that, data privacy laws vary greatly around the world. For instance, the European Union (EU) arguably has the most stringent rules, and in the United States it can vary from state to state. It is therefore vital that any HR team gathering sensitive personal data makes sure it is operating within the laws of its country. Even within the relatively strict EU, it is fair to say that legislation has failed to keep pace with the speed at which technology has advanced and our ability to gather, store and analyse huge volumes of data. But that situation is changing. New EU regulation coming into effect in May 2018 – called GDPR, or the General Data Protection Regulation – is designed to enhance data protection and the right to privacy for EU citizens, giving them greater control over their personal data and how they are used.[1]

What about Brexit, I hear you ask. Well, at the time of writing, the indications are that GDPR still will be implemented into UK law – although, as with anything involving Brexit, this is a complex issue that is subject to change. However, I stress that GDPR covers the data of *EU citizens*, so, regardless of what happens with UK law, if your company touches data related to any EU citizens, you will absolutely have to comply with GDPR.

Looking at the impact of GDPR on HR teams

GDPR represents a complete overhaul of the legal requirements that must be met by any company handling the personal data of EU citizens, including employee data. Designed to give EU citizens greater control over what businesses can do with their personal data, the law states that companies can only use personal data for the *express purpose* for which it was given. Consent is therefore a critical pillar of GDPR. Customers and employees must explicitly opt in to allow a company to use their personal data, and they must be made fully aware of how those data will be used. Privacy policies will also have to be updated as there is a requirement for companies to make individuals aware of their new rights under GDPR.

The need for data consent

In light of the changes, it is vital you ensure the correct permissions are in place that allow you to use your people-related data in the way you intend – and *only* in the way you intend. More than one company has been tripped up in the past by invasive data collection strategies, collecting all manner of data that seemingly were not relevant to the service or product users had signed up to. Spotify is one such example. In 2015, the company released a new privacy policy that read more like the demands of a jealous partner than a music service. Among the new terms, Spotify claimed the right to go through your phone and access your photos, media files, global positioning system (GPS) location, sensor data (like how fast you are walking) and your contacts. It also announced it would share these data with advertisers, music rights holders, mobile networks and other 'business partners'.[2] Of course, the free version of the service is supported by advertising revenue, but these terms also applied to the platform's many millions of paid users. The reaction from users was swift and negative. A huge outcry erupted on Twitter and other social-networking sites, with users saying they would leave the service rather than agree to the new terms. Part of the problem stemmed from the fact that the new privacy policy was extremely vague about exactly which data were being collected, when, why and with whom they were being shared. The huge backlash against this lack of transparency prompted the company's CEO, Daniel Ek, to issue an apology and clarify the company's position and intentions.[3] This included the promise that: 'We will ask for your express permission before accessing any of this data – and we will only use it for specific purposes that will allow you to customize your Spotify experience'.[3]

Total transparency is therefore important when it comes to using people's data, and that is something I talk about in more detail later in the chapter. From a consent and GDPR point of view, however, what this means is being upfront with your employees about which data are being collected and for what purpose, and how those data will be used in practice. This can be clarified through a simple data privacy statement distributed to employees.

As stated, you also need to get employees' express permission to collect and use the data in question. It used to be that consent was assumed as part and parcel of employment, but that is no longer the case. Under GDPR, HR teams will now need to get employees' specific consent (eg a signed consent form) for processing personal data. Crucially, you can then only use the data for the purpose for which they were handed over. If you want to use the data for a different purpose, new permission will be required. Companies which fall foul of this regulation and are found to be misusing personal information face stiff fines of up to 20 million euros or 4 per cent of annual worldwide turnover, whichever is the greater of the two.

Other GDPR considerations

Under GDPR, employees also have the right to be forgotten and to withdraw their consent, so you will need to think through what this means for your systems. Do you have procedures in place for deleting employee data, for instance? How many systems would be affected? Can you be sure you are removing all traces? Does your team understand how important it is to comply with this regulation? These are all things that need to be considered as part of your data-driven HR strategy.

It is also very important you keep records of consent for gathering, storing and using employee data, as well as being able to demonstrate a clear business case for using the data. As another key point of compliance, companies must appoint a designated data protection officer (DPO), who should be properly skilled (or trained) and have an 'expert' level of understanding of the organization's responsibilities regarding GDPR. You should therefore involve your DPO in discussions about your plans for data-driven HR and they will be able to advise you on compliance and consent issues.

GDPR also sets out strict mandates concerning reporting the theft or loss of personal data. While, for most companies, this is more of an issue for customer data, be aware that employee-related data are still highly personal in nature. So, in the event of any breach that affects employee data, you will need to inform the supervising authority (in the United Kingdom that is the Information Commissioner's Office) within a maximum of 72 hours. You will also have to inform those individuals whose data are affected. There is more on data security and breaches later in the chapter.

What about those outside of the EU?

In the United States, regulation concerning the use of personal data may be a little less stringent, but there are still many things that can trip a company up. As Felix Wu, professor of law at the Benjamin N Cardozo School of Law, told me: 'Unlike Europe, the US does not have comprehensive privacy regulation, but this may actually make things more difficult for companies, which must comply with a patchwork of varying state and federal laws'.[4]

There are also specific things to consider if your business transfers data related to EU citizens to the United States. Say, if your company has a US office, or if a data analytics provider is based in the United States, or if your data travel through the United States as part of a distributed storage system, you will be affected by these data transfer rules. The transfer of personal data between the United States and EU used to be covered under something called the Safe Harbor Framework. This provided a set of principles for transferring data between US and EU companies, and was designed to streamline business interactions by ensuring minimal business interruptions. Unfortunately, it also arguably relaxed attitudes to privacy, which is why, in 2015, the Court of Justice of the European Union ruled that the Safe Harbor agreement was no longer valid.[5] The proposed solution is called Privacy Shield, and it provides a framework for US-based companies to demonstrate they can provide adequate protection in line with GDPR for EU citizens.[6] For HR teams, the takeaway is to ensure that any personal data flowing through the United States are being handled by companies which are compliant with Privacy Shield and GDPR policies.

Privacy implications in practice

Let us look at a specific example of employee data and the privacy implications for HR teams. If a company has the ability to analyse e-mail data, it can get at all sorts of valuable insights – not just about who is planning their Saturday night out on work time, but much more valuable information such as how happy and engaged people are with their work and with the company as an employer. Monitoring e-mails for sentiment allows a company to gather much more accurate information than, say, an employee survey, and it also allows for much more frequent analysis than only once a year. In the United States, such use of employee e-mail data may be subject to state-specific laws but, in the main, employees in the United States have no general right to privacy in the workplace. Things are a little stricter in the EU, and will tighten up further in 2018 when GDPR comes into effect.

As we have already seen in this chapter, under GDPR, employees who are EU citizens have a right to privacy and consent must be obtained before you can capture and use their data. And companies which ignore these rules face huge fines (not to mention potential backlash and damage to their reputation). But even in the EU, employers can monitor staff e-mails, other electronic messages and the websites visited during work hours, providing they have a good reason for doing so. In 2016, this was challenged in the European Court of Human Rights when a Romanian employee took his employer to court after they fired him for sending private Yahoo Messenger messages during work time.[7] The court ruled in favour of the employer, stating that it was not 'unreasonable' for the company to monitor the employee's communications, and that the employer's legitimate interest in carrying out such monitoring outweighed the individual's right to privacy.[7] But this decision does not give you carte blanche to read all employee communications just because you feel like it, or without telling them. Crucially, in this case, the court ruled that the employer's actions were 'limited in scope and proportionate'.[7] In other words, they had a legitimate reason for monitoring the employee's communications and their activity was limited to company resources, tied to a company policy regarding private communication and proportionate.

Telephone calls also may be monitored for business purposes. So, if your company operates a customer service or helpdesk call centre, you could be using the data gathered from those calls to assess and improve performance. Obviously, you need to obtain consent for monitoring calls, both from your customers and from your call-centre employees.

What this means for HR teams is that any monitoring of staff communications must be clearly explained in a privacy policy, employee handbook or contract and you should get employee consent for that monitoring. You need to make it very clear which data you are gathering in terms of e-mails, instant messages, website usage etc and *why* you are doing that. If there is no clear business reason for gathering the data, you should not be doing it. I would also steer well clear of messages that are obviously of a very personal nature and are not related to the business. Essentially, you should seek to strike a balance between the privacy of your employees and the needs of the business, and be transparent about what you are doing at all times.

Ethical issues and the need for transparency

As well as sitting on the right side of the law, HR teams also need to ensure their data usage sits within the ethical boundaries set by the company. Most companies these days emphasize a culture of openness and honesty, and your data-driven HR activities should not fly in the face of that culture. Clumsily implemented or poorly communicated data projects can do far more damage than good ones, potentially leading to serious issues with staff trust and morale. So it is important not to gloss over this aspect of data-driven HR. On the whole, we are all getting a lot more used to the wealth of data being collected and generated about us. When we sign up for a free online e-mail service, we acknowledge the e-mail provider's right to read those e-mails. When we use an app, we agree to the provider's right to use our location data, among other things. Or when we wear a fitness tracking band, like the Up band that I wear, we accept that the band will be gathering all sorts of data on our activities. The Internet of Things (IoT) – particularly the use of sensors being built into products – means we are all getting used to our everyday activities being tracked.

Why transparency is still important, even in this big data age

For a long time, I have been expecting a widespread backlash against large-scale data collection activities. In some cases, there have been complaints or protests against particularly dubious uses of data, usually when privacy policies are wilfully vague or when unethical companies misuse data. But it seems likely that, as we get more used to cameras, sensors, smart devices and other means of data collection, concerns will ease and people (employees included) will be more comfortable with companies collecting and using their data; however, this does not mean generating or gathering people-related data can be a free-for-all. As I have emphasized elsewhere in this chapter, you must have a clear business case for collecting data on your employees and this must be properly communicated. Transparency is one of the key pieces of advice I give to every company I work with. What this means in practice is employees need to be made aware of which data are being collected, why and what the company will use them for, ideally with a positive tone that emphasizes the benefits of these data. What you want is to achieve widespread buy-in for the use of data, from the top-level executives to frontline employees. It is easy for people to get on board with data when they understand how they will benefit the company and them as employees. Just as hundreds of millions of people are seemingly happy for Google to scan their e-mails in return for a free e-mail service, your employees are more likely to be happy with you using their data if they understand that information will be used to improve their working environment, for instance.

Getting buy-in for using data

Of course, how successful you are at gaining buy-in depends not just on how well you communicate the reasons and benefits for gathering data, but also the way in which you intend to use the data. If it is clear that the data are going to be used to whip people into working harder or as a disciplinary tool, you are facing an uphill battle. But that is not what intelligent, data-driven HR is about. It is not about creating a Big Brother culture and berating employees when they spend five minutes too long in the bathroom. It is about helping to drive the company forward and meet its strategic goals, which benefits everyone within the company. So, if you are looking to use sensor badges, for instance, to get an overview of how a job gets done or how interactions with colleagues or customers create a happier, more productive environment, that is a much more positive message for employees to buy into. Remember the bank in Chapter 5 which used Sociometric Solutions badges to identify that call-centre workers who took breaks together performed better? When the company instituted group breaks based on this insight, the whole team benefitted. This added value for the employees concerned as well as the company as a whole. And that is a critical point to make about data: transparency is vital, but so is adding value for employees. People are far happier for their data to be used when they feel they are getting something valuable in return, whether it is better working conditions, more effective management, a safer environment or something else.

In the same way, I do not mind Jawbone, the manufacturer of my Up fitness band, analysing my sleeping patterns, because the system helps me to monitor my health and wellbeing in real time. I also use the data from my band to recover faster between time zones, which actually is really helpful when I travel for business. And although I do not mind that Jawbone is collecting data on me, I do want to know the truth about what the company is doing with those data. If the data are aggregated with data collected from other people and not necessarily connected to me as an individual, I am fine with that because it can help us to understand more. For example, the data that Jawbone has collected on sleep alone are making huge in-roads into our collective understanding of sleep, insomnia and how sleep is impacted by various factors, and this has the potential to help a lot of people.[8–10]

The key to success in data-driven HR therefore is to be open about how you want to use the data you collect, to operate ethically and offer genuine value to your employees in return. When you provide value and can demonstrate a clear business case, most people will be happy, especially if the data are anonymized, that is, stripped of any personal markers that link an individual to the information (more on this later in the chapter).

Data democratization promotes transparency

Another aspect of data transparency is the democratization of data, as in sharing data with people within the organization wherever possible. This works on a couple of levels. First, if certain performance-related data can help to improve decision making across the business, it makes sense that the people who need those data have access to it. Second, sharing data promotes a more open culture, which, in turn, promotes greater buy-in. So, if you have the opportunity to share relevant data with areas of the business that can benefit from them, providing good data governance policies are in place, you should do so because it is a win-win situation. This could be as simple as sharing insights from data in the form of reports of visualizations (eg sharing insights from recruitment channel analytics or competency acquisition analytics with hiring managers). Or it could mean investing in dashboards or other reporting tools that allow people throughout the company to access, interrogate and manipulate data that are relevant to their job (eg managers having access to data from short pulse surveys on employee satisfaction, rather than waiting for the results of a lengthy annual survey).

Looking at security and data protection

An important part of data-driven or intelligent HR is making sure your data are secure and adequately protected from threats.

The devastating impact of data breaches

Data breaches can lead to huge losses for businesses, in terms of legal costs and financial compensation, as well as the damage done to a company's reputation. These days, it seems like barely a week goes by without reports of yet another large-scale loss or theft of personal data. The biggest headlines tend to focus on customer or user data, as opposed to employee data. The 2015 Ashley Madison hack is one example. The website is effectively a dating site for people who want to have extra-marital affairs (its own tagline is 'Life is short. Have an affair'). Back in 2015, hackers famously published personal details (including names and e-mail addresses) of 32 million of the site's members.[11] What is interesting about this example is that it was probably the first time the public at large became aware of the potential social consequences (as opposed to financial or political consequences) of poor data security. But even this particularly juicy example pales into insignificance compared to the kinds of breaches that could happen in the future.

Google, for example, has dedicated itself to learning how to build profiles of people from the information they input into its services. In reality it has done this by conditioning us to enter as many data as we possibly can. Our phones constantly report our location. Speech recognition systems store recordings of our vocal commands which can be analysed for insight into our emotional state and stress levels after they have filled their primary purpose of letting us tell Google what to do. The possibility of a data set such as this existing at all may be scary enough for many of us, but the consequences of it falling into the wrong hands could be catastrophic. Just considering the implications of a data leak on this scale is enough to make any business take data security extremely seriously.

If you think that no one would be interested in stealing your employee-related data (as opposed to, say, customer credit card details), think again. If they contain personally identifiable information, data of any kind can be valuable. Think about the types of data the average HR team has access to: names, addresses, passport or ID numbers, bank account details, employment histories, health information etc. If this got into the wrong hands, it not only could be potentially damaging and inconvenient for your employees, but also it could seriously tarnish your employer brand.

Keeping IoT threats in mind

The IoT and its ever-expanding network of connected devices present an extra layer of security concerns. The notion that computers need to be kept secure is now pretty much commonplace, but it is not quite so commonplace with smart devices and other IoT-enabled products. With the explosion in IoT devices like fitness bands, sensors in machinery etc, businesses are inevitably becoming more vulnerable to hacking. Many are now arguing that the same level of precautions that apply to computers also should apply to smart devices. The theory is simple: more devices mean more possible attack vectors for intruders who want data. The how and the why are a bit more complicated: what benefit would an attacker gain from taking control of a smart thermostat, for instance? Well, aside from causing mischief (which is certainly the main motive for a good deal of IoT hacking activity), the likelihood is that the hackers want to use it to take advantage of network vulnerabilities which would allow them to get at the real jackpot: other devices such as personal computers or phones which are far more likely to hold sensitive and valuable information. Another angle of attack would be faked faults and prompts to make service calls or download software patches designed by hackers. These software patches could be malware designed to access other devices on the network through the supposedly faulty appliance. Ransomware is another potential danger. These viruses are already used to infect computers and make valuable data unusable unless a ransom is paid. Last year researchers at Symantec showed that this sort of virus could be programmed to spread from one device to another, locking the user out of their phone, then their watch and, in the future, perhaps their car, fridge or entire house. And new vulnerabilities are being found every day, as quickly as manufacturers can patch them, which is why any HR team using IoT-related devices to gather data needs to take its security very seriously.

What this means for HR data

Obviously, the HR department needs to operate within the data governance and data security guidelines set by its company, as well as legislation. GDPR sets strict rules on data protection and what to do in the event of a breach, so it is important you get up to speed on this or consult the GDPR expert within your organization. The downside of generating increasingly more data is that they introduce new vulnerabilities for the organization by creating more data that someone could potentially steal. The world of sport gives us a good indication of where HR teams might be going with data in the future. Data are now thoroughly embedded in most major sports, and it is now commonplace to minutely track every aspect of an athlete's performance, wellbeing, diet etc. While this is great for those sports and teams which are benefitting from greater insights than ever before, there is a darker side: the main concern is data falling into the wrong hands.

Formula One (F1), for instance, is intensely data driven, as well as sports professionals, the teams are effectively technology teams. The threat level in F1 has been intense and teams have suffered losses following data theft, as well as malware infection. Even in lower-tech sports like rugby and football, analysts will analyse almost every aspect of games. Players wear GPS trackers to monitor every move they are making and a massive amount of data are generated in training. If this information got into the wrong hands, it could have serious competitive consequences, which is why teams are now putting measures in place to protect their data.[12] While HR-related data may not be as valuable as data from an F1 team, they are still important. These are personal data, after all, covering everyone from the CEO down to frontline staff, and they need to be protected, just like any other business asset.

Bringing all this together into good data governance

So far, we have uncovered a lot of pitfalls to working with data, which can be daunting. But these pitfalls can be managed and mitigated. How? The answer lies in good data governance. Data governance refers to the overall management and caretaking of data, covering their usability and integrity (ie making sure the data are of good quality and that you have the individual's consent to use their data as you need), and security. Practising good data governance means being aware of the moral and legal requirements concerning every aspect of your data-related activities to make sure you are not breaking any laws and that you are operating in an open, ethical and transparent manner. Data governance also extends to having policies in place to determine exactly who has access to data, and who is responsible for maintaining the quality and accuracy of those data. Always there should be an emphasis on taking care of data and treating them as the valuable asset that they are.

Creating a data governance programme

At its heart, data governance is about managing data as one of your business assets. Just as you have processes and systems in place to facilitate managing your staff, the same applies to your data. Assuming your organization has a data governance policy already in place (and it really should have), you need to ensure your intelligent HR activities operate within the scope of that policy. You may also need to put in place various data governance policies that are specific to your HR remit. This may include defining exactly who owns the various people-related data within the organization and who is accountable for various aspects of the data. Consider who is responsible for data accuracy, who is responsible for controlling access to the data and who is responsible for updating the data. You should also appoint a data steward or data champion from within your team to coordinate with others in the company on data governance, quality and privacy issues.

A good data governance programme also should set out clear procedures for how the data can be used and ensure that all staff who come into contact with your people-related data are aware of the privacy and permissions issues surrounding those data. Remember, you will not be able to use personal data for any other purpose than that which you originally got consent for. It is vital your people know and fully understand this. As we have seen in this chapter, legislation is certainly tightening up when it comes to misuse of personal data, and fines can be enormous.

Making sure you have got consent

Getting proper consent is a vital part of good data governance and, with the implementation of GDPR, is a strict legal requirement. Therefore, whenever you intend to capture, store and analyse employee personal data, you must ask permission first. And whenever you ask individuals for consent, it is imperative you explain which data you require and what you intend to do with them, and get their express consent for that usage. Further down the line, if you want to use the data for other purposes, additional consent will be needed.

Practising data minimization

My fear is that many companies will spend too much time crunching all the things they can so easily collect data on, including how much time employees sit in their office chairs or how many people they have interacted with, rather than the more meaningful qualitative measures of what they did when sat in those chairs and the quality of their interactions with others. It is therefore important for HR teams to follow data minimization practices, which basically means gathering only the very essential data, ie data that can help to meaningfully improve the company and add value.

I firmly believe the 'collect it all and analyse it later' approach used by some companies should be a thing of the past, because it is a strategy that poses far too many risks. Any piece of personal datum which can potentially be stolen or leaked should be thought of as a security risk to your company and employees, particularly in light of the forthcoming GDPR legislation. This is why, even when I am talking about 'big data', I am still a big fan of the 'less is more' approach. With regulations tightening up, the days of big corporations collecting every speck of datum they can on their employees just in case it proves useful one day (or as Jeff Bezos, CEO of Amazon, put it: 'We never throw away data'[13]) are gone. Not only is this an expensive approach – since the more data you collect, the more you will have to invest in data storage and analysis – it may land you in legal trouble.

GDPR insists that any personal data collected must be 'adequate, relevant and limited to what is necessary in relation to the purposes for which those data are processed'.[14] In effect, this means collecting and holding only the minimum amount of personal data needed to fulfil your purpose. This is exactly what is meant by the term 'data minimization', or limiting the collection of personal information to that which is directly relevant and necessary to accomplish a specified purpose. Particularly as the IoT continues to grow, organizations are faced with increasingly more ways to collect ever-more kinds of data, including (and especially) private, personally identifiable data. Instead of a 'save everything' approach, any good data-driven HR approach should embrace a data minimization policy, collecting and storing only what you really need. After all, data collection and storage cost money, and no HR team in the world has a bottomless budget. In addition, too many data (especially personally identifiable data) bring big risks. A major leak of sensitive personal information can easily destroy a business's reputation or even land it in court. You can imagine how much more galling this would be if you did not even need the data that you lost in the first place!

Anonymizing data

When you have decided that you absolutely do need to collect certain data, one great way to minimize risk is to anonymize those data as much as possible. This means removing any personally identifiable markers that are not essential to the task at hand before you store and analyse the data. For instance, when Jawbone analyses the data it gathers about me while I wear its fitness band, those data are aggregated and any markers that link the data to me as an individual may be removed. Say, for example, you are analysing the performance of sales colleagues to identify the key traits of successful salespeople in order to inform future recruitment decisions. In this case, what you are really aiming to do is hire the best talent for your sales team and remove some of the guesswork from the recruitment process. If that is the goal, do you really need the data you gather to identify individual sales colleagues? Answer: not really. Obviously, it is not always possible or desirable to anonymize data and there will be times when the data do need to be linked to individuals. In these cases, it is vital you take the necessary steps, like encryption and other data protection measures, to protect that information.

Protecting and securing your data

Given the impact of data breaches, as outlined in this chapter, it is vital your data-driven HR strategy takes account of data security considerations, ie the need to prevent data loss and breaches. When you are dealing with personal data (as in data by which an individual can be identified), you are responsible for their protection and you need to take measures to ensure those data are secured. There are certain safeguards any business can put in place to secure data and prevent data breaches. Such measures can include encrypting your data, having systems in place to detect and stop breaches while they are happening and training your staff so they never give away secure information. Do keep in mind that data security is a specialist field and it is always a good idea to consult with a data security expert, either inside or outside your organization.

Key takeaways

I am well aware that we have covered a lot of information in this chapter and that data privacy, security and governance comprise one of the drier, less interesting aspects of big data. The following is a quick rundown of what we have covered in this chapter:

- The new EU regulation coming into effect in May 2018 – called GDPR, or the General Data Protection Regulation – enhances data protection and the right to privacy for EU citizens.

- As well as legal considerations, HR teams need to ensure their data usage sits within the company's ethical boundaries, which generally means being transparent with employees about what data you are collecting and why.

- Data breaches can lead to huge losses for businesses in terms of legal costs and financial compensation, as well as the damage done to a company's reputation.

- Data governance refers to the overall management and caretaking of data, covering its usability, integrity (ie making sure the data are of good quality and that you have the individual's consent to use their data as you need) and security.

- Getting proper consent is a vital part of good data governance and, with the implementation of GDPR, is a strict legal requirement.

- HR teams should practise data minimization, which basically means gathering only the very essential data, ie data that can help to meaningfully improve the company and add value. Data also should be anonymized where possible.

- Measures to secure data and prevent breaches include encrypting your data, having systems in place to detect and stop breaches while they are happening and training your staff so they never give away secure information.

With transparent privacy policies and good data governance processes in place, and by keeping abreast of the latest regulations, there is no reason why any HR team cannot use data to its full advantage. This brings us neatly to the next part of the book, which looks at how HR teams can use data in practice across the various HR functions. Up first: data-driven recruitment.

Endnotes

1 EUGDPR [accessed 23 October 2017] GDPR Portal: Site Overview [Online] http://www.eugdpr.org

2 Mason, P (2015) [accessed 23 October 2017] The Spotify Privacy Backlash: What Is My Personal Data Really Worth? [Online] https://www.theguardian.com/commentisfree/2015/aug/23/the-spotify-privacy-backlash-what-is-my-personal-data-really-worth

3 Ek, D (2015) [accessed 23 October 2017] Sorry [Online] https://news.spotify.com/us/2015/08/21/sorry-2

4 Marr, B (2016) [accessed 23 October 2017] Big Data: How a Big Business Asset Turns into a Huge Liability [Online] https://www.forbes.com/sites/bernardmarr/2016/03/09/big-data-how-a-big-business-asset-turns-into-a-huge-liability/#5a5aa8917761

5 Sayer, P (2015) [accessed 23 October 2017] EU-US Safe Harbor Agreement Is Invalid, Court Rules [Online] http://www.cio.com/article/2989732/eu-us-safe-harbor-agreement-is-invalid-court-rules.html

6 PrivacyTrust [accessed 23 October 2017] Privacy Shield Certification [Online] https://www.privacytrust.com/privacyshield

7 Collins, E C, Ornstein, D and Tarasewicz, Y (2016) [accessed 23 October 2017] European Court of Human Rights Rules Employers Can Read Employees' Emails [Online] http://www.internationallaborlaw.com/2016/02/09/european-court-of-human-rights-rules-employers-can-read-employees-emails

8 Wilt, B (2014) [accessed 23 October 2017] In the City That We Love [Online] https://jawbone.com/blog/jawbone-up-data-by-city

9 Goode, L (2013) [accessed 23 October 2017] Men Sleep Naked and Other Useful Stuff Jawbone Up Can Tell Us [Online] http://allthingsd.com/20131023/men-sleep-naked-and-other-useful-stuff-jawbone-up-can-tell-us

10 Mandel, E (2014) [accessed 23 October 2017] How the Napa Earthquake Affected Bay Area Sleepers [Online] https://jawbone.com/blog/napa-earthquake-effect-on-sleep

11 Hackett, R (2015) [accessed 23 October 2017] What to Know about the Ashley Madison Hack [Online] http://fortune.com/2015/08/26/ashley-madison-hack

12 Marr, B (2017) [accessed 23 October 2017] The Big Risks of Big Data in Sports [Online] https://www.forbes.com/sites/bernardmarr/2017/04/28/the-big-risks-of-big-data-in-sports/2/#4ea1879a6809

13 Davenport, T H (2014) [accessed 23 October 2017] What It Takes to Succeed with Big Data [Online] http://data-informed.com/takes-succeed-big-data

14 Gabel, D and Hickman, T (2016) [accessed 23 October 2017] Chapter 6: Data Protection Principles – Unlocking the EU General Data Protection Regulation [Online] https://www.whitecase.com/publications/article/chapter-6-data-protection-principles-unlocking-eu-general-data-protection

Data-driven recruitment 07

Recruitment is one area of HR that is particularly rich in data, and it is also an area that has undergone a lot of change. Particularly with platforms like LinkedIn and Glassdoor, every employer – no matter how big or small – now has access to valuable big data. I believe that those HR teams which understand and work with big data are the ones which will recruit most successfully in the coming years and see the greatest ROI for their recruitment activities. Plus, as we will see throughout this chapter, automation is becoming a bigger consideration in intelligent recruitment, from automating aspects of candidate assessment and selection, to the need to recruit people with the right kinds of skills to manage data and automation in the workplace. For me, there are three key strands of intelligent, data-driven recruiting (see Figure 7.1):

- boosting your employer brand;
- identifying the best recruitment channels;
- identifying and assessing the most suitable people for your organization.

Each of these topics could fill a whole book in its own right, and things are developing fast. But in this chapter I look at each of these three strands in turn to identify some of the main ways in which data can help to boost your recruitment activities. Innovative real-life examples are included throughout the chapter (and, indeed, this whole part of the book) to demonstrate how data are already transforming the work of HR teams.

Figure 7.1   Intelligent, data-driven recruiting

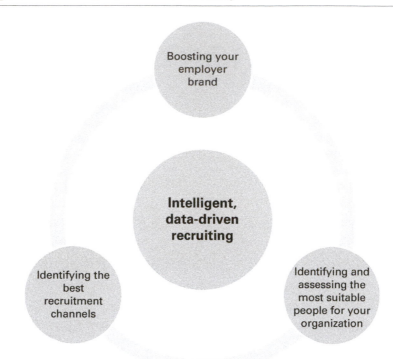

Boosting your employer brand

Effectively, your employer brand is how people (both current, ex- and potential future employees) view your company as an employer. As any marketing colleague will tell you, branding is absolutely vital when it comes to attracting and retaining customers (in this case, employees) and, indeed, your employer brand should ideally align with your overall company, service or product brand. If the two are sending different messages – ethical manufacturer with questionable employee ethics, for example – you could struggle to attract the best talent. One recent paper by Risesmart stated that nearly 70 per cent of unemployed job seekers would not take a job with an employer which had a dubious reputation.[1] On the flip side, the same paper stated that 84 per cent of employees would consider quitting their current job to move to an employer with an excellent reputation, even if the salary increase was less than 10 per cent. Your employer brand tells employees what you are as a company, what you stand for, what it is like to be part of the company and what makes you different from other employers. When creating your employer brand, you will want to consider what kind of talent you want to attract. Or, to put it another way: what kind of people best fit with your company's culture and goals?

Measuring your employer brand

Having identified your employer brand, you need to be sure this brand image chimes with reality, and this is where data come in. You should look to test your employment brand at regular intervals. Sentiment analysis of interview and survey responses, as well as social-media posts, can really help to establish how successful your employer brand is. And if your company goes through major changes, such as a restructuring, you should absolutely look to assess the impact of such changes on your brand. Measuring sentiment before, during and after the changes will give vital insights that will help you to manage the transition and maintain a positive employer brand.

Finding out what your employees (current and otherwise) think

You may already have heard of the *net promoter score*. This is a key performance indicator (KPI) commonly used by sales and marketing departments to assess how willing customers are to recommend the company's service or products to others. Using data, you can apply the same thinking to your employer brand. Indeed, 'how likely are you to recommend the company?' is a common question on employee surveys. Rather than taking the temperature of this once a year, many companies are using 'pulse' surveys: asking just this one simple question on a weekly, monthly or quarterly basis. For this type of survey to be truly useful, responses must be anonymous. Employees may not answer truthfully if they think a negative response could have negative repercussions for them.

Creating and maintaining a positive employer brand is not just about keeping your current employees happy; it is also about how attractive your company appears to outsiders. In this way, social media and employer review sites like Glassdoor are particularly helpful when it comes to assessing your employer brand, especially among ex-employees. One severance and workforce transition study showed that more companies are mining social media and review sites after laying off an employee than three years ago.[2] But this need not apply only to employees who have been let go (although it is a good way to monitor progress in a large-scale restructuring where many employees are being made redundant in stages); feedback from anyone who has left the company voluntarily will also give vital insight into people's perception of your brand.

What makes your employer brand attractive?

What factors do you think attract potential employees to a company or make an employee more likely to recommend your company? Salary? Flexible working? The answers are: 'no' and 'no', according to data. *Human Resources Today* analysed Glassdoor data from more than 6,000 companies and 2.2 million employees to get some interesting findings on employer brand.[3] The biggest factor affecting whether employees would recommend their company as a place to work was 'culture and values'. In fact, an employee's rating on 'culture and values' is almost five times more predictive of a company being recommended than 'salary and benefits'. Among those under the age of 35, 'career opportunities' was the top driver of employer brand. This demonstrates the need for any employer to consider culture and employee development as much as, or even more than, the usual salary and benefits. I am not saying decent salaries and benefits do not impact on employer brand, but it is clear that people want to feel truly at home in a company. They want to enjoy the culture, they want to be proud of the company they work for and they want their input to be valued through good development opportunities. These are all elements to focus on when it comes to boosting your employer brand and promoting that brand to those outside the organization.

Promoting your employer brand

Another key element of branding of course is raising the profile of your employer brand among potential employees. This is especially worthwhile if you are in a highly competitive industry, like the technology world, where you are struggling to attract talent. A strong employer brand gives candidates a definite feel for what it is like to work for your company. As we have already seen, this is often more important to potential employees than salary and benefits, which is great for any company unable to compete on salary. Some innovative organizations are using data-related technology like virtual reality (VR) to capitalize on this idea, delivering 360-degree videos that show people what it is really like to work at the company. This helps employers to show off their culture, give an authentic feel for everyday life within the business and attract the best candidates.

One of my favourite recent examples comes from the unlikely world of US college football. The University of Minnesota's (UM's) Golden Gophers team has been using a slick VR experience to sign up in-demand players.[4] The team's VR pitch is watched using Google cardboard glasses or other VR goggles, and includes footage of practices, games, workouts, those all-important UM campus experiences, city life and even the Minnesota weather. Described as a 'day in the life of a Golden Gopher', it serves to immerse candidates in UM life and tell a compelling story about what it is really like to be part of the team. In the competitive world of college football, it can be hard to stand out and convey the benefits of signing with a smaller team. VR is a great way to do this authentically, which is why VR is fast becoming an increasingly popular tool among college recruiters, and I think the trend is likely to filter through to businesses.

Identifying the most effective recruitment channels for you

Most companies use a mix of recruitment channels, including newspapers, headhunters, social-media campaigns and LinkedIn searches. Different channels will work better for different industries, or even different positions within the same company. Given the diversity of recruitment channels, it is important to know which deliver the greatest return on investment (ROI). In my work with clients, I would estimate that maybe 50 per cent of recruitment spend is wasted. If a channel is not driving actual recruitment, you should stop recruiting through that channel immediately and focus on those channels that deliver the most value for your money.

Getting maximum bang for your recruiting buck

The beauty of data is that they allow you to test your recruitment channels and measure their success rate. These days, it is possible to measure everything minutely. So, rather than focusing on obvious indicators like how many CVs you get in response from different channels (which only tells you volume, not quality), you could look instead at more valuable indicators like how many offers were made to candidates from particular channels. You could even take this further and assess your most successful employees in particular roles and pinpoint which channels they came from. The point is to target your recruitment appropriately and only spend precious resources to reach exactly the kinds of people you want to attract. A good example of this comes from Marriott Hotels, a chain which employs hundreds of thousands of people all around the globe in positions as diverse as cleaning and management. Marriott has an impressive social recruiting strategy, and ranks as more effective at recruiting through a social platform than even Facebook itself.[5] Marriott Hotels has the largest recruitment page on Facebook, with, at the time of writing, more than 1.1 million likes and around 50,000 people interacting with the page every week. The page obviously lists available jobs, but it also beautifully demonstrates what it is like to work for the chain through photographs and videos of life behind the scenes in the hotels. It also celebrates success by congratulating teams and employees for achievements. Perhaps more importantly, the page actively encourages constant engagement through likes and comments, and this is a two-way street, with Marriott responding to comments. Everything is designed to attract users to Marriott's employer brand and show the company off as a desirable place to work. It then builds on that desirability through interaction, which encourages users to progress to searching and applying for positions.

It makes sense that a hospitality business like Marriott wants to attract the classic 'people person'. This explains why Facebook is the most appropriate social recruitment channel for Marriott, as opposed to LinkedIn, which would perhaps be more appropriate for attracting professionals like marketers or lawyers. It is an excellent lesson for any company looking to maximize its employment channels: go with the channel most used by the type of people you want to attract. Building on its Facebook success, Marriott also created an online Facebook game (like Farmville) where potential employees can learn how to manage hotels. The game, called MyMarriottHotel, involves players doing all the things involved in running a hotel, such as: keeping guests happy, managing the kitchen, delivering room service etc. The happier they keep the guests, the more points the players score. The specific idea behind the game is to help to recruit more young people in the 17–24 age group in the Chinese and Indian markets[5] – a group that research shows is spending a lot of time playing games on social media. The game reportedly has been very successful, and it certainly demonstrates new approaches to engaging prospective employees and giving them a taste of the job on offer.

Identifying new recruitment channels

Sometimes you may need to think a little further outside the recruitment box and look for entirely new channels to recruit talent, particularly in areas where there is a lot of competition to hire the best talent. Data scientists are one such group in great demand for all kinds of businesses, yet there just are not enough people with the required skills to work with big data. One survey recently carried out by researchers at Gartner found that more than half of the business leaders queried felt their ability to carry out analytics was restricted by difficulty in finding the right talent.[6] To overcome this problem, Walmart decided to get creative. Rather than advertising through traditional channels, it turned to crowdsourced analytics competition platform Kaggle to find the talent it needed.[7] At Kaggle,[8] an army of 'armchair data scientists' apply their skills to analytical problems submitted by companies, with the designer of the best solution being rewarded, sometimes financially – in this case, with a job at Walmart. Candidates were provided with a set of historical sales data from a sample of stores, along with associated sales events, such as clearance sales and price rollbacks. They were asked to come up with models showing how these events would affect sales across a number of departments. As a result, several people were hired for the analytics team, and the competition was held again the following year, with candidates then being asked to predict how weather would impact on sales of different products. Mandar Thakur, senior recruiter for Walmart's Technology division, told me: 'The Kaggle competition created a buzz about Walmart and our analytics organization. People always knew that Walmart generates and has a lot of data, but the best part was that this let people see how we are using it strategically'.[7] The crowdsourced approach led to some interesting appointments of people who, as Thakur said, would not have been considered for an interview based on their CVs alone. For example, one had a very strong background in physics but no formal analytics background: 'He has a different skillset – and if we hadn't gone down the Kaggle route, we wouldn't have acquired him'.[7]

Walmart also ran a recruitment campaign across social media using the Twitter hashtag #lovedata, to raise its profile among the online data science community and avert their eyes away from Silicon Valley and towards Bentonville, Arkansas – the retail giant's headquarters – when scoping for job opportunities. Another valuable source of job applicants for Walmart is referrals. Data fans – academic, industrial or armchair – are as active in online communities and social networks as any other breed of techies. Provide one with a great job and they are likely to spread the word to their associates.

The world of motorsport gives us another example of recruiting through unusual channels. Nissan and Sony have joined forces to create the GT Academy, a global annual contest designed to find the best racers from the world of videogames.[9] The idea is to find the best racing gamers who play the popular Gran Turismo game and turn them into real-life racing drivers. In the contest, players drive around a track and the competitors with the best times get an in-person try-out. The winner of that try-out gets to race, in real life, for Nissan.

Hundreds of thousands now enter the contest each year. All of the winners selected in the past few years are still racing – three of the winners have even raced for Nissan at Le Mans – which goes to show how successful this recruitment channel is for Nissan.

While you may not be looking to recruit an army of data scientists like Walmart or the next Michael Schumacher, these examples show why it is important to consider some of the more unusual recruitment channels, find out where your talent socializes and use that knowledge to focus on recruitment channels that deliver the biggest return for your money.

Identifying and assessing the best people for your business

It used to be said that employers made up their minds whether or not to hire a prospective candidate within five minutes of sitting down to interview them. It is hard to say if this is true or not, but many HR professionals or hiring managers would probably admit that they had made appointments based on a gut feeling: simply whether or not they felt the person was the right fit for the vacancy. As it is in many other areas of business, data and analytics are helping to take the guesswork out of recruitment. Rather than relying on the famous gut feeling, those teams taking a more scientific approach to appointing staff are finding it leads to more suitable people who stay happy and on the job for longer.

Employers in every industry are turning to data, and tools such as Evolv and TalentBin allow them to crunch data in more ways than ever before to find the right candidate for the right position. Tools like these allow employers to find the best person for any given job, whether that person is actively searching for a position or not, based on their skills, interests and actions. Big data and artificial intelligence (AI) tools are increasingly being offered by vendors like LinkedIn to sift through candidates' profiles and identify the most suitable candidates for a position, which is just as well when you consider that 52 per cent of talent acquisition leaders state the most difficult part of recruitment is identifying the right people from a large pool of applications![10] In my opinion, this is where the future of recruitment lies: using data and algorithms to identify talent and take the guess-work out of recruiting.

Predicting personality

Crucially, when recruiting a new candidate, personality and fit are as important as skill set. These can sometimes be tricky to judge, but not with the help of data and predictive analytics. Companies like Facebook and Google now can predict an awful lot about our intelligence, behaviour and personality attributes based on our profiles and online activities. For example, did you know that your Facebook 'Likes' can expose a great deal about your personality traits and preferences? A study by researchers at Cambridge University and Microsoft Research Labs showed how the patterns of Facebook Likes can be used to automatically predict a range of highly sensitive personal attributes.[11] Using the Like data of 58,000 volunteers, the study also illustrated that the Likes can have little or nothing to do with the actual attributes they help to predict and often a single Like is enough to generate an accurate prediction. So, for example, the study found that Likes for curly fries, science, Mozart, thunderstorms or *The Daily Show* predicted high intelligence, while Likes for Harley Davidson, Lady Antebellum and 'I love being a mom' predicted low intelligence. Meanwhile 'so so happy', 'dot dot curve', *Girl Interrupted, The Adams Family* and Kurt Donald Cobain predicted being emotionally unstable or neurotic, while business administration, skydiving, soccer, mountain biking and parkour predicted being emotionally stable or calm and relaxed. It is pretty scary stuff for anyone who clicks Like without thinking about what they are potentially giving away!

So how do you turn this predictive capability to your advantage when it comes to identifying the right employees? It sounds obvious, but the first step is to identify exactly what you are looking for. What does your ideal employee look like? Throughout the book we have seen examples of how certain attributes were found to be linked to success in certain roles, and those kinds of insights may inform your decision. So think about the skills, qualifications and experience you are looking for. You will also want to think about culture, fit and personality attributes. Armed with this 'shopping list' if you like, it is relatively easy to use analytics software to sift through potential candidates to identify certain data points in applications, CVs or profiles and find the candidates with the best fit in a far more efficient, effective way, which often just takes minutes. And while the final hiring decision will always come down to a human, the algorithms will save a lot of time by narrowing the field down from maybe hundreds of candidates to the most suitable 10 or 20.

Machine learning and AI in recruitment

There are many AI-driven tools that can be used to narrow down, test and assess candidates by, for example, asking them common questions about the job. But some assessments go way beyond this to create immersive gamification experiences, a bit like the Marriott game discussed earlier in the chapter. Using machine learning and AI techniques, the process of attracting, sourcing, matching, screening and assessing candidates is automated using data from all sorts of sources, including the employer's own data, social-media data, employee history etc. Machine learning and AI algorithms like those offered by HR software company Restless Bandit help companies to filter out much of the 'noise' when it comes to selecting candidates. While this used to be a slow process of humans reading every CV and sorting them into piles of 'yes', 'no' and 'maybe', now algorithms can model patterns of hiring to find exactly the right people quickly and easily. Crucially, this process removes the biases that humans inevitably bring to the recruitment process, meaning candidates hopefully will no longer have to hope that they will not be overlooked because the interviewer does not like the tie they are wearing, or because they went to the wrong school.

Connectifier is one company aiming to revolutionize the recruitment process through AI technology, and build up more than 300 million online profiles to help employers find the perfect candidate.[12] The company – which was founded by ex-Google workers – collates data from across the Internet to help find people who are ideal for specific jobs, whether those people are currently searching for jobs or not. Connectifier's platform sorts and combines data to create a complete profile of potential candidates, then lets employers feed in the types of skills and expertise they are looking for to find perfect matches based on that information.

JetBlue Airlines gives us a great example of data analytics being used to boost recruitment processes.[13] Previously, the company had focused on 'niceness' as the most important attribute for flight attendants. Then, after carrying out some customer data analysis with the Wharton Business School, JetBlue was interested to find that, in the eyes of its customers, being helpful is actually more important than being nice, and can even make up for people being not so nice. The company was then able to use this information to narrow down candidates more effectively. This just goes to show that you do not have to be a data powerhouse like Google to use talent analytics to boost your recruitment processes.

Of course, there are a lot of costs involved in hiring an employee, including advertising and the selection process itself. And when an employee turns out not to have the required skills or to be a poor fit with the company's culture, this can be an incredibly expensive mistake (not to mention a waste of time). While there is obviously a cost involved in implementing machine learning systems, over time they are likely to save money, effort and resources, ultimately freeing up HR's time to focus on more valuable activities than sifting through hundreds of applications.

Identifying candidates for top-level positions

While a lot of the focus of talent analytics focuses on filling low and mid-tier vacancies (like the Xerox call-centre example we saw in Chapter 4), data and analytics in fact can be used to identify the best candidates for any position, even right up to the CEO. US-based mattress company Purple, for example, used talent analytics in the search for its current CEO, Sam Bernards.[14] The 'C-suite' of CEOs, CFOs, CMOs and other chiefs in the company are the people who are going to guide the direction of the business. They carry a large amount of responsibility and in return often take home a sizeable chunk of a business's earnings. When mistakes are made in appointing people at this level, disaster is a distinct and clear likelihood. So of course it makes sense that filling these vacancies should be done with as little guesswork as possible.

Corporate headhunter Korn Ferry has taken steps to ensure C-level recruitment is firmly rooted in data and analytics.[15] The firm has specialized in finding candidates for the highest level jobs for almost 50 years. In recent years it has started to apply big data analytics to the wealth of data it has acquired, in order to find the best people for the best jobs. This has allowed the firm to draw up detailed profiles of the competencies, traits and experiences needed to succeed at the top level. In partnership with data scientists at the University of Southern California, the company began to build its analytics-based people placement platform (which it refers to as the Korn Ferry 4 Dimensions of Leadership and Talent – or KF4D for short). Dana Landis, Korn Ferry's vice president of global talent assessment and analytics, told me: 'The biggest discovery was that there are some real universals playing out – more than we expected would be the case'.[15] The data revealed some strong patterns about the importance of traits and qualities required for C-level positions, including being a lifelong learner and having higher levels of emotional intelligence (eg empathy), communication skills and a tolerance for risk.

Along with traits and competencies, experience is obviously a core necessity for success in many roles. This can be covered with analytics too. Comparative analytics can show what skills a person has picked up in previous positions, and which of those they will be likely to need to carry with them as they move up the career ladder.

Another key element which the system is designed to assess is how well the candidate will fit within the culture of the organization. Mike Distefano, chief marketing officer and president of Korn Ferry's research and analytics arm, the Korn Ferry Institute, told me: 'One thing I always say is that people get hired for what they know and fired for who they are. So we have spent a lot of time making sure we can check that the person is a good cultural fit'.[15] Clients looking to fill positions have the ability to choose whether they are happy with their organizational culture – in which case the system will find someone who is likely to fit in – or are looking to change it. If this is the case, then candidates will be suggested who are likely to be agents of change.

But is there one quality – or attribute – that stands out above all others as essential for leadership? The answer is 'yes', according to Distefano: 'If I had to pick one individual indicator of success, then it would be agility. The data analysis has shown that candidates who score highly for agility also tend to deliver well on delivering increased profitability'.[15] His advice is therefore to: 'hire the agile, but check for fit'.[15]

Appointing a new CEO is undoubtedly one of the biggest challenges a business will ever face. Most companies would not make decisions about which products or services to offer without solid data analysis, so it makes sense to bring the same in-depth, analytical approach to hiring for top-level positions. The claim is that, by making the move to evaluating top talent on quantifiable data, backed by comparative analysis, companies can make sure their leadership positions are filled by the people most likely to take the business – and everyone inside it – onwards to bigger and better things.

Sourcing virtual workers

In this data-rich and connected world, it is now increasingly common for companies to draw in talent without actually recruiting people. As increasingly more businesses and applications head for the cloud, it is becoming much easier for companies to agree to hiring remote workers as and when they need them. In fact, a remote workforce can drastically cut down on a company's overheads. In the United Kingdom, there are around 5 million 'crowdworkers' – people working as part of the 'gig economy' – often through digital platforms like CrowdFlower and Upwork.[16] The obvious advantage for workers is they can work wherever and whenever they like. For employers, they can tap into talent without the expense of hiring people full-time. It is a brave new world.

Even when companies do want to hire full-time talent, increasingly more are letting employees work remotely. As the types of information stored in the cloud increase, the more jobs there are that can be worked remotely. Data entry, programming, writing, design, translating and customer service: these types of jobs are already heavily remote. But soon more teachers, nurses, researchers, psychologists and others will find their work headed to the cloud as well. Online education providers are using virtual professors to mark work, law firms are outsourcing document processing and some researchers are even experimenting with using untrained crowdworkers to analyse medical imagery. Remote working – working from somewhere *other* than a business's office building – is one of the fastest-growing segments of the jobs market. One survey of business leaders reported that more than a third of those surveyed stated that over half of their company's full-time workforce would be working remotely by 2020.[17]

What does this mean for recruitment? Well, the analytical techniques we have talked about in this chapter can be incredibly useful when identifying and assessing candidates who may never set foot in your offices. Also, when someone works remotely, they may not have access to the same level of one-to-one mentorship that an in-house employee may have. This may mean you need to focus your hiring on highly experienced people who already have all the core attributes needed to succeed in the role. Analytics can help you to pinpoint such candidates quickly and easily.

Identifying and promoting suitable candidates inside the company

As a final word on identifying candidates, it is often said that it is more cost-effective to promote from within than to recruit from outside the company. Another obvious advantage is that internal candidates are already well versed with the company's systems, processes and culture. So it makes sense to keep in mind the benefits of applying the same sort of talent analytics to identifying suitable candidates from within the company. As we saw from the *Human Resources Today* finding discussed earlier in the chapter, the opportunity to progress and grow within a company is hugely attractive to millennials, so promoting from within is another great way to boost your employer brand. Talent analytics can help HR teams to identify the top performers in roles across the company, as well as those who are already in the best position for them.

Key takeaways

As we have seen in this chapter, it is essential that recruiters are able to understand data and analytics and use them to their advantage in boosting their employer brand, maximizing recruitment channels, and identifying and assessing candidates. Intelligent HR means using technology to automate processes where possible, freeing up time for more valuable activities. The following is a quick summary of what has been covered in this chapter:

- Your employer brand tells employees who you are as a company, what you stand for, what it is like to be part of the company and what makes you different from other employers.

- Data provide a way to measure and truly understand your employer brand, and help to promote your employer brand to potential employees.

- Given the diversity of recruitment channels, it is important to know which deliver the greatest ROI. Data allow you to test your recruitment channels and measure their success rate.

- Data and analytics are helping to take the guesswork out of recruitment and find more suitable people who stay happy and on the job for longer.

- Data and analytics can help to predict personality and fit, assess candidates, narrow down a lengthy list of candidates, identify the best candidates and attributes for certain positions (at every level of the company) and more.

- AI is beginning to play a key role in recruitment, and many recruitment-related tasks now can be automated.

For me, recruitment is one area in which analytics, particularly machine learning, offers lots of opportunities for streamlining, improving and even automating processes, which allows HR teams to save time (and, ultimately, money), as well as fill positions with the best possible candidates. Of course, once you have found the right people, you need to keep them engaged and satisfied with the company, which is what we will look at in the next chapter.

Endnotes

1   RiseSmart [accessed 23 October 2017] The Connection between HR Analytics and Employer Brand [Online] http://info.risesmart.com/wp-rg-insight-whitepaper?utm_campaign=2017.5.1_WP_Insight_Whitepaper&utm_source=website

2   RiseSmart [accessed 23 October 2017] 2017 Guide to Severance and Workforce Transition [Online] http://info.risesmart.com/2017-guide-to-severance-and-workforce-study

3   Bersin, J (2016) [accessed 23 October 2017] Data Proves That Culture, Values, and Career Are Biggest Drivers of Employment Brand [Online] http://www.humanresourcestoday.com/data/employer-branding/recruitment/?open-article-id=5366961&article-title=data-proves-that-culture--values--and-career-are-biggest-drivers-of-employment-brand&blog-domain=joshbersin.com&blog-title=josh-bersin

4   Heitner, D (2016) [accessed 23 October 2017] Golden Gophers Go with Virtual Reality to Tempt Football Recruits [Online] https://www.forbes.com/sites/darrenheitner/2016/11/23/golden-gophers-go-with-virtual-reality-to-tempt-football-recruits/#6fd4880722e4

5   Slezak, P (2013) [accessed 23 October 2017] How Marriott Hotels Is Beating Facebook at Their Own Game in Social Recruiting [Online] http://www.recruitingblogs.com/profiles/blogs/how-marriott-hotels-is-beating-facebook-at-their-own-game-in

6   Gartner (2015) [accessed 23 October 2017] Gartner Survey Highlights Challenges to Hadoop Adoption, press release [Online] http://www.gartner.com/newsroom/id/3051717

7   Marr, B (2015) [accessed 23 October 2017] Walmart: the Big Data Skills Crisis and Recruiting Analytics Talent [Online] https://www.forbes.com/sites/bernardmarr/2015/07/06/walmart-the-big-data-skills-crisis-and-recruiting-analytics-talent/#7857e8f56b55

8   Kaggle [accessed 23 October 2017] The Home of Data Science and Machine Learning [Online] https://www.kaggle.com

9   Golson, J (2015) [accessed 23 October 2017] The Best Way to Spot Great Racing Drivers? Videogames [Online] https://www.wired.com/2015/08/best-way-spot-great-racing-drivers-videogames

10 Ideal [accessed 23 October 2017] AI for Recruiting: a Definitive Guide for HR Professionals [Online] https://ideal.com/ai-recruiting

11   Baldwin, R (2013) [accessed 23 October 2017] Study: Facebook Likes Can Be Used to Determine Intelligence, Sexuality [Online] https://www.wired.com/2013/03/facebook-like-research

12   Connectifier [accessed 23 October 2017] Hire In-demand Talent, Faster [Online] https://www.connectifier.com

13   Aslan, B (2016) [accessed 23 October 2017] To All Recruiters – Use Machine Learning to Hire Better Candidates [Online] https://medium.com/@deadlocked_d/to-all-recruiters-use-machine-learning-to-hire-better-candidates-c5aad22f3319

14   Olenski, S (2016) [accessed 23 October 2017] Using Talent Analytics When Hiring for Your Brand [Online] https://www.forbes.com/sites/steveolenski/2016/10/05/using-talent-analytics-when-hiring-for-your-brand/#141ff19b1f97

15   Marr, B (2015) [accessed 23 October 2017] Can Big Data Find Your Next CEO? [Online] https://www.forbes.com/sites/bernardmarr/2015/07/27/can-big-data-find-your-next-ceo/2/#4e1b1e19407b

16   Huws, U and Joyce, S (2015) [accessed 23 October 2017] Crowd Working Survey [Online] http://www.feps-europe.eu/assets/a82bcd12-fb97-43a6-9346-24242695a183/crowd-working-surveypdf.pdf

17   Global Leadership Summit (2015) [accessed 23 October 2017] What If… ? [Online] https://gls.london.edu

Data-driven employee engagement

08

With employees being frequently touted as the most valuable asset of a business, it makes sense that keeping those employees engaged, happy and committed to the company is a critical activity for any organization. Indeed, a 2015 Deloitte report revealed that 87 per cent of business leaders are very concerned about employee engagement and retention.[1] Data and analytics, and particularly AI-based technology like machine learning, are beginning to have a significant impact on every aspect of maintaining and improving employee engagement. In intelligent or data-driven employee engagement, HR teams are looking to connect with employees more seamlessly, measure and improve their experience of working for the company and, in turn, drive employee satisfaction – as well as drive productivity and improve the company's employer brand (see Chapter 7). In this chapter I explore why employee engagement is ripe for change and look at three key strands of data-driven employee engagement:

- driving employee satisfaction (or how happy your people are);
- measuring and improving employee loyalty and retention;
- improving compensation and benefits with data.

Why employee engagement is ripe for change

Employees who are engaged tend to go 'above and beyond' for the company they work for, meaning companies with the most engaged employees outperform companies with disengaged workforces. We know

Figure 8.1   Data-driven employee engagement

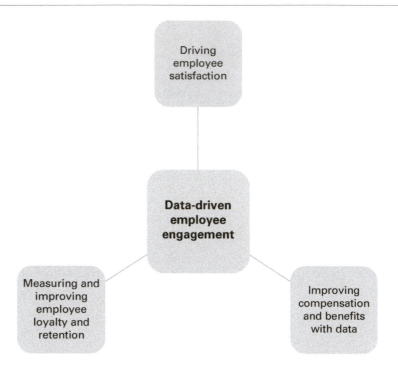

this, and yet companies are not necessarily giving employee engagement the attention it deserves. In fact, one global study found that only 40 per cent of employees feel engaged.[2] Why is this percentage so low when the effects of disengaged employees are clearly known? In the United States alone, disengaged employees cost the economy US $500 billion every year in lost productivity. In the United Kingdom, one report claims disengaged employees could be costing the economy as much as £340 billion.[3]

It is clear that employee engagement is in need of a shake-up. In this age of social media, transparency and connectivity, where people freely share their experiences of the world (including work) online, I believe employee engagement will become a far more critical issue for employers. With advances in data and analytics, companies now can begin to clearly understand their level of employee engagement (including underlying reasons for disengagement) and put these critical insights to use. Most businesses are already using big data in one form or another to assess how satisfied their customers are and drive customer engagement and retention. It is time the same applied routinely to employees, who, let us not forget, are a core customer of the business.

Determining employee satisfaction – how happy are your people?

Measuring employee satisfaction is something companies have been doing for a long time, largely using employee surveys and benchmarking information. More than 80 per cent of companies conduct employee surveys;[4] however, I believe this approach is now completely out of date. An annual employee survey is not agile or granular enough to give most businesses the timely, detailed insights they need to monitor and improve employee engagement. After all, employee opinions shift constantly, and change can happen very rapidly in a lot of organizations. There is also the issue that most people hate filling out these lengthy surveys or, worse, they are worried their answers could be traced back to them so they simply say what they think the company wants to hear. It is therefore questionable how useful the feedback even is.

Knowing what people are really thinking and feeling

Data and analytics, particularly AI-related technology, are promising to help organizations really understand what their people are thinking and feeling. These tools are not perfect yet, but the field is developing extremely fast. For me, the real promise lies in measuring employee satisfaction and happiness in far more accurate and agile ways that are less onerous for employees. As well as working out how satisfied (or not) your employees are, data and analytics also can help you to understand exactly what it is that employees do and do not care about and, therefore, what will boost their engagement. There are already many systems on the market that make engaging with employees easier and more successful, and more are being developed all the time. Beyond 360's system, for example, automates the collection of employee feedback, helping employers take the temperature of employee sentiment and satisfaction quickly and easily. Another service, this time from Veriato, uses artificial intelligence (AI) technology to analyse employees' e-mails and other messages to work out whether they are happy in their jobs. The system analyses the words and phrases workers use and applies a score for sentiment: positive or negative. By measuring sentiment over time, the system can even create a daily score for each individual employee. In addition, alerts can be sent if a change in tone is detected in a particular team or group. Programmes like these allow HR teams and managers to more accurately assess how the workforce is feeling right down to a team or individual level, meaning they can quickly spot when satisfaction is taking a turn in certain areas of the business and take steps to address this issue.

Getting continuous feedback

In Chapter 7 I briefly mentioned how short 'pulse' surveys can take the temperature of employee satisfaction with a quick question delivered at regular intervals, maybe even daily. Tools like these allow companies to get instant, granular feedback on topics as diverse as how much people like the food in the canteen or how well staff understand the company's strategy.

Feedback in real time

HighGround has developed a platform that mines real-time data directly from employees, providing HR teams and business leaders with better, continuous feedback from their people. The idea behind the platform is to create a continuous dialogue with staff, for example, by asking employees how they feel at work that day. The system works as a simple app downloaded onto employees' phones; this ease of use promotes employee buy-in, making staff more likely to engage with the system and provide accurate, regular feedback. Another such company, Glint, has produced an app that works alongside HR systems and can be used to ask employees for feedback in real time (which is particularly useful when certain events occur, like a change in leadership). Working with clients like United Airlines and Sky, Glint uses natural language processing and sentiment analysis (more on this in the next section) to analyse employees' open-ended responses to questions, and can then turn those responses into a visual map of key topics and issues. Glint and HighGround are just two examples of the many continuous feedback systems available today that aim to develop more of a dialogue between an organization and its people. While these systems often use short, simple questions, one company has taken the idea to a new level of simplicity: using smileys.

Employee satisfaction in the emoji age

You may already have encountered HappyOrNot's terminals in somewhere like an airport or bank, encouraging you to give quick, easy and anonymous feedback on your experience that day. HappyOrNot kiosks are used by approximately 2,000 retail and service providers around the world. Now, the company that made its name in gathering customer feedback is turning its eye to staff feedback. Using HappyOrNot terminals, organizations can get daily feedback on their employees' experiences. When placed in high-traffic areas like meeting rooms or the canteen, the kiosks ask an employee a simple question and the employee responds by choosing between one of four smiley faces that best demonstrates how much they agree with the question. It is that simple: just one press of a button. HR then can use the data gathered (which are all anonymous) to get a clear picture of staff reactions to things like new initiatives, company policies, overall strategy and direction, facilities... pretty much anything. The beauty of simple, continuous feedback systems like these is not only the quick access to insights, but also the ability to monitor changes and initiatives made in response to the feedback to see how well those changes improve employee satisfaction. What exactly you measure will depend on your company and its goals but some of the key metrics to keep an eye on include, among other things:

- the extent to which employees approve of leadership;
- how happy they are with their working environment;
- how likely they are to recommend the organization as a good place to work;
- the extent to which they understand and approve of new initiatives, policies and strategies.

Measuring employee sentiment

Conducting regular surveys is all well and good but, if you ask your employees open-ended questions (as opposed to hitting a smiley-face button), you could end up with a mountain of unstructured text data that can prove tricky to analyse. Text analytics provides the answer to this problem. Text (specifically, sentiment) analytics and AI capabilities are now beginning to play a big role in measuring employee sentiment. Forward-thinking organizations are already using sentiment analysis to mine social media and other messages for positive and negative phrases that show what customers really think about their company. Applying the same thinking to employees is perhaps the logical next step. Sentiment analysis potentially can be used on any kind of written text, including survey answers, e-mails, intranet posts, internal messaging systems, social media etc. For example, sentiment analysis could show that members of a division with a new manager have shown a dramatic increase in the number of negative wordings used over the past month, which may alert HR to a manager that is struggling to settle in.

Weighing up the pros and cons of sentiment analysis

One of the real advantages of sentiment analysis is that it does not take up any of the employee's time, as opposed to filling in extensive annual surveys that may be out of date by the time they are analysed. There are obvious privacy concerns surrounding analysing employee communications (see Chapter 6), so it is important you view sentiment analysis as a means to gain a broader picture of employee engagement, and not to police what individuals say or single out employees for punishment. Therefore, implementing any kind of sentiment analysis programme will require careful thought and communication with employees so as not to have a detrimental effect on morale, which is the very opposite of what you want. Making employees aware of the benefits of such analysis is the best way to promote buy-in; for example, you could make it clear that, if the majority of employees disagree with a new policy, it is important for leaders to know this so they can act accordingly to fix issues. In this way, sentiment analysis gives companies the opportunity to gather broad pictures without asking individuals to 'speak out' on their own, which may make them uncomfortable.

Real-life examples of sentiment analysis in action

Although sentiment analysis is in its early days in an HR capacity, large organizations like Intel, Twitter and IBM are already using it to better understand their employees.[5] Twitter has used Kanjova software to analyse employees' answers to monthly surveys (with open-ended questions) about their experience of the workplace. Using sentiment analysis, Kanjova ploughs through the narrative answers, identifying patterns and useful insights. At IBM, sentiment analysis is applied to employee posts on its internal social-networking platform. In one example, when IBM was overhauling its performance review system, the company turned to the internal network to ask employees for feedback on ideas for a new review system.[5] The company received tens of thousands of responses. Using its Social Pulse text analysis software, IBM surfaced one prevalent concern: employees did not like their performances being graded on a curve. The company was then able to discount this method from performance reviews. Notably, IBM does not mine e-mails, chats or private group messages for insights, preferring to focus on the internal network posts shared with the whole company.[5]

It is not just about written text

Of course, sentiment analysis does not necessarily apply just to text. We show how we are feeling through our facial expressions, body language, tone of voice and many little ways. With this in mind, two computer scientists at Sathyabama University in India have proposed using facial scans to assess employee attitudes.[6] They have developed a system that snaps images of employees' faces as they enter the premises, and uses these to work out whether those employees are happy, angry, sad etc.

Happy employees are productive employees

I look at performance management in more detail in Chapter 11 but, for now, it is important to highlight again the link between happy, engaged employees and increased productivity. One study by the

University of Warwick found that happiness led to a 12 per cent productivity bump.[7] Yet, despite evidence that happy employees perform better, studies have shown that up to 71 per cent of employees describe themselves as uninspired or unengaged in a work context.[8] This lack of engagement can have a significant effect on productivity; one study found a 30 per cent difference in absenteeism between companies with high versus low employee engagement.[9] The message is clear: happy employees are more engaged and perform better, and companies that can harness this knowledge to ensure their employees stay happy will, in turn, perform better.

How organizations can best make (and keep) their employees happy is still up for debate, and there is no clear one-size-fits-all approach that works for all businesses across all industries and geographies. What is clear, however, is that technology is likely to play a greater role in boosting employee happiness in the future. One US-based start-up company, Happybot.ai, has developed an AI-powered robot that serves as an automated Chief Happiness Officer. The bot communicates with employees to help ease pressure and boost their happiness and productivity. Founder Aaron Cohn, who spent years as a 'people and change' consultant at PricewaterhouseCoopers, based the bot on his observation that employees continually feel overwhelmed by everyday pressures at work. By communicating with employees and empathizing about those pressures, the Happybot.ai aims to help lift their spirits.[10]

Measuring and improving employee retention

Employee satisfaction and retention are intrinsically linked. Glint data from over 500,000 employees show that the attrition rate of employees with low engagement or satisfaction scores is 12 times higher than those with positive engagement scores.[11] We also know that losing employees is costly (not to mention disruptive and time-consuming). US businesses lose an estimated US $11 billion a year due to employee turnover.[12] Therefore, if a company is able to identify who is likely to leave and why, it is then able to take action and address those issues with a view to retaining those critical staff members who are a flight risk. With data and analytics, it is now possible to predict overall retention rates, including when certain individuals are likely to leave the company based on factors like how long they have been in the job.

Workday's AI-based retention risk tool, for example, uses algorithms based on 25 years' worth of data from 100,000 individuals. Based on around 60 factors (such as job title, salary, time off and how long it has been since they were promoted), the tool can calculate a risk score for each individual employee.[13] But intelligent employee engagement is not just about getting at critical insights like this, it is also about using that knowledge to make improvements. Many retention risk tools also suggest what actions to take to retain valuable workers. Workday's program, for instance, can suggest next steps in an individual's career, based on the data showing what others in comparable circumstances have done.

Inspiring loyalty

Businesses talk a lot about customer loyalty and how to encourage customers to remain loyal to a particular brand, product or service. Yet employee loyalty is just as important to a business's success; in fact, there is a proven link between employee loyalty and retention and customer retention.[14] It is therefore vital that companies apply the same level of attention to keeping their employees satisfied as they do to keeping their customers satisfied. Unhappy employees lead to high turnover (which, in turn, can affect customer retention, among other things). I mentioned HighGround's employee engagement tool earlier in the chapter, which gathers regular feedback from employees about their experience of working for a company. HighGround says that its service actively reduces turnover, citing an example of cutting turnover by 5 per cent at a company called Echo Global Logistics.[15] Some HighGround clients have installed the software at every retail store across a national chain to gather daily information on how happy employees are around the country. When stores that have previously shown stable moods begin to show a drop in happiness, management can investigate the cause of that and take necessary action.

Improving your levels of employee loyalty starts right at the time of hiring. In Chapter 7 we looked at how data are revolutionizing the recruitment process. By using some of the machine learning methods outlined, companies can not only find candidates with the best-fitting skills and attributes, but also those who are most likely to commit to the company on a long-term basis (based on their employment history and patterns from other employees who have demonstrated high levels of loyalty). Data and analytics can help you to identify the employees that are more likely to enter into a long-lasting relationship with the company and demonstrate loyalty and commitment. Of course, it is then up to you to ensure they stay that way. Luckily, data can help with this too. As the Xerox example from Chapter 4 shows, data can drastically reduce employee attrition – in Xerox's case, by an impressive 20 per cent.[16]

Many people make the mistake of thinking employee retention is all about compensation, but it is not. There are many factors besides salary that inspire and maintain employee loyalty. So, once you have found the people that are the best fit with the organization, you then need to implement all the good practices that keep those employees happy, engaged and loyal. These include communicating and rewarding successes, offering plenty of training and development, providing career progression opportunities etc.

Predicting employee churn

For many companies, being able to accurately predict when someone may be about to jump ship is the holy grail of employee retention, and there are many tools on the market now that claim to be able to do just that. The idea is not a new one. Google has been using algorithms for many years to predict who among its employees are most likely to leave the company. Competition for talent in Silicon Valley is incredibly intense, and while Google remains one of the most popular employers in the United States, it still needs to put the work in when it comes to retaining its talent. Google first developed its algorithm back in 2009, which worked from data including employee surveys and peer reviews.[17] The algorithm was a quick success, identifying that 'feeling underused' was one of the biggest reasons people left the company. Speaking at the time, Google's Laszlo Bock said the algorithm could 'get inside people's heads even before they know they might leave'.[17]

Of the tools on the market, you will need to assess which is the best option for your needs. Unless you are a very large organization, it is a good idea to opt for a tool that is based on external data as well as your own internal data (such as employee performance data, employment history, performance review data, survey responses, compensation data, and possibly employee e-mails and communications). Some sort of capability for taking regular pulse surveys and conducting sentiment analysis also, in my opinion, is a must, as the results will feed into your employee churn analytics. The best tools will work right down to an individual level, delivering an alert when a certain employee shows signs of disengaging, or when they become a flight risk. Of course, once you understand your employee churn patterns and can pinpoint those who might be at risk of leaving the company, you can then take steps to turn the situation around. Again, a salary bump is not necessarily going to keep an employee in their job. As we saw in Chapter 7, for many people, career progression opportunities are far more important.

Data-driven compensation and benefits

It is fair to say that, in terms of data and analytics, compensation and benefits comprise the less-developed area of employee engagement. But it is developing fast and more tools and services are coming onto the market to help companies take a more intelligent, data-driven approach to their compensation and benefits structures. Offering a fair compensation and benefits package remains an important part of successful employee engagement. Having found the right people, it is up to you to create a package that engages employees and makes them more likely to remain committed to the company, and therefore more likely to stay with the company. If you bargain down candidates to pay them the lowest possible salary you can get away with, it does not exactly inspire loyalty. And, as we have already seen in this book, different factors will be more important to some people than others. Millennials, for instance, typically want great career progression opportunities.[18] The ability to tailor your compensation and benefits packages to individuals, based on what the data tell you about certain demographics, will inspire greater long-term employee engagement.

Focusing on fair market value

Salaries and market value typically have been very secretive, both from the employer and from the employee side. Some companies may not want employees to know their true market value so that they can get away with paying them less. And employees may not want to share their salary data for fear of repercussions from management or co-workers. But such secrecy is not good for anybody. Employees are at a disadvantage when negotiating because they do not know what salary to ask for. And while certain employers might *think* they are getting a good deal by paying less than market value, it is actually more likely to limit their talent pool and increase staff turnover. Things are changing, however, and it is now far easier for people and companies to discover the fair market value for particular jobs. We are all used to searching price comparison sites for good flight or insurance prices, now the same mentality applies to salary. Glassdoor may have started out by posting employee-generated reviews of companies so that jobseekers could get a feel for what working for a particular company was really like, but now it also provides a tool aimed at making salaries and market value more transparent. Employees and employers can type in a job title and location and clearly see what the average salaries are for that area and position. The site also offers personalized salary reports for individuals based on more detailed information about their skills and experience. Glassdoor claims to have the most complete market salary information because it is based on thousands of users reporting their real salaries anonymously. This means that it is increasingly likely that candidates will go into salary negotiations armed with a very good idea of their fair market value. This allows them to negotiate from a position of power, with the facts on their side. Employers therefore need to raise their own game to ensure they are armed with the same level of knowledge and are prepared to offer fair market value to get the right talent for the company. HR managers should therefore stay up to date with the market value of their employees. Not only does this data-based approach help you to budget appropriately for new hires, it also ensures salaries remain competitive, thereby improving employee morale and loyalty and reducing turnover.

Determining market value

Unless you have an in-house compensation expert – and many small and medium-sized companies do not – it can be difficult to accurately calculate employee compensation. But, thanks to now widely available information on salary and benefits trends, it is becoming easier for any organization to calculate employee compensation in line with market value. Tools like salary.com or payscale.com, for instance, help employers to understand whether they are paying competitively or not. This data-based approach, where you calculate the value of employees and new hires based on external research (as opposed to internal historical data or gut feeling), is the most sensible approach for ensuring your compensation package is fair. But remember to get a complete picture by drilling down into detailed demographics (such as your specific location) rather than just grabbing a general figure for a certain job title. Having determined the fair market value for new hires, you then need to ensure you stay competitive. Be sure to reassess compensation levels on a regular basis. I would say to do this at least every two years, but do it annually if you can or if you are in a field with a lot of fierce competition for talent.

Combining data to create your compensation and benefits packages

Clearly, the realm of compensation and benefits ties in with a number of other areas of HR and the wider business, including performance management, learning and development, and payroll. It is therefore important to create a full picture by combining multiple data sets for the greatest strategic effect, and advances in data and analytics technology make this easier than ever.

Real-life examples

The University of Lincoln, for example, has implemented a new system that integrates HR and payroll in one place to create a comprehensive reporting tool. Speaking to *HR Magazine*, Ian Hodson, reward and benefits manager at the university, said: 'the data becomes more powerful when it is overlaid with other information. Our new system has fed data triggers in to populate other systems, and we have a much more cross-function approach to data collation and production than ever before'.[19] Using this system, Hodson and his team have been able to draw a correlation between pay and consistently strong performance.

When two giant publishing companies – Penguin and Random House – merged in 2013 to form Penguin Random House, the new company faced significant challenges in redesigning its compensation and benefits offering. Also speaking to *HR Magazine*, Neil Morrison, group HR director at the publisher, explained how the company used a vast amount of data to determine how benefits and compensation should be structured. In one example, the company used broad data on the take-up levels of benefits, but also drilled down into how take-up varied among different demographic groups, and whether salary played a role in this. According to Morrison, this involved: 'everything from understanding people with different backgrounds but the same job titles, to the take-up of benefits and the specific value of certain ones. Whether they have the value you think they do and whether that has links with turnover and retention, and whether therefore the investment is adding value'.[20] In a specific example of how these data helped the publisher to redesign its benefits offering, Morrison explained how the data showed that young people did not take up private medical care. Based on this knowledge, the company was able to offer 'the flexibility of a lower-value product'.[20] Penguin Random House is working with reward consultancy firm Innecto to look at its salary and incentives schemes, using both internal and external data. According to Morrison: 'Being able to take external data and analyse and compare it with our internal data and make decisions on pay structures will hopefully take us forward for the next five years rather than just working on individual pay structures'.[20]

Gaining feedback on schemes

Once a scheme or benefit has been introduced, data and analytics allow you to accurately assess how successful that scheme is and whether certain benefits are influencing engagement. Exactly what kind of compensation and benefits platform you go for will depend on your company's needs, but key functionality to look out for includes the ability to look at skills and experience within the organization and compare these both internally as well as against national levels. It is also important to be able to assess correlations between salary and specific benefits and employee satisfaction levels. In addition, survey tools are increasingly being built into benefits platforms to gain employee feedback on various rewards, which gives the employer valuable data on how well benefits are being received, and further engages staff by giving them a chance to voice their opinions. Where possible, it is a good idea to build this functionality into your platform at the outset.

The role of AI in compensation and benefits

AI is changing every aspect of business, and compensations and benefits are no different. Just as AI can be used to easily find the most suitable candidates for a particular role and the best fit for the company culture (Chapter 7), it can also help to enhance and automate various aspects of compensation and benefits. One area of benefits that gets a lot of attention is flexible working and the ability to work remotely. While this may not appeal to everyone, there are certain demographics, such as parents and millennials, who prize flexible working above many other benefits. To give you an idea of how highly prized flexibility is, 59 per cent of millennials say flexibility improves their productivity, and 49 per cent say it enhances their happiness.[21]

It is very likely that, as our workplaces become more flexible, so too will our compensation and benefits structures. Traditional schemes are highly likely to be replaced by flexible, variable compensation and benefits programmes that are tailored more to individuals' needs. Those companies that are able to adapt and offer flexible compensation and benefits schemes may well find themselves at the forefront of the industry. AI, and analytics in general, will help to make this flexible approach a reality. Think about it: having to manually analyse and tailor compensation and benefits packages to each individual employee would be completely unfeasible without data and analytics, taking up far too much time and resources to be workable. AI-based platforms, on the other hand, make it possible to understand and accurately predict trends, understand the relevance and take-up of various benefits among different demographics and easily create tailored solutions that work on a personal level. What this means for HR professionals who focus on compensation and benefits is that their role is likely to change dramatically. They will probably need to upskill from an in-depth support role to a more strategic role, looking at how to apply AI-based analytics to both internal and external data sets to gain valuable insights on compensation and benefits. In fact, this is an important point that applies to the whole area of employee engagement, not just compensation and benefits. As the technology develops rapidly, it becomes HR's role to provide strategic direction for the company on how best to apply all of these tools and systems to employee engagement in order to get maximum value.

Key takeaways

In this chapter we have looked at three core strands of data-driven employee engagement – employee satisfaction, employee retention, and compensation and benefits – and explored the following key points:

- Disengaged employees cost the global economy billions in lost productivity. Happy employees, on the other hand, are productive employees.

- Most businesses are already using data to assess how satisfied their customers are and drive customer engagement and retention. It is time we applied the same level of care to our employees.

- Annual employee surveys are nowhere near agile or granular enough to deliver the timely, detailed insights needed to monitor and improve employee engagement.

- Data and analytics technology allow us to measure employee satisfaction and happiness in far more accurate and agile ways, such as by using very brief but regular pulse surveys.

- Sentiment analysis makes it possible to analyse open-ended responses, or any written or spoken text, to determine what your employees are really thinking and feeling.

- High employee turnover is costly for any business. Data-driven employee retention means identifying insights on employee churn, identifying who might be about to leave the company and making evidence-based changes to inspire employee loyalty.

- Data and analytics also help you to determine a fair market value for employees, assess how successful your compensation and benefits programmes are in influencing employee satisfaction and create programmes that chime with what is really important to your employees.

Keeping your people engaged, satisfied, loyal and well compensated is one thing, but you also need to look after their safety and well-being if you want them to stay happy, engaged and productive. In the next chapter I explore the fascinating world of data-driven employee safety and wellness, and see how data-related technology is transforming how we look after our employees.

Endnotes

1 Deloitte [accessed 23 October 2017] 2017 Deloitte Global Human Capital Trends [Online] http://www2.deloitte.com/us/en/pages/human-capital/articles/introduction-human-capital-trends.html

2 Zarkadakis, G (2015) [accessed 23 October 2017] Next Generation Employee Engagement [Online] https://www.towerswatson.com/en-GB/Insights/Newsletters/Europe/HR-matters/2015/12/next-generation-employee-engagement

3 Hay Group [accessed 23 October 2017] Employee Disengagement Costs UK £340bn Every Year, press release [Online] http://www.haygroup.com/uk/press/details.aspx?id=7184

4 Galagan, P (2015) [accessed 23 October 2017] Employee Engagement: an Epic Failure? [Online] https://www.td.org/Publications/Magazines/TD/TD-Archive/2015/03/Employee-Engagement-An-Epic-Failure

5 Waddell, K (2016) [accessed 23 October 2017] The Algorithms That Tell Bosses How Employees Are Feeling [Online] https://www.theatlantic.com/technology/archive/2016/09/the-algorithms-that-tell-bosses-how-employees-feel/502064

6 Subhashini, R and Niveditha, P R (2015) [accessed 23 October 2017] Analyzing and Detecting Employee's Emotion for Amelioration of Organizations [Online] http://www.sciencedirect.com/science/article/pii/S1877050915006407

7 University of Warwick (2014) [accessed 23 October 2017] New Study Shows We Work Harder When We Are Happy, press release [Online] http://www2.warwick.ac.uk/newsandevents/pressreleases/new_study_shows

8 Pepperdine University [accessed 23 October 2017] 7 Ways Managers Can Keep Employees Engaged [Online] http://mbaonline.pepperdine.edu/resources/news-articles/7-ways-managers-can-keep-employees-engaged/?utm_campaign=elearningindustry.com&utm_source=%2Femployee-engagement-and-artificial-intelligence-elearning&utm_medium=link

9 Flink, C [accessed 23 October 2017] Engaged Employees: the Key to a Thriving Brand [Online] http://www.marketforce.com/blog/engaged-employees-key-thriving-brand?utm_campaign=elearningindustry.com&utm_source=%2Femployee-engagement-and-artificial-intelligence-elearning&utm_medium=link

10 Happybot [accessed 23 October 2017] A Bot That Surprises & Delights You. At Work [Online] http://happybot.ai

11 Glint (2016) [accessed 23 October 2017] Glint Raises $27 Million to Boost Employee Engagement with Help from Artificial Intelligence [Online] http://www.marketwired.com/press-release/glint-raises-27-million-boost-employee-engagement-with-help-from-artificial-intelligence-2154186.htm

12 Lipman, V (2013) [accessed 23 October 2017] Why Are So Many Employees Disengaged? [Online] https://www.forbes.com/sites/victorlipman/2013/01/18/why-are-so-many-employees-disengaged/#3a29b5081e22

13 Greenwald, T (2017) [accessed 23 October 2017] How AI Is Transforming the Workplace [Online] https://www.wsj.com/articles/how-ai-is-transforming-the-workplace-1489371060

14 Carter, B (2017) [accessed 23 October 2017] Employee Engagement = Customer Engagement [Online] http://blog.accessdevelopment.com/index.php/2014/03/employee-engagement-customer-engagement

15 White, S K (2016) [accessed 23 October 2017] How Big Data Can Drive Employee Engagement [Online] http://www.cio.com/article/3023311/careers-staffing/how-big-data-can-drive-employee-engagement.html

16 Walker, J (2012) [accessed 23 October 2017] Meet the New Boss: Big Data [Online] https://www.wsj.com/news/articles/SB10000872396390443890304578006252019616768

17 Morrison, S (2009) [accessed 23 October 2017] Google Searches for Staffing Answers [Online] https://www.wsj.com/articles/SB124269038041932531

18 Adkins, A and Rigoni, B (2016) [accessed 23 October 2017] Millennials Want Jobs to Be Development Opportunities [Online] http://news.gallup.com/businessjournal/193274/millennials-jobs-development-opportunities.aspx

19 Giles, H (2015) [accessed 23 October 2017] Where's the Evidence for Performance-related Pay? [Online] http://www.hrmagazine.co.uk/hro/features/1150736/helen-giles-wheres-the-evidence-for-performance-related-pay

20 Beagrie, S (2015) [accessed 23 October 2017] The Growing Role of Big Data in Reward Strategies [Online] http://www.hrmagazine.co.uk/article-details/the-role-of-big-data-in-reward-strategies

21 Staples [accessed 23 October 2017] Staples 2017 Workplace Survey [Online] https://www.staplesadvantage.com/sites/workplace-index

Data-driven employee safety and wellness

09

Employee safety and wellness are critical areas of any HR team's work. Intelligent, data-driven HR is about using data and analytics to better manage employee safety, improve working conditions for staff, and boost employee wellbeing and wellness. Technology, particularly sensors, has helped to make the work environment safer for a long time now – including smoke alarms, gas sensors, security and entry systems etc – but the emergence of big data, and especially the Internet of Things (IoT), has taken this to a completely new level. A big part of intelligent employee safety and wellbeing is about humans and machines working together. It is incredibly powerful when workplace systems are aware of the people in the workplace – what they are doing, how they are performing and how they are feeling – and this is perhaps one of the main driving forces in making our workplaces safer and our employees happier. We will see examples of humans and technology working together throughout this chapter. In particular, this chapter will explore how employee safety is improving all the time thanks to data and analytics technology, as well as ways in which companies can better look after their employees' physical and mental wellness. I will also take a look at some of the main pitfalls concerning data-driven employee safety and wellness, particularly the need to protect employees' health data.

Improving employee safety with data and analytics

I believe that making sure people are safe at work is a critically important role of big data. Obviously, there is a sliding scale of data-related technology, from completely automated robotics-driven factories at one end of the scale to the more realistic (for most businesses, at least) end of the scale where sensors and other technology are deployed as part of a safety programme. This chapter assumes that your business sits at the latter end of the scale.

Embracing technology, not abdicating responsibility to technology

I am not talking about companies relinquishing all responsibility for employee safety over to machines. There was an interesting story in 2016 about how participants in a Georgia Tech study were found to trust safety robots over their own common sense, even when it was obvious the robot was leading them into a dangerous situation.[1] In the experiment, people were guided to a room by a clearly faulty robot; it either took them via an obviously inefficient route to the room in question or broke down in the process – all of which was set up by the researcher. Once the participants were settled in the room, the smoke alarm was triggered and the unreliable robot then guided them through corridors filled with artificial smoke. Here is the scary part: even though the robot was clearly leading people the wrong way, away from emergency exit signs, most people in the study still chose to follow the robot. A few even followed the robot into a dark room blocked by furniture – again all set up by the researcher. People trusted the robot, despite the fact that it had proven itself to be faulty or unreliable at the start of the experiment. This crazy outcome shows how we need to marry technology with human experience and common sense, rather than just turning over all responsibility for our safety to machines.

In today's data-driven world, almost everything can be measured, and it is now possible for companies to measure a great deal about what their employees are doing and how they are feeling. One of my favourite examples of just how much we can measure comes from the world of healthcare. Cloud-based health monitoring, which is at the cutting edge of modern medicine, enables healthcare professionals to monitor people's health from afar and provide help or advice when needed. One wearable device developed by Philips Healthcare Informatics, for example, helps elderly people continue to live in their own homes, rather than moving into a care home.[2] The device – a small plastic fob that is worn around the neck – contains a tiny mobile phone, motion-sensing software and an accelerometer. Not only can the wearer call for help by pressing a button on the fob, the device itself can alert people if the wearer has fallen over. In systems like this, data are transmitted from the wearable device to the cloud, where analytics programs pore through the data looking for signs of concern and alerting medical professionals when needed. Wearable devices can even detect subtle changes, like a deterioration in the wearer's gait, which may be a cause for concern and require therapy. They can also seamlessly track blood pressure, heart rate, blood sugar levels, blood oxygen levels and much more. As we will see in this chapter, this kind of wearable technology can play a huge role in employee safety and wellbeing, and the technology is advancing all the time.

How the IoT is making workplaces safer

Of course, most employers want their workplaces to be safe environments where no one gets hurt. Yet, workplace accidents and work-related health issues remain a problem. The Health and Safety Executive estimates that, annually in the United Kingdom, an average of more than 600,000 workers are injured in workplace accidents and a further 500,000 suffer ill health believed to be related to their work. It also estimates the total cost of workplace injury and illness to be over £14 billion.[3] Much of this cost is borne by the individuals affected, but almost £3 billion is borne directly by employers. The impact of work-related accidents and health problems is huge, not only for the individuals and their families, but also for the employer in question and their reputation. Clearly, something needs to change.

Changing employee behaviour

Today, the IoT is transforming the way we think about and deliver employee safety. One of the challenges in workplace safety is getting employees to change their behaviour in line with existing company safety rules or to adopt new safety initiatives. And this can be particularly helpful in industries or companies that rely on contract or temporary employees, like the construction industry. The IoT helps to encourage employee adoption of safety initiatives by providing much clearer monitoring and insights into safety-related behaviour. IoT devices, particularly wearables but also sensors, now can generate a mountain of real-time data on workplace safety and employee activities. Not only can these data show whether safety rules and initiatives are being properly adopted, they also can lead to insights that help to improve safety programmes in the future. And the more these data improve safety programmes, the greater the employee buy-in and the more likely employees are to adopt new or improved safety initiatives in the future. Crucially, because IoT devices can be used to transmit real-time data for on-the-fly analysis, managers then can be alerted when unsafe practices are taking place and take appropriate action. A couple of examples of this were given in Chapter 4, including the use of video data to detect that an employee was not wearing the appropriate safety gear, prompting a notification to be sent to the employee's supervisor. Analytics like this can help to significantly reduce workplace accidents and injuries in the future. Indeed, our ability to predict workplace accidents is improving all the time. A few years ago, researchers at Carnegie Mellon University used real-world data to create predictive safety models that had accuracy rates of between 80 and 97 per cent.[4] The model, which is now in use at a number of companies, takes workplace safety inspection data and uses these to predict not just the number, but also the location of safety incidents over the next month.

The role of wearables

Throughout this chapter we will see plenty of examples of IoT devices, such as sensors, tracking bands and smart helmets, being used across a variety of industries. Clearly, wearable technology will have a huge impact on the field of employee safety, and the vision of a 'connected worker' is starting to become reality in many different industries. The beauty of IoT devices is that they make employees (and their supervisors) more aware of what they are doing and the environment around them, whether that means alerting someone when they are close to over-exerting themselves and need to take a break, or raising the alarm when the proper safety equipment is not being used. This awareness in itself can dramatically improve safety, because more aware workers are likely to behave in a much more safety-conscious manner.

One example of IoT technology in action comes from steel producer North Star BlueScope Steel. The company has been working with IBM to design a safety programme that incorporates IBM Watson's cognitive computing power and sensors in wrist bands and helmets.[5] The programme, called IBM Employee Wellness and Safety Solution, delivers alerts in real time to workers and supervisors in the event that proper safety protocols are not being followed, or when an employee's physical safety is in question. For example, if the technology detects a worker is not moving and they have an increased heart rate and high temperature, it could mean they may be suffering from exertion or even extreme heat stress, in which case a supervisor could be alerted, or the employee advised to take a break. What is really exciting is the ability not only to monitor individuals in real time, but also to personalize advice and actions to individuals based on what the data are reporting.

Similarly, the Honeywell 'Connected Worker' solution, developed in partnership with Intel, uses sensors to gather data on workers' heart rates, movements and gestures to deliver personalized advice that can help to prevent accidents or injury[6] – more on this later in the chapter. The same sort of sensor technology also can be used to monitor the environment in which someone is working. Data can be gathered on temperature, noise levels, humidity, light levels, toxic gases and radiation. Robots can effectively 'smell' now, and can use sensors to detect chemical signatures like blood or alcohol in the air. Blanca Lorena Villarreal, a researcher from the Tecnológico de Monterrey in Mexico, has developed an 'electronic nose' that can be built into robotic devices.[7] And this is not the first time this type of technology has been used. Örebro University in Sweden has developed a 'Gasbot mobile robot' that has been used to detect methane leaks in landfill sites. In fact, robots can detect such leaks much faster and more accurately than humans.[8] I will look at more examples from different industries later in the chapter but, for now, it is clear that the IoT is the future of employee safety.

Making driving safer

Driving remains one of the most dangerous things humans do, whether it is simply driving to and from work, taking to the road to visit clients or driving machinery as part of their job. One US company has now turned its iris-scanning technology towards making driving safer. Delta ID's collaboration with Gentex Corporation, known for its rear-view-mirror technology, has resulted in a rear-view mirror that scans the iris of a driver and authenticates that the driver is authorized to drive the vehicle. While this technology is primarily aimed at security for now, it is feasible that this sort of driver-scanning technology incorporated into rear-review mirrors could be used in future to identify when a driver is feeling tired or is even under the influence of alcohol or drugs.[9]

Driver fatigue is a huge issue and may contribute to up to 20 per cent of road accidents. What is more, road accidents caused by driver fatigue are roughly 50 per cent more likely to result in death or serious injury.[10] If your employees are driving vehicles as part of their job, it pays to make sure they are not struggling due to fatigue. And this does not just apply to transportation companies or individual employees taking to the roads in cars (like sales people, for instance). Driver fatigue can be an issue when driving any kind of vehicle. A report by Caterpillar has estimated that operator fatigue is one of the main causes of accidents involving earth-moving equipment, like diggers and bulldozers.[11] For those companies in the mining and construction industries, for example, driver fatigue is therefore a key aspect of employee safety.

One Australian company, Seeing Machines, has developed technology designed to tackle driver fatigue by tracking the driver's eyes.[12] The tracking system, designed specifically for vehicles used in the mining industry, incorporates a camera, global positioning system (GPS) and accelerometer. It tracks eye and eyelid movement, such as how often a driver blinks, how long those blinks last and how slowly the eyelids are moving, and it can do all this even if the driver is wearing sunglasses. It can even analyse the position of the driver's head and whether it has started to drop. When a driver closes their eyes for longer than 1.6 seconds, an alarm is triggered inside the truck – both a noise and a vibration within the seat. Then, if the alarm is triggered for a second time, a dispatcher or supervisor will be contacted, so that they can make contact with the driver via radio. If a third alarm is triggered, the driver would generally be taken off their shift. Speaking to *Wired* magazine, Seeing Machines CEO Ken Kroeger said the system could reduce 'fatigue events' by 70–90 per cent.[13] Caterpillar has been so impressed, it is now introducing the technology into some of its mining trucks. Interestingly, the system also can be used to detect when a driver is distracted and taking their eyes off where they should be, again triggering an alarm in the cab.

Seeing Machines is not the only company offering this technology; there are many other devices available for monitoring fatigue and attention, including the Maven Co-Pilot, a headset-style device that measures fatigue and distraction in drivers.[14] It is easy to see how this technology has applications far beyond vehicles used in mining and, potentially, it could be integrated into any kind of delivery vehicle, company car, heavy goods vehicle (HGV) or even aeroplane.

Making industrial and manufacturing settings safer

This vision of a connected worker may soon become reality in many industrial and manufacturing settings. Earlier in the chapter I mentioned the Honeywell and Intel 'Connected Worker' solution, and I believe this is the sort of wearable technology that will revolutionize employee safety. The technology comprises a number of wearable sensors that gather data on heart rate, breathing, motion, posture and even the presence of toxic gases. All this information is pulled together into a dashboard display that gives supervisors and safety professionals an accurate picture of what employees are experiencing in real time and enables them to respond to dangerous situations and flag potentially unsafe conditions to prevent injury or illness. Of course, most industrial and manufacturing settings involve humans working with machinery. The IoT, particularly sensors, plays a vital role in increasing machine safety and efficiency. Sensors can be used to assess machinery compliance, safety anomalies, machine stoppages (and their causes) and much more – all of which helps companies to better understand what is going on in real time on the floor, better understand the safety risks, accurately pinpoint machinery misuse and reduce safety-related stoppages. This blend of machinery and IT systems is often referred to as the 'connected enterprise'.[15]

Despite the fact that technology plays a critical role in most industrial and manufacturing settings, safety management traditionally has relied on rather dated methods and information, often based on what has happened in the past or at other locations. The ability to gather real-time insights therefore makes a huge difference. One way in which data are proving particularly valuable is in identifying discrepancies between the way machinery and safety systems are designed to be used, and the way in which they are actually used in practice. For example, data may highlight that emergency stop buttons on machines are not in fact being used in emergencies, but to clear routine jams. This misuse could reduce the efficiency of the safety system and cause it to fail when it is really needed, thus putting people at risk. Insights like this highlight when additional safety training is needed for employees. Without understanding what is really going on and why, those in charge of ensuring worker safety are effectively working in the dark. Data and analytics provide the guiding light. Plus, with the predictive capabilities of analytics, machine safety systems can predict risk through a detailed risk calculator.

Making construction sites safer

Construction sites present many safety hazards for employees, and construction workers can experience a number of work-related health problems, such as exposure to hazardous substances, vibrations and noise. One start-up company, SmartSite, has developed a hardware and software solution to help. The system, which is currently being trialled with construction companies, uses sensors to measure noise levels, ultraviolet light levels and air quality to tell bosses when workers may be at risk. The aim is to accurately measure actual conditions on the ground at construction sites instead of identifying risks based on previous jobs.

Thanks to IoT technology, even hard hats are now being made 'smart'. SmartCap have produced hard hats fitted with sensors that detect (with almost 95 per cent accuracy) fatigue in those operating machinery. Originally developed for truck drivers, the hats are already being used by construction company BAM Nuttall on rail projects in Wales, with roll-outs expected in Scotland soon.[16]

Another construction company, VINCI Construction UK, has been using ViSafe sensor technology to gather real-time data on how construction workers move as they do their jobs. These data have proved that one particular mortar board (those boards with a handle underneath used by bricklayers) actually reduced the risk of bricklayers suffering lower back injury. The EcoSpot mortar board system reduced the amount of time workers spent with their backs bent more than 20 degrees by as much as 85 per cent. Not only that, but the company found the EcoSpot system led to a 17 per cent increase in productivity, ie the number of bricks laid per minute.[17]

Keeping people safe in the heat

In recent years, the United Kingdom has experienced a number of heatwaves with temperatures above 30°C. That may not seem high to those who work in places like the Middle East or the Australian outback, but for the United Kingdom it is extreme! Even sitting at my desk writing can feel like an exertion in this level of heat. But particularly for those who work outdoors or do very physical jobs, extreme heat can present serious risks.

Engineering company Laing O'Rourke, which operates in the Australian outback, uses IoT technology to keep its employees safe in such extreme conditions.[18] The company uses a smart hard hat fitted with a sweatband sensor that measures the heart rate and temperature of wearers, as well as the external temperature around them. The data are uploaded from the hard hats to the cloud, where they are analysed to look for patterns that suggest a worker might be at risk of heatstroke. If an employee is in danger, the hard hat itself receives a sound and vibration alarm that alerts the worker to take a break in the shade. This technology is clearly applicable beyond outback conditions, and heat sensors could be used in a number of different settings, ranging from fruit farms or vineyards to construction sites.

Researchers at the University of California-Berkeley have now gone a step further to develop a device that can be easily incorporated into wristbands and headbands to monitor sweat chemicals, which could be a far more accurate way to predict when someone may be at risk of dehydration, heat exhaustion etc. The sensors detect sweat but, critically, adjust the reading according to changes in skin temperature. These signals are then uploaded to an accompanying app that can give real-time information on dehydration levels.[19]

Looking at the link between connectivity, employee safety and productivity

While it is clear that increased connectivity of both workers and machines can help to dramatically increase safety, it can also significantly boost productivity. Think about the factory machinery example outlined earlier in the chapter: if machinery or safety systems are not being used in the way intended, this can lead to earlier failure or extended shutdown for unscheduled maintenance, which obviously impacts on productivity. Detailed insights on safety-related issues can improve troubleshooting and resolve downtime issues much faster, and even prevent them from happening in the first place through improved staff training. The same is true of connected individual workers. We have already seen in this chapter how connectivity helped to improve bricklayers' productivity by 17 per cent. Other studies have shown that connected workers are typically 8–9 per cent more productive, and that having connected workers actually reduces costs by around 8 per cent.[20] With benefits like these, it is no surprise a study of around 500 manufacturing bosses found that 85 per cent believed connected workers will be commonplace in their operations by 2020.[21]

Improving employee wellbeing and wellness

As well as ensuring working environments are safe, sensors are also commonly used to ensure workplaces are pleasant environments to be in – think temperature sensors, windows that open automatically to control ventilation etc. This sort of technology is commonplace in many organizations, so, in this section, I am going to look at some of the newer or more up-and-coming ways in which companies are looking after their employees. Much of this focuses on employee health or wellness, and how many organizations, such as BP, are providing data-driven employee wellness programmes.

Why is wellness important?

It makes sense that the healthier employees are, the happier they are and, therefore, the better they perform for the company. Some of the most common work-related illnesses include mental health issues (like stress and anxiety) and musculoskeletal problems (such as back pain), and these health issues are costing companies increasingly more through employee absence and lost productivity. One report shows workplace absence currently costs the UK economy £18 billion a year, and this is predicted to rise to £21 billion by 2020.[22] In this landscape, wellness programmes are becoming increasingly more popular among employers, in an effort to encourage employees to be healthier and, therefore, happier. But such programmes are not just about reducing absence, wellness programmes also have been shown to boost employee engagement and retention.[23]

Data and analytics are beginning to play a key role in improving the effectiveness of wellness programmes and encouraging employees to engage with such programmes. Wearable fitness tracking bands such as the Fitbit brand are increasingly being offered to employees either for free or at a subsidized rate in order to help them monitor their activity levels and encourage them to be more active. There is more on this later in the chapter.

At the organizational level, analytics allow employers to analyse data on their wellness programmes – such as data from wearable devices or responses to pulse surveys to help them better design and manage aspects of employee wellness. For example, if pulse surveys highlight that one aspect of a wellness programme has a take-up that is lower than expected, the company can either modify and improve that part of the programme or replace it with something new.

Looking after your employees' mental health

As we have seen throughout this book, artificial intelligence (AI) is also playing an increasing role, particularly when it comes to employees' mental health. In Chapter 8 we looked in detail at the use of pulse surveys and sentiment analysis to identify how employees are feeling. This sort of technology, particularly sentiment analysis, can even pinpoint signs of stress, depression or anxiety in employees. With more than 400,000 people suffering from stress-related illnesses that stem directly from work every year, stress should be an especially big concern for employers.[24] According to the Health and Safety Executive, in 2015–16, stress was responsible for 37 per cent of all work-related illness cases and 45 per cent of all working days lost due to illness.[25] Digital health company BioBeats recently conducted a trial with BNP Paribas on the use of data to help employees better manage their health and wellbeing through personalized, AI-based recommendations. As part of the trial, 560 BNP Paribas employees wore a Microsoft Band 2 that continuously gathered biometric data and transmitted those data for analysis by BioBeat's AI engine. According to the findings, the programme was able to identify perceived and actual stress, and links between stress and ruminators.[26]

Improving physical health with the IoT

As well as identifying when employees are in physical danger, or suffering from stress or anxiety, technology is now able to help employees lead healthier, more active lives. The IoT has played a huge role in this – for example, how many people do you know who wear a fitness tracking band or use an app on their phone to track their activity or number of steps a day? The answer is a lot, I bet.

Reducing the risk of back problems

I was shocked to learn that 12.5 per cent of all sick days in the United Kingdom are down to back pain.[27] Increasingly, this can be attributed to how many of us sit down at a desk all day. We are simply not designed to sit down for seven hours a day, even if we do sit correctly with perfect posture the whole time. Most of us struggle to maintain great posture all day; come to think of it, most of us are not even aware of our posture a lot of the time. Yet poor posture can have serious long-term health effects and should not be overlooked.

While workstation risk assessments and ergonomic products like back supports and foot rests go some way towards protecting employees against back problems, it is clear that more could be done. Part of the solution may lie in the IoT. We have already seen many examples of how products and people are becoming increasingly connected, now even your office chair has undergone an IoT makeover. Even with a super fancy ergonomic chair, it is still possible to sit badly because we are generally not aware of our posture while we are busy working. With this in mind, the Axia Smart Chair, produced by BMA Ergonomics, has been designed to monitor your posture as you sit at your desk and provide feedback where appropriate on how to improve your posture to avoid back problems.[28] Sensors in the seat register the user's posture and make them aware when they are sitting incorrectly; vibrations let the user know when they have been sitting down too long in a bad position. A 'smart label' also enables users to actually see their current posture or how they have been sitting for the last hour, and accompanying software provides practical advice to help workers improve their posture. The idea is that, by increasing awareness of posture throughout the day, employees can modify their posture as needed and avoid back problems in the future.

The role of fitness tracking bands

The IoT is also impacting on employee health and wellness in more obvious ways: wearable fitness tracking bands. These are increasingly becoming part of corporate wellness programmes around the world, and Fitbit, one of the largest fitness tracking providers in the world, counts BP and Bank of America among its corporate clients. Target has given over 300,000 Fitbit bands to its employees, IBM gave out 40,000 Fitbits to staff over a period of two years and Barclays has given 75,000 employees subsidized Fitbit trackers.[29] Fitbit's corporate wellness offering now includes a suite of tools and resources for employers, including dashboards to monitor how employees are doing. And the trackers themselves do far more than encouraging staff to get up and walk more; Fitbit claims they also increase engagement in wellness programmes and improve health outcomes. And, particularly in the United States, these trackers are also being used to reduce health insurance costs, by allowing employers to leverage employee health and activity data to negotiate with insurers. As part of BP's 'Million Step Challenge', the company gives employees a Fitbit and challenges them to walk a million steps in one year to earn a discount off their insurance premiums for the following year. Reportedly, the programme has an impressive participation rate of 75 per cent. Furthermore, 81 per cent of employees in 2015 reached the 1 million step target.[30] This is not to say that you must rush out and buy thousands of fitness trackers for your staff, but it does point to how employees are willing to engage with IoT-enabled wellness programmes. As increasingly more people are investing in their own fitness tracking bands, and as mobile apps are increasingly offering similar capabilities to track activity and other health metrics, it is possible wellness programmes could leverage these developments to their advantage.

Predicting health issues in the future

The next logical step in IoT-enabled employee wellness is using predictive analytics to pre-empt health conditions. Intel's COVALENCE Health Analytics Platform combines wearable technology with predictive analytics to help companies identify early warning signs of illness and take action.[31] The platform uses data gathered from fitness trackers (such as heart rate, activity levels, sleep patterns etc), as well as historical health data and self-reported health data. By analysing these data, the system can pinpoint trends and flag up warning signs of potential health issues or lack of progress towards an employee's health goals.[32] Employees who are identified as being at risk then can be helped with tailored support and coaching in order to help to delay or eliminate altogether the onset of health issues.

Looking at the potential downsides of data-driven employee safety and wellness

It is clear that we can monitor an increasing number of data about employees' activities and health. The question is, perhaps, how much monitoring is too much? Particularly when it comes to employees' health data, these are obviously highly sensitive and personal data and employers need to tread carefully and act in an open and transparent way (see Chapter 6).

Health data are valuable data

Shockingly, health data are reportedly 10 times more valuable on the black market than credit card data.[33] In 2014, one of the largest healthcare providers in the United States, Community Health Systems Inc, was targeted by hackers who stole personal information on 4.5 million patients;[34] and this is in line with a wider trend of cyber criminals targeting health data. Large batches of personal health data are incredibly valuable because they can be used for medical fraud. And because medical fraud is typically slower to detect than, say, banking fraud, that makes health data far more tempting prospects for criminals. Plus, health data are frequently not as well protected as credit card data or other obvious sources of fraud, which makes them an easier target. While this is more of an issue for healthcare providers who are often operating on old legacy computer systems in desperate need of an update – as the 2017 WannaCry malware attack on the UK National Health Service shows[35] – it still needs to be considered by employers who are working with employee health data. It is imperative you guard these valuable employee data with the same level of protection as you would your customer data.

How much should employers know about their employees?

We know that tracking employee data can have a whiff of Big Brother about it, and sometimes employee scepticism is well warranted. One 2016 article showed how employers are already using data to identify when employees might be pregnant or considering becoming pregnant before those employees were ready to divulge the news to their employer.[36] Not only is this an invasion of privacy, it also opens up the potential for employers to slyly discriminate against pregnant or soon-to-be pregnant women (such as overlooking them for promotion) before they have been officially informed of the pregnancy.

The article describes how healthcare analytics company Castlight Health, which works with employers like Walmart, has the ability to mine workers' health data and identify particular segments of the employee population according to the data. 'We can tell who's at risk for being diagnosed with diabetes, who's considering pregnancy, who may need back surgery', Castlight senior product manager Alka Tandon told *Fortune*.[37] And while Castlight makes it clear it does not disclose the names of individual employees in the data it shares with clients (it only shares top-line numbers), it is easy to see how employers potentially could still work out who the data are referring to. Or, if the data highlighted that, say, 20 per cent of female employees were considering starting a family, the employer might begin to discriminate against women in its hiring practices.

There is also the issue that employees may simply be uncomfortable with their bosses knowing how fit (or not) they are, or their employer having the ability to identify when they might be at risk of health issues. Back in 2012, Ohio healthcare provider The Cleveland Clinical announced that employees who were overweight or at risk in other ways (such as being a smoker) and who did not join the company wellness programme would have to pay more for their health insurance – over 20 per cent more, in fact. And those who did join the programme but did not meet health targets set by programme administrators for them also saw their premiums rise by almost 10 per cent. Pennsylvania State University faced a similar controversy when it tried to get employees to undergo mandatory health check-ups and fill out a health risk questionnaire that asked them whether they had recently been divorced or were planning to become pregnant. Under the plan, anyone who refused to fill in the questionnaire would be fined a whopping US $100 per month. The school was forced to abandon the plan after significant staff protest.

Navigating these challenges

The challenge for HR teams is therefore to encourage participation in wellness programmes and use data to help employees live healthier lives (which, in turn, financially benefits the company) without making employees uncomfortable. BP's 1 million steps challenge gave bosses access only to aggregated data, not the ability to drill down into individual activities, and that is a smart way of doing it. Crucially, BP's programme is also voluntary. When participation in wellness programmes becomes mandatory, or when employers feel their health data may be used to punish them in some way, buy-in for wellness programmes is reduced. In addition, as we saw in Chapter 6, when you offer employees an incentive in return for their data, they are far more likely to get on board, and that is exactly what BP did when it offered lower insurance premiums to those who hit a million steps in a year. There are of course many non-data ways in which to facilitate employee wellbeing, such as providing on-site exercise facilities or discounted (or free) gym membership and serving up healthy food in the canteen. Data in no way replace good practice like this. But, used well, data and analytics can give HR teams precious insights into how to manage and improve employee wellbeing and safety.

Key takeaways

I think employee safety and wellbeing comprise one of the most exciting and fast-developing areas in relation to data and analytics, and I hope this chapter has inspired you to use data to improve your own safety measures and wellness programmes. Key points from this chapter are:

- Over half a million UK workers are injured in workplace accidents each year, and a further half a million suffer ill health believed to be related to their work.

- Data-related technology, especially wearable technology and sensors, is making workplaces safer and more comfortable places to be, ranging from construction sites and factories to regular offices.

- Because IoT devices can transmit real-time data for on-the-fly analysis, managers can be alerted when unsafe practices are taking place and take appropriate action.

- While increased connectivity of both workers and machines can help to dramatically increase safety, it can also significantly boost productivity.

- Wellness programmes are becoming increasingly more popular among employers, in an effort to encourage employees to be healthier and, therefore, happier.

- Wearable fitness tracking bands such as Fitbits are increasingly being offered to employees either for free or at a subsidized rate.

- It is important to take proper precautions to protect employee health and wellness data. Also, remember that employees may be uncomfortable with their bosses knowing how fit (or not) they are.

- The challenge for HR teams is to encourage participation in wellness programmes and use data to help employees live healthier lives without making those employees feel uncomfortable.

In the next chapter I move from making sure employees are safe and healthy to giving them the opportunities to grow, learn and develop in their careers, with a little help from data and analytics, of course.

Endnotes

1 Alphr [accessed 23 October 2017] People Trust Safety Robots over Common Sense, Even When It Puts Them in Danger [Online] http://www.alphr.com/robotics/1002840/people-trust-safety-robots-over-common-sense-even-when-it-puts-them-in-danger

2 New Scientist (2015) [accessed 31 January 2018] How Cloud-connected Sensors will Provide 24/7 Healthcare [Online] https://www.newscientist.com/article/dn28342-the-internet-of-caring-things/

3 Health and Safety Executive [accessed 23 October 2017] Costs to Great Britain of Workplace Injuries and New Cases of Work-related Ill Health – 2015/16 [Online] http://www.hse.gov.uk/statistics/cost.htm

4 Schultz, G (2013) [accessed 23 October 2017] The Era of Big Data Analytics in Safety [Online] http://www.naylornetwork.com/ngc-safetyMatters/articles/index.asp?aid=241739&issueID=38258

5 O'Connor, C (2016) [accessed 23 October 2017] Improving Worker Safety with Wearables [Online] https://www.ibm.com/blogs/internet-of-things/worker-safety-and-wearables

6 Honeywell (2015) [accessed 23 October 2017] Honeywell & Intel Demonstrate Wearable IoT Connected Safety Solutions for Industrial

Workers & First Responders [Online] https://www.honeywell.com/newsroom/news/2015/11/honeywell-intel-demonstrate-wearable-iot-connected-safety-solutions-for-industrial-workers-first-responders

7   Science Daily (2014) [accessed 23 October 2017] Electronic Nose Could Aid in Rescue Missions [Online] http://www.sciencedaily.com/releases/2014/07/140723110403.htm

8   Gasbot [accessed 31 January 2018] The Gasbot Project [Online] http://www.aass.oru.se/Research/mro/gasbot/index.html

9   Cision PR Newswire (2017) [accessed 31 January 2018] Delta ID Introduces Iris Scanning Technology for In-car Biometrics and Secure Autonomous Driving at CES 2017 [Online] https://www.prnewswire.com/news-releases/delta-id-introduces-iris-scanning-technology-for-in-car-biometrics-and-secure-autonomous-driving-at-ces-2017-300386174.html

10 RoSPA [accessed 23 October 2017] Driver Fatigue and Road Accidents [Online] https://www.rospa.com/road-safety/advice/drivers/fatigue/road-accidents

11 Caterpillar (2008) [accessed 31 January 2018] Operator Fatigue: Detection Technology Review [Online] https://www.slideshare.net/willred/cat-fatigue-technology-report-2008

12 Solon, O (2013) [accessed 23 October 2017] Eye-tracking System Monitors Driver Fatigue, Prevents Sleeping at Wheel [Online] http://www.wired.co.uk/article/eye-tracking-mining-system

13 Ludwig, S (2017) [accessed 23 October 2017] Reimagining Safety with the Industrial Internet of Things [Online] http://ehstoday.com/safety/reimagining-safety-industrial-internet-things

14 Maven Machines [accessed 31 January 2018] The Maven Co-Pilot [Online] https://mavenmachines.com/maven-co-pilot/

15 Kolodny, L (2016) [accessed 23 October 2017] Smartsite Uses Sensors to Monitor Construction Workers' Health and Safety [Online] https://techcrunch.com/2016/08/22/smartsite-uses-sensors-to-monitor-construction-workers-health-and-safety

16 BAM Nuttall (2017) [accessed 23 October 2017] BAM Nuttall and SmartCap Technologies Collaborate to Monitor Construction Workers Fatigue Levels, press release [Online] http://www.bamnuttall.co.uk/images/editor/BAM%20SmartCap%20Final%20draft%20(3).pdf

17 Smith, S (2016) [accessed 23 October 2017] IoT: Reducing Back Injuries and Costs, Improving Productivity [Online]

http://ehstoday com/construction/iot-reducing-back-injuries-and-costs-improving-productivity

18 Microsoft News Center (2015) [accessed 23 October 2017] Doffing the Hat to an Innovative Safety Solution [Online] https://news.microsoft.com/en-au/2015/11/17/doffing-the-hat-to-an-innovative-safety-solution

19 Yang, S (2016) [accessed 23 October 2017] Let Them See You Sweat: What New Wearable Sensors Can Reveal from Perspiration [Online] http://news.berkeley.edu/2016/01/27/wearable-sweat-sensors

20 Hobbs, M (2017) [accessed 23 October 2017] The Connected Industrial Worker: Achieving the Industrial Vision for the Internet of Things [Online] http://www.telegraph.co.uk/business/digital-leaders/horizons/telegraph-horizons-connected-industrial-worker

21 Accenture [accessed 23 October 2017] Disrupting the Enterprise [Online] https://www.accenture.com/t20170227T211435__w__/us-en/_acnmedia/PDF-43/Accenture-Enterprise-Disruption-Driving.pdf

22 FirstCare (2017) [accessed 23 October 2017] Cost of Absence to UK Economy Rises to £18 Billion [Online] http://www.personneltoday.com/pr/2017/03/cost-of-absence-to-uk-economy-rises-to-18-billion

23 Wright, A D (2015) [accessed 23 October 2017] How Fitness Trackers Can Boost Employee Wellness [Online] https://www.shrm.org/ResourcesAndTools/hr-topics/technology/Pages/Fitbits-and-Workplace-Wellness.aspx

24 Trades Union Congress [accessed 23 October 2017] Rep Guidance: Stress [Online] https://www.tuc.org.uk/union-reps/stress

25 Health and Safety Executive [accessed 23 October 2017] Work-related Stress, Depression or Anxiety Statistics in Great Britain 2017 [Online] http://www.hse.gov.uk/statistics/causdis/stress/stress.pdf

26 [Accessed 23 October 2017] [Online] https://biobeats.com

27 Shafizadeh, M (2016) Movement coordination during sit-to-stand in low back pain people, *Human Movement*, **17** (2), 107–11

28 BMA Ergonomics [accessed 23 October 2017] Axia Smart Chair [Online] https://www.bma-ergonomics.com/en/product/axia-smart-chair/#ad-image-0

29 Farr, C (2016) [accessed 23 October 2017] How Fitbit Became the Next Big Thing in Corporate Wellness [Online] https://www.fastcompany.com/3058462/how-fitbit-became-the-next-big-thing-in-corporate-wellness

30 Wellable (2015) [accessed 23 October 2017] BP's Wellness Program Produces 2:1 ROI by Asking Employees to Take a Million Steps [Online] http://blog.wellable.co/2015/02/04/bps-wellness-program-produces-21-roi-by-asking-employees-to-take

31 Young, E (2015) [accessed 23 October 2017] Do You Want Your Company to Know How Fit You Are? [Online] http://www.bbc.com/news/business-33261116

32 McKinsey and Company (2015) [accessed 23 October 2017] Realizing the Benefits of Health Analytics and Wearables for Population Health [Online] https://www.intel.com/content/dam/www/public/us/en/documents/solution-briefs/benefits-health-analytics-wearables-brief.pdf

33 Humer, C and Finkle, J (2014) [accessed 23 October 2017] Your Medical Record Is Worth More to Hackers Than Your Credit Card [Online] http://www.reuters.com/article/us-cybersecurity-hospitals-idUSKCN0HJ21I20140924

34 Pagliery, J (2014) [accessed 23 October 2017] Hospital Network Hacked, 4.5 Million Records Stolen [Online] http://money.cnn.com/2014/08/18/technology/security/hospital-chs-hack/index.html

35 Graham, C (2017) [accessed 23 October 2017] NHS Cyber Attack: Everything You Need to Know about 'Biggest Ransomware' Offensive in History [Online] http://www.telegraph.co.uk/news/2017/05/13/nhs-cyber-attack-everything-need-know-biggest-ransomware-offensive

36 Zarya, V (2016) [accessed 23 October 2017] Employers Are Quietly Using Big Data to Track Employee Pregnancies [Online] http://fortune.com/2016/02/17/castlight-pregnancy-data

37 McGee, S (2015) [accessed 23 October 2017] How Employers Tracking Your Health Can Cross the Line and Become Big Brother [Online] https://www.theguardian.com/lifeandstyle/us-money-blog/2015/may/01/employers-tracking-health-fitbit-apple-watch-big-brother

Data-driven learning and development

10

Learning and development (L&D), a core function of HR, is being transformed by big data technology. Even just a quick glimpse at the digital transformation happening right now in the world of education points to how data can facilitate learning at all levels, from schools and universities to corporate learning. Nowadays, everything in education can be measured, from how well a student performs in tests, to how well they engage with and understand the pages in an online course. For example, data have been used extensively in education, even in primary schools, to give a better understanding of skills levels, thereby helping to identify those who may be struggling and need extra support. And, as we saw in Chapter 7, Facebook is even able to predict our intelligence based on what we 'like'. Developments like these can all feed into a corporate L&D programme that is intelligently designed around the organization's and its employees' needs.

I start this chapter by outlining the dramatic transformation happening in the world of education (both in schools and in universities), to give an idea of how HR could benefit from data-driven learning. Then I explore some of the changes beginning to take place in corporate L&D and how big data technology can help you to identify learning gaps in your organization, deliver data-driven learning programmes, and measure how learners are doing and how your L&D programme impacts on wider company performance. I also spend time looking at some of the more cutting-edge developments in L&D, namely virtual reality (VR) and augmented reality (AR). Finally, I close the chapter with an outline of the key pitfalls to be aware of when applying big data technology to your L&D activities.

How data are positively disrupting education in schools and universities

With learning now coordinated online and often taking place via a laptop or tablet, even when the student is in a traditional classroom environment, increasingly large amounts of data are being generated about how students learn. Technological innovators working with educational establishments are learning to transform these data into insights that can identify better teaching strategies, highlight areas where students may not be learning efficiently and transform the delivery of education.

Learning that is tailored to individual students

Education has always fundamentally been about feedback loops. A teacher presents a problem and the student attempts to solve it. From that attempt, the teacher can learn what the student understands and does not understand, and can adjust their instruction accordingly. Likewise, the student understands more about the problem they attempted. When a teacher is faced with a classroom overflowing with students, data and technology help to facilitate this feedback process. With hundreds of students to monitor, in the past it may have been difficult for teachers to identify which pupils were in need of an extra helping hand, and many of these decisions may have been based on gut feeling. In the past, the first sign that a pupil was in danger of failing might have been when they scored poorly in a test. A data-based approach to ongoing analysis and assessment of individual students' achievements means that more personalized learning can be delivered, taking each student's individual interests, prior knowledge and level of academic ability into account.

Any teacher can walk students through a course, but to pinpoint and develop the specific problem areas of each student in a classroom of many is a tough undertaking. This is why numerous adaptive learning companies like Knewton have sprung up, offering services that analyse the progress of students, from the nursery class to university level, to create better test questions and personalized learning materials. Crucially, these data-driven courses adapt to each individual student. Technology now makes it possible to assess, in real time, whether a section is too easy, too hard, or just right for that student, and to adjust the remaining course materials accordingly. Personalized learning like this also allows students to learn at their own pace, regardless of what the other students around them are doing. Then, the teacher can receive that information and understand where any one student might be struggling, or analyse the performance of a class as a whole.

In another development, IBM recently unveiled its vision of 'smart classrooms': online learning systems that use machine learning to help teachers pinpoint students most at risk of dropping out of a class, as well as guiding teachers on the best interventions to stop that from happening.[1] The system also identifies individual students' learning styles and guides the teacher on what kind of content is best for which students, and how best to deliver that content. Other systems like IBM's Watson content analytics help to organize and optimize content for learners.

The impact of AI in schools

But what does all this technology mean for the teachers themselves? The best teachers go into the profession because they are passionate about educating young people and they thrive on seeing a student's eyes light up when they understand a subject. The idea of effectively becoming a data administrator may not appeal to most teachers. It is the classic human versus machine scenario: as artificial intelligence (AI) gets better at teaching and providing educational assistance, the question inevitably turns to whether (or when) human teachers will be replaced by computers. Students across the United States are currently enrolled in online schools that provide the benefits of a teacher and curriculum with the comfort and convenience of home-schooling and, although these schools still have human teachers ready to answer questions from students, much of the teaching is done by computer programs. Now, I do not believe cyborgs are going to take over our classrooms. Instead, teachers and AI computers will team up to provide stronger and better educational experiences for students at every level. Following are just some of the ways in which AI is positively disrupting education:

- *AI can automate basic, repetitive activities like marking papers.* Today's essay grading software is not up to par with human teachers, but computer programs can accurately grade all kinds of multiple choice and fill-in-the-blank-style homework.

- *Educational software can adjust to meet each student exactly where they are.* Educational programs can adjust the speed at which individual students go through coursework, provide additional help when a student is getting stuck or provide additional enrichment when a student is working ahead of the rest of the class.

- *AI can go beyond the classroom and support students at home.* As any parent knows, it can be a huge challenge when a child struggles with homework. Educational programmes that can be accessed from home can provide support at any time of the day or night, and can even provide additional tutoring to students who need it.

- *AI can help the teacher provide better learning experiences.* If educational software notes that a large percentage of students are missing a particular question, it can flag that question, which can provide important feedback to the human teacher that their lesson may need additional details or clarity.

- *Computer systems can provide valuable feedback to parents, educators and administrators.* This could reduce the need for separate standardized testing and provide a level playing field for helping to assess teacher and school performance.

This dramatic transformation of education should not come as a surprise. Computers were born in colleges and universities, and, by the 1980s, they had become common in primary and secondary schools too. You may well have had your first experience on the Internet at school or college. IT and education have always gone hand in hand. Data just add another dimension.

Real-world examples from the education sector

I have encountered many cutting-edge uses of data and analytics in education, and there are numerous examples of how technology is helping both teachers and students to get the most out of their school days. In Wisconsin's Menomonee Falls School District, for example, data have been put to use for everything from improving classroom cleanliness to planning school bus routes, after department leaders were encouraged to attend classes themselves on how to gain insights from data and analytics.[2] The following are just a few other examples from the real world.

Improving student behaviour

One US middle school found that, for some reason, the number of pupils being sent to the principal's office for disciplinary reasons had grown by a worrying amount. On examining the data, they realized that this had coincided with a reduction in school excursions such as ice skating and sledding trips. When these were reinstated, behaviour among students improved, leading to a noticeable reduction in the number being sent to see the principal.[3]

Reducing cheating

Schools are also finding themselves armed with new technologies aimed at cutting down on exam cheating and plagiarism among students. The Proctortrack system aims to prevent cheating by using webcams and microphones to monitor students while they sit for online exams. By building profiles of cheating behaviour, it is able to recognize and flag suspicious activity. Proctortrack also uses facial recognition to ensure that the correct student is taking the test, monitors computer activity to make sure that unauthorized sources are not being consulted and even tracks eyeball movement during the assessment. The system can be used for tests taking place in traditional exam-room environments as well as remote learning.

Improving the education experience for students

In universities, too, big data technology is being put to use to improve the education experience. Lectures in higher education establishments, by their nature, are less interactive than school lessons, perhaps based on the flawed assumption that older, more advanced learners will need less prompting to pay attention in class. This means that lecturers often get very little feedback on the efficiency of their teaching before students either graduate or fail based on their final exams.

One Michigan University professor developed the LectureTools software to combat this problem. The program allows students to follow lecture presentations on their laptops, annotating them as they go along. It also lets them ask anonymous questions while the talk is in progress, and these questions flash up on the lecturer's screen. This makes it easier for students who may be embarrassed about speaking in public or their lack of understanding. The system also includes an 'I'm confused' button. Lecturers can look at usage statistics for all of these features and use them to fine-tune their delivery and engage with students when individual attention is required.

Beyond the classroom

Of course, not all education takes place in the classroom. Increasingly, thanks to the Internet, remote learning is making it possible for people of all ages whose geographical location, income level or general lack of free time make attending traditional educational establishments difficult. These massive online open courses (MOOCs), which deliver all of the learning materials and exams via a computer or tablet, are providing a wealth of insights into the ways in which people learn. Harvard University has recently developed Harvard X Insights, a tool that allows data gathered from these courses to be examined in real time.[4] This means data from the millions of people around the world who take these courses (and the far smaller number that actually complete them) can be analysed to find the stumbling blocks that cause learners to fail. As we will see in this chapter, online learning and the ability to track and measure progress is having a significant impact on the world of L&D.

Introducing the digital transformation of L&D

One survey of senior L&D officers found that most respondents expected corporate learning to change dramatically over the next few years, and more than 60 per cent planned to increase L&D spending and the number of training hours for each employee.[5] It is no surprise that, like the education sector, corporate L&D is also evolving quickly thanks to data and analytics. As technologies like online

Figure 10.1   Digital transformation of L&D

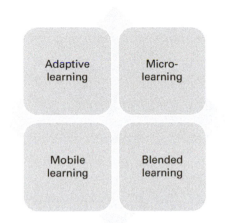

learning have developed, the notion of individuals learning at their own pace at a computer screen (as opposed to being part of a group training programme delivered at a set pace) has become increasingly popular. Below I briefly look at some of the ways in which L&D is being transformed by data (see Figure 10.1). I will explore the most important of these trends later in the chapter.

Learning that is adapted to individual employees

Thanks to online learning, data and analytics, L&D is becoming increasingly personalized to individual learners. 'Adaptive' learning technology allows courses, segments of courses, activities and test questions to be personalized to suit the learner's preference, pace of learning and best way of learning. As well as allowing individuals to learn at their own pace, online learning also offers the same big advantage seen in the education sector: the ability to measure how individual participants are progressing, how well they are retaining the information and where additional guidance or information might be required. Individual, self-paced online learning is also arguably more cost-effective than pulling employees out of their job for a day or week to send them on expensive training courses. Self-directed learning like this also helps to integrate ongoing development into workers' everyday routines. Danone's online Danone Campus 2.0 is one example of this in action.[6] The food giant has created a user-friendly online platform where employees can boost their development and share best practice and knowledge with other staff.

Micro, mobile and blended learning

Running with this idea of employees learning when it best suits them, 'micro-learning' has become a bit of a buzz phrase in L&D. Micro-learning involves very short bursts of learning, often delivered through short videos of just a couple of minutes. These are typically delivered as part of a wider course, and are used to help learners absorb information more quickly and easily. We all know how information is easier to absorb in small chunks at a time, rather than in one massive go. Micro-learning capitalizes on this. Mobile learning is another up-and-coming trend in L&D, as increasingly more learning and training providers support mobile devices in their programmes. Mobile access to learning content allows employees the flexibility to learn when and where it suits them, for example, when there are minimal distractions. It also fits with the increase in remote working that many companies are experiencing. Finally, 'blended learning' – commonly used to describe the marriage of online learning and classroom learning – is proving very popular as companies transition away from traditional L&D models. So remember, what works for your company indeed may be a blend of traditional training courses and self-directed learning.

Identifying and closing gaps in learning

Before we delve further into delivering data-driven L&D programmes, you need to be able to understand exactly what kind of content is needed. As we will see in Chapter 11, data can significantly improve a company's ability to assess performance and pinpoint exactly where employees are performing well and where they may need some extra assistance. In this way, data help HR teams to identify gaps in learning, so that they can plug those gaps through appropriate training. Clearly, with data, analytics and automation developing at the pace they are, and with no sign of that exhausting pace letting up, one major function of L&D professionals is to help fill the digital skills gap. HR teams have a responsibility to ensure more people in the organization have the necessary skills to prepare for the data-driven transformation of the business. There is no doubt in my mind that the ability to tap into and nurture digital skills is going to be critical to the success of most businesses in the future. Yet, more than 12 million employees in the United Kingdom do not have the necessary digital skills.[7] As well as attracting talent with the right digital skills, companies also need to invest in delivering accessible and effective training where needed. Without this, employees will not be properly equipped to help the business thrive in the future. Online learning is perfectly placed to help companies fill the digital skills gap, and those that invest now will reap the rewards in the future.

Delivering data-driven L&D

With 68 per cent of workers saying L&D is the most important workplace policy, and with 40 per cent of employees who receive poor training leaving the company within the first year, it is vital companies get L&D right.[8] In addition, L&D has a significant impact on employee engagement, and companies that use e-learning or online learning achieve an 18 per cent increase in employee engagement.[8] As we have already seen in this chapter from just a quick glimpse at recent developments in education and L&D, learning is now moving away from traditional models where participants go to a specific place for a set duration of time to learn at a predefined pace. Now, for workers, learning is becoming something to dip into much more frequently, but perhaps in more bite-size pieces, and at their own pace. Learning is essentially becoming a core part of the day-to-day job. In this section, I explore in more detail some of the key trends in data-driven L&D that were identified earlier in the chapter (see Figure 10.2).

Figure 10.2   Key trends in data-driven L&D

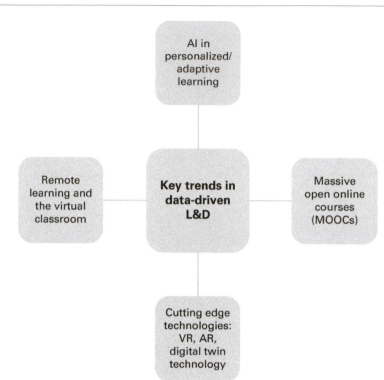

Remote learning and the virtual classroom

One of my favourite examples of just how much learning has transformed comes from Harvard Business School (HBS). The school has created a digital classroom as a template of the classroom of the future.[9] In this virtual classroom, the lecturer teaches in a specially designed broadcast studio. Cameras follow the lecturer as they address a huge screen made up of faces: live-feed videos (with audio) of all the students participating in the lecture, connected to the class simply by their standard computers or laptops. Even though these students could be anywhere in the world, it is as though they are in the same room. This virtual classroom, which HBS has called HBX Live, took three years of planning and development, and is designed to integrate seamlessly with HBS's online teaching programmes.

Inspired by TV

Much of the HBX Live experience was apparently inspired by visits to NBC Sports in New York, and it is clearly a big production in the same vein as a TV show. Four production staff are required to assist the teacher, operating the camera, managing the live feed, cueing up slides and videos etc. Speaking to *Fortune* about his experience of teaching in HBX Live, Harvard professor Bharat Anand said: 'You can see someone who is up at 3 am in the Philippines, someone in Seattle and another in Mumbai. This feels like you are literally in the classroom, and the feedback we're getting is that this is every bit as engaging as being in the classroom – but more intense'.[9] Students participating in the virtual classes have noted how it encourages participation because no one can hide in the back row of the class.

Recreating an authentic classroom experience

One thing that is really striking about this virtual classroom is the extent to which it feels like a real classroom experience to the lecturer and students participating. The system was designed so that all microphones would be on all the time, including the students', and no one was muted. This makes for a much more collaborative, authentic learning experience, where students can laugh along if the professor makes a joke and agree verbally when someone makes a good point. When a student wants to interject with a question or point, rather than raising their hands, they simply click a button on their computer and their nameplates on the screen turn red, letting the lecturer know that they have something to say. Students can also type comments via a chat bar, and the comments then scroll along the bottom of the huge video screen like a news ticker. And, even more impressively, up to 60 students can participate in these virtual classes at a time, which is quite a feat when you consider that is 60 separate video feeds being managed in real time without any delay whatsoever. The system also allows for up to 1,000 additional students to observe the virtual lesson with a short time delay. HBS began testing the virtual classroom back in 2014 and launched it officially in 2015. It is now also being offered as part of HBS's custom solutions for corporate clients. For example, the school, fittingly, offers corporate clients access to an HBX course by disruption innovation expert Clay Christensen. For me, this example points to the future of education and gives us a hint as to where corporate L&D may be going in the future, either by companies developing their own version of virtual learning or tapping into services provided by forward-thinking schools like Harvard.

The use of AI in personalized learning

Online learning allows for much greater measurement, because learners leave behind digital traces of everything they do within the parameters of the course they are taking. These traces include how quickly the learner moved through a particular element of the course, where they paused, where they got a test question wrong, which material they revisited and even potentially what time of day the learner best assimilated information. Learning management systems allow providers to track these data and use the insights gained to tailor courses to individuals' needs, thereby making them much more engaging. AI is critical in this ability to provide adaptive, personalized learning. It is AI, and particularly machine learning, technology that allows providers to identify where a learner might be struggling and what areas need extra emphasis for that individual. Analytics company Zoomi, for example, uses AI capabilities to analyse each learner's behaviour, performance, engagement and comprehension to improve learning content and create a uniquely individual learning experience. Zoomi claims its solution can shorten training hours by up to 60 per cent.[10]

The evidence for an AI or machine learning-based approach is clear. A 2016 paper published by Pearson and UCL set out how AI creates learning programmes that are more flexible, efficient and inclusive.[11] In particular, the authors cite how AI effectively allows personalized, one-to-one learning to be provided on a large scale, which is especially beneficial for larger companies with a diverse network of employees all with different training needs. Naturally, this works both ways: not only can personalized learning track how individuals are progressing, it also allows learners to provide instant feedback on course content and features.

Making use of MOOCs

Because of their vastness ('massive' being the big clue in the name), MOOCs provide a unique opportunity for data. Huge amounts of data can be gathered not only on individuals but also across multiple learners to pick up broader patterns and insights. These courses allow providers to map an individual's learning trajectory, identify trouble spots and provide targeted interventions where needed. MOOCs from the likes of Coursera and Khan Academy provide accessible learning opportunities for millions of people around the world, covering anything from vocational learning to degree-level courses. In MOOCs, learners undertake self-directed learning when it suits them, engage with bite-size micro-learning content like short videos, and participate in collaborative discussions with other learners. Now, many corporate L&D programmes are making use of MOOCs to deliver training to their employees. Companies like Microsoft are creating their own custom MOOCs for employees. For example, global steel manufacturer Tenaris has created MOOCs on various topics, including technical topics like 'Introduction to steel' and broader business topics like 'International trade'.[12] Tenaris is now offering the MOOCs externally to attract university students and boost its employer brand. Other organizations, such as Bank of America, are leveraging content from existing MOOCs to deliver training on core competencies. This strategy allows businesses of all sizes to curate a wide range of content that suits their needs in a simple, cost-effective way. Both strategies are innovative ways of rethinking L&D and capitalizing on the latest advances in learning technology.

Measuring how learners are doing and how L&D impacts on performance

When learners work through the content in a digital course, they leave a digital trace of all their actions. This ability to track leaners' journeys gives training providers and L&D professionals the opportunity to understand a great deal about the learning experience. Indeed, most learning providers incorporate some sort of learning management system that tracks how learners progress and provides insights that can help both individual learners and the company-wide L&D programme.

The importance of learning analytics

Learning analytics should therefore underpin every aspect of employee learning, from developing better learning programmes, to delivering them in the most engaging way and tracking how employees interact with the programme. Data and analytics can also dramatically improve the measurement of L&D by showing how effective (or not) it is in practice. Currently, assessing the effectiveness of corporate training often comes down to little more than trainees completing an evaluation questionnaire after a course. Data allow us to go so much further, such as showing how trainees respond to each section of a course, which areas they struggle with and which trainees are ready for more advanced materials. With the in-depth insights available from data like these, L&D professionals can pinpoint exactly what is working and what is not.

Two specific data points that every company should be measuring are employee comprehension (eg are people struggling with various aspects of the content?) and employee engagement with content (eg are they taking up opportunities for learning and are they then participating in courses all the way through or are they ignoring various aspects?).

Demonstrating value by linking training to performance

Data also allow HR teams to create clear, evidence-based links between training and performance, which is helpful for improving future L&D, establishing return on investment (ROI) and securing leadership buy-in for training programmes. There is more on measuring and driving performance in Chapter 11. This detailed measurement and assessment is already commonplace in the education sector, where students, teachers and whole schools are commonly assessed according to various metrics and benchmarks. Sometimes this has proven problematic, such as the argument that standardized testing (such as statutory assessment tests or SATs) provides just a snapshot of what has really been learned. The development of learning analytics therefore has dramatically improved the ability to measure, understand and improve teaching and learning right down to an individual level.

Purdue University in the United States previously developed the Signals learning analytics programme, which uses a coloured traffic-light system to tell students whether their learning is going well or whether they may need more help.[13] Not only do systems like this help measure learners' progress, they also encourage self-reflection and monitoring in order to improve performance while undertaking a course. This benefits the individual, but also helps the company to get the utmost out of its training programmes.

The cutting edge: incorporating VR and AR into L&D

Interestingly, VR and AR are becoming more common tools in corporate L&D and, in particular, many vendors are now offering VR-enabled training programmes.

Stepping into a virtual world

VR creates an interactive environment by generating realistic images, sounds and other sensations to fully immerse the user in that environment. It is easy to imagine how this technology could be used to provide immersive training experiences in fields as diverse as medicine, the armed forces, engineering etc. This is not a new idea – just think of flight simulators, for example – but the ever-decreasing cost of VR hardware (headsets, gloves etc) has made the technology more accessible to a far wider audience. VR technology even can be used on smartphones, although that tends to be less immersive than the VR hardware.

Some current uses of VR include Medical Realities' education platform for surgical trainees.[14] Using the Oculus Rift VR system, Medical Realities' platform provides a collection of modules, each offering immersive 360-degree videos of real operations. VR training is also available for armed forces and law enforcement personnel in the form of the VIRTISM VR system, created by US defence contractor Raytheon.[15] The system, which comprises full-body motion capture, VR headsets and fake guns, provides simulations of realistic combat environments, where squads of trainees are pitted against each other.

The applications of this technology can reach far into the world of business too. For example, one global manufacturer has created a virtual model factory, where employees are completely immersed in a 3D experience that lets them 'see' and 'feel' equipment in the companies' factories.[5] And even softer business skills can be learned with VR technology. VirtualSpeech's app makes use of Google's Cardboard VR smartphone technology to allow users to practise their public speaking and interpersonal communication skills.[16] Combining practical experience, online reading materials, videos that teach basic skills and instant feedback, the course aims to help people to develop quickly and build their confidence in a safe environment. It is easy to see how VR technology like this could be incorporated into an L&D programme to boost individuals' presentation skills.

'It's reality, Jim, but not as we know it'

While VR plunges the user into a simulated world, AR is rooted firmly in reality, and adds an extra layer of information to the real world that the user sees in front of them. Google Glass is based on this technology. Although AR is, for now, less commonly used in training, there are certainly many potential uses for AR in L&D. For example, an engineer in training could be able to look at an aircraft engine with Google Glass and be given information on each part of the engine.

Creating digital twins

'Digital twin' technology is closely related to AR because it pairs the virtual and physical worlds. The digital twin concept is now so imperative to business, it was named one of Gartner's Top 10 Strategic Technology Trends for 2017.[17] Quite simply, a digital twin is a virtual model of a process, product or service that allows analysis of data and monitoring of systems to head off problems before they even occur, preventing downtime and even planning for the future by using simulations. How do digital twins work? First, smart components that use sensors to gather data about real-time status, working conditions or position are integrated with a physical item. The components are connected to a cloud-based system that receives and processes all the data that the sensors monitor. This input is then analysed and lessons are learned and opportunities are uncovered within the virtual environment that can be applied to the physical world. Digital twins are powerful tools for driving innovation and performance. In fact, IDC predicts that, by 2018, companies which invest in digital twin technology will see a 30 per cent improvement in cycle times of critical processes.[18] One example of this in action comes from GE's 'digital wind farm'. GE uses digital twin technology to inform the configuration of each wind turbine prior to construction in order to generate efficiency gains. As Ganesh Bell, chief digital officer and general manager of Software & Analytics at GE Power & Water, told me: 'For every physical asset in the world, we have a virtual copy running in the cloud that gets richer with every second of operational data'.[19] While digital twins are largely used to drive performance and efficiency, it is not a huge leap to imagine how this technology could be used to enhance training for a wide range of employees, particularly in the field of engineering.

Looking at the downside of data-driven L&D

As with almost any application of data, there are ethical concerns concerning working with individuals' learning data, particularly when it comes to data privacy and security. There is more on this in Chapter 6.

Key pitfalls to look out for

Data breaches are always a legitimate concern, and rightly so. In 2009, one school district in Tennessee inadvertently left the names, addresses, birth dates and full social security numbers of

18,000 students on an unsecured server for months.[20] Therefore, ensuring your employees' data are private and secure is a critical concern for any HR team. These days, it is incredibly naive to think you do not have to worry about protecting your employees' data. Where possible, anonymizing employees' L&D data will help. Where anonymizing data is not possible, you will need to ensure the data are kept secure.

There is also the concern, particularly in the world of schools and universities, that education providers can simply know too much about their students. In a brilliantly titled 2014 article – *Blowing off Class? We know* – the author, Goldie Blumenstyk, stated: 'the stuff some colleges know right now about their students, thanks to data mining of their digital footprints, boggles the mind'.[21] With the latest advances in technology, it is possible for education providers and companies to gather huge amounts of data on an individual's performance, activities and behaviour, whether they are a student or an employee. And I can certainly see how that would be a concern for many people.

Navigating these pitfalls

Good practices of data minimization and transparency help to steer the way here. As with any use of data, there is no point gathering data for data's sake. Therefore, if you do not intend to use L&D data to make improvements, then do not gather them – it is as simple as that. And when you do intend to gather them, make sure you are upfront with your employees about what information you are gathering and why. If it is clear these data are being analysed to help improve the delivery of learning programmes in the future, and to facilitate individuals' development within the company, staff are much more likely to get on board.

Key takeaways

Helping employees to grow and develop is a critical part of any HR team's function – perhaps even one of the most rewarding parts – and it is clear that data have a big role to play in this field. Following is a rundown of what we have covered in this chapter:

- With 40 per cent of employees who receive poor training leaving the company within the first year, it is vital companies get L&D right.

- Corporate L&D is undergoing a massive digital transformation, with key trends being adaptive learning, micro-learning, mobile learning and blended learning.

- Data help HR teams to identify gaps in learning, so that they can plug those gaps.

- AI is critical to providing adaptive learning. It allows companies to identify where a learner might be struggling and which areas need extra emphasis.

- Many corporate L&D programmes are making use of MOOCs. Some companies like Microsoft are creating their own custom MOOCs for employees, while others are leveraging content from existing MOOCs.

- Learning analytics should underpin every aspect of employee learning, from developing better learning programmes, through delivering them in the most engaging way, to tracking how employees interact with the programme.

- Data also allow HR teams to create clear, evidence-based links between training and wider company performance, which helps to improve future L&D, establish ROI and secure leadership buy-in.

- VR and AR are becoming more common tools in corporate L&D and these areas are definitely worth keeping an eye on.

- Take necessary steps to protect your employees' learning data and minimize data collection wherever possible.

As we will see in the next chapter, the use of data and analytics extends even further, helping companies better measure and drive employee performance and identify where employees may need extra assistance to perform at their best, which links back to these data-driven L&D activities.

Endnotes

1 Davison, M (2016) [accessed 23 October 2017] AI and the Classroom: Machine Learning in Education [Online] http://blog.trueinteraction. com/ai-and-the-classroom-machine-learning-in-education

2 Rich, M (2015) [accessed 23 October 2017] Some Schools Embrace Demands for Education Data [Online] http://www.nytimes.com/ 2015/05/12/us/school-districts-embrace-business-model-of-data-collection.html?smid=tw-share&_r=1

3 Marr, B (2016) [accessed 23 October 2017] Big Data and the Evolution of Education [Online] http://data-informed.com/ big-data-and-evolution-education

4 Harvard University [accessed 23 October 2017] Harvard X Insights [Online] http://harvardx.harvard.edu/harvardx-insights

5 van Dam, N and Otto, S-S (2016) [accessed 23 October 2017] Corporate Learning's Transformation in the Digital Age [Online] http://www. clomedia.com/2016/12/05/corporate-learnings-transformation-digital-age

6 YouTube [accessed 23 October 2017] Danone Campus 2.0 [Online] https://www.youtube.com/watch?v=oBJAvsl6gRI

7 Cellan-Jones, R (2015) [accessed 23 October 2017] More Than 12 Million Fall into UK Digital Skills Gap [Online] http://www.bbc.com/ news/technology-34570344

8 Olenski, S (2017) [accessed 23 October 2017] Why C-Levels Need to Think about eLearning and Artificial Intelligence [Online] https://www. forbes.com/sites/steveolenski/2017/02/06/why-c-levels-need-to-think-about-e-learning-and-artificial-intelligence/#76748552ff70

9 Byrne, J A (2015) [accessed 23 October 2017] Harvard Business School Really Has Created the Classroom of the Future [Online] http:// fortune.com/2015/08/25/harvard-business-school-hbx

10 Zoomi [accessed 23 October 2017] Artificial Intelligence for Learning [Online] http://zoomiinc.com

11 UCL Institute of Education (2016) [accessed 23 October 2017] Why We Should Take Artificial Intelligence in Education More Seriously [Online] https://www.ucl.ac.uk/ioe/news-events/news-pub/april-2016/ New-paper-published-by-pearson-makes-the-case-for-why-we-must-take-artificial-intelligence-in-education-more-seriously

12 Franceschin, T [accessed 23 October 2017] Case Study: How Tenaris University Built a Successful MOOC for Employee Training [Online] http://edu4.me/en/case-study-how-tenaris-university-built-a-successful-mooc-for-employee-training

13 Arnold, K (2010) [accessed 23 October 2017] Signals: Applying Academic Analytics [Online] http://er.educause.edu/articles/2010/3/signals-applying-academic-analytics

14 Medical Realities [accessed 23 October 2017] Learn Surgery in Virtual Reality [Online] http://www.medicalrealities.com

15 Lang, B (2012) [accessed 23 October 2017] VIRTSIM is the Virtual Reality Platform That Gamers Crave but Can't Have [Online] http://www.roadtovr.com/virtsim-virtual-reality-platform

16 VirtualSpeech [accessed 23 October 2017] Communication Skills Courses with VR [Online] http://virtualspeech.com

17 Panetta, K (2016) [accessed 23 October 2017] Gartner's Top 10 Strategic Technology Trends for 2017 [Online] http://www.gartner.com/smarterwithgartner/gartners-top-10-technology-trends-2017

18 IDC [accessed 23 October 2017] IDC FutureScape 2016 [Online] http://www.idc.com/idcfuturescapes2016

19 Marr, B (2017) [accessed 23 October 2017] What is Digital Twin Technology – and Why Is It So Important? [Online] https://www.forbes.com/sites/bernardmarr/2017/03/06/what-is-digital-twin-technology-and-why-is-it-so-important/2/#683fd24c3227

20 SC Media [accessed 31 January 2018] School District Contractor Exposes Student Information [Online] https://www.scmagazine.com/school-district-contractor-exposes-student-information/article/556679/

21 Blumenstyk, G (2014) [accessed 23 October 2017] Blowing off Class? We Know [Online] https://www.nytimes.com/2014/12/03/opinion/blowing-off-class-we-know.html

Data-driven performance management

11

Generally speaking, measuring and reviewing the performance of employees is done poorly by many companies. Traditional methods such as annual performance reviews are often disliked by both the employees being reviewed and the managers conducting the reviews, and can be a huge waste of time. Intelligent, data-driven HR teams, however, take advantage of data and analytics to better monitor *actual* performance on a more regular basis (even in real time) and provide feedback to employees in a more constructive, continual and consistent (ie without bias) way. As we have seen throughout this book, it is now possible to measure pretty much everything an employee does in the course of their daily working life. That is not to say you would necessarily measure absolutely everything, as most companies simply do not have the budget and data capabilities to measure everything an employee does, and the risk of alienating your workforce in that scenario would be high. But, with well-chosen metrics, it is certainly possible now to gather an accurate picture of how your people are actually performing and use that information to provide recognition and feedback to help employees grow.

A word of warning before we start

Clearly, measuring people performance with data and analytics can offer a great deal, but it must be applied carefully. There is a fine line between performance improvement and employee surveillance, and companies that have overstepped this mark have faced huge backlashes. Most people do not want their boss to monitor their every move and, in fact, this can be hugely demoralizing for staff, particularly the most self-motivated members of the workforce. To avoid your company coming across as some sort of Orwellian tyrant, you will need to tread a fine line, gathering the data that you really need to give people genuinely useful feedback, without upsetting your workforce or damaging your employer brand. Undoubtedly, this is a difficult balance to achieve and maintain, and my concern is that many employers will not get this delicate balance right. I hope this chapter will help you to chart a course that is appropriate for your organization.

So what can you expect from this chapter? I start by exploring a few key developments in the world of sport, which may give us some hints about where data-driven employee performance may be heading in the future. I then look at two key strands of data-driven employee performance: intelligently measuring employee performance and intelligently reviewing how employees are performing. Finally, I look at the potential backlash concerning using performance data and look at two in-depth case studies: one that demonstrates how *not* to handle employee performance, and one where the company managed to strike the right balance.

Lessons from the world of sport

Sport is often at the cutting edge of data and analytics, and it provides a useful glimpse of how data can be used to drive very real performance improvements. Coaches across a whole range of sports, from cycling to football, are using data to assess and improve individual performance.

Measuring physical performance and sleep

A number of US National Football League (NFL) teams use an athlete tracking system called OptimEye, developed by Catapult Sports.[1] A lightweight wearable device (worn in a small top that looks a bit like a sports bra) tracks metrics such as players' speed, motion and heart rate, and calculates player exertion. Having these data helps coaches and support staff to identify which players are working hardest in practice and who could work harder, as well as preventing illness or injuries from players pushing themselves too hard. It also means workouts and practice drills can be tailored to each individual on the team. Plus, if a player does get injured, the historical data will help to ensure the player does not reinjure themselves during recovery. OptimEye devices are also used in UK football by many Premier League teams during practice sessions to monitor and design individual training routines, and spot early warning signs of injury. Looking to the future, devices are being developed to monitor things like adrenaline and cortisol (the stress hormone) levels, as well as perspiration levels.

But sport performance is not just about physical exertion; good quality sleep is another critical factor in getting athletes to perform at their best. A Stanford University study found that basketball players who slept for an extra 90 minutes improved both the accuracy of their shots and how fast they could run.[2] In football, many clubs give players wristbands to assess sleep quality, in order to assess any potential problems and find solutions that will help to boost the players' performance.

Moving to real-time analysis

When it comes to analysing player performance in matches, most analysis traditionally was done post-match using video analytics. That is starting to change though as, in 2015, the International Football Association Board agreed to change the rules governing the use of wearable devices, opening up the potential for league and competition organizers to allow players to wear such devices during matches themselves.[3] This provides coaching teams with a wealth of new possibilities to track actual player performance during a match and potentially make changes at half-time based on what the data are telling them. The hope is that the use of tracking devices would also help to reduce the number of deaths from cardiac arrest. While in-depth monitoring like this clearly goes way beyond what the average company is capable of, the use of cheap and readily available fitness trackers could change this situation. For example, it is not inconceivable for employers to use sleep data to understand who may be too tired for a certain job, especially if it is a dangerous task. Even in a typical office setting, a critical sales pitch or meeting could be allocated to the employee who is the most rested.

Intelligently measuring employee performance

There is clear evidence that measuring performance delivers real operational and financial improvements, as the UPS example later in this chapter shows; however, 'performance' is the critical word in that sentence and companies need to make it clear they are monitoring performance and not individual behaviour. Think about what motivates you as an employee and what would send your satisfaction and engagement plummeting. Personally, I am very self-motivated: give me a goal and I will achieve it, without needing to be hit with a big stick. If I felt my boss was watching my every move to make sure I achieved that goal, I would hardly thrive.

It is a tough balance to strike

If we think of the publisher of this book as my boss for a second, I know I would not be happy if my boss was monitoring how many minutes I spent typing at my computer. On paper, those minutes spent 'idling' and not typing would look unproductive, and yet those minutes are critically important for research and organizing my thoughts. If my every keystroke was monitored, I would feel extremely demotivated and disengaged. Not only that, while such monitoring may lead me (at least in the short term) to produce more words a day, the quality of my output would be likely to go down, not up. This is the danger with monitoring employees: self-motivated employees could well be put off and you could end up with the opposite effect to what you intended.

We know that it is now possible for HR teams to understand more about their employees – how they think, what they are feeling, who they interact with, how productive they are etc – than ever before. The opportunities are endless, in fact. So, to improve people performance in a meaningful way without alienating your workforce, it is important to drill down to the right metrics that will drive performance while maintaining employee engagement. Intelligent HR is likely to involve looking at metrics such as what motivates employees, what stops them performing at their best, where people are dissatisfied in the organization etc, rather than metrics like how many hours employees spend at their desk or how long they spend in the bathroom. In this way, data-driven, intelligent employee performance is about finding a more grown-up way of measuring performance, where intelligent people understand exactly what they need to do to help the company succeed, and data are used to see how this is going in reality. Crucially, it is not, and should never be, about punishing individuals.

The IoT and how happy, connected employees are more productive

The rise of Internet of Things (IoT)-enabled devices, particularly wearables, plays a huge role in HR's ability to effectively measure performance. This can mean measuring physical movements, such as how staff are coping in challenging physical conditions (there is more on employee safety and wellbeing in Chapter 9), or how people are interacting with each other, such as the IoT-enabled badges we have discussed already in this book. Using technology to drive efficiency is not a new thing. In the 1990s, telecommunications company Bell Canada gave phone technicians devices to wear on their wrists that let them enter repair data without having to go back to the computer in their vehicle. And this reportedly saved each technician almost an hour a day.[4] But this technology has leapt forward with modern wearables. Research from Tractica predicts more than 75 million wearable devices will be used in the work environment by 2020.[5]

Creating happier, more productive employees

What particularly interests me is how wearables can help to measure and improve both productivity and wellbeing. As we saw in

Chapter 9, happy employees are more productive, and connectivity plays an important role in this – one standout statistic from Chapter 9 being that connected workers are typically 8–9 per cent more productive. One innovative example of this link between connectivity, wellbeing and, ultimately, productivity comes from video-game publisher Ubisoft. The company has trialled measuring employees' stress levels with a finger-clamp sensor that is linked to a gaming interface. During the test period, the stress levels for one group of users decreased by over 50 per cent.[4] Hitachi employees wear badges that house sensors to effectively measure employee happiness.[6] The badges gather data on employee movements, such as time spent sitting, talking and nodding, and the company has used these metrics to develop an algorithm to measure happiness. Bank of America used similar technology to identify that call-centre workers who took breaks together were happier and, after instituting a group break policy, saw a double-digit increase in productivity.[7]

It is about working smarter, not necessarily faster

Wearables are also helping employees to work smarter, and one example of this in action comes from Tesco.[8] Workers at the retail giant's distribution centre in Ireland wear armbands that track the products they are picking, saving employees time having to check those goods off a list, thereby improving their productivity over the course of a day. Wearables also allocate tasks to Tesco staff, telling them what they need to pick next, and prompting staff when an order is short, with the idea being to help employees work smarter, not just faster.

Helping workers complete tasks in a smarter, quicker and safer way is a critical pillar of data-driven people performance management. Digital consulting company Accenture has written about how its collaboration with Airbus helped to boost productivity in one specific area by a whopping 500 per cent.[9] The company deployed the latest wearable technology (devices that it calls 'heads-up displays') to help component assembly workers access assembly information quickly, whenever they needed it. As a result, workers were able to assemble more components, more quickly, and with dramatically fewer errors.

Other data-driven performance measurement systems

Aside from wearable devices, there are a number of different technologies to help you measure performance. Once again, I want to stress that the idea behind this should be to help individuals and the company as a whole perform better, not to punish individuals who are not performing well. If someone is not performing a task as well as expected, there may be a very good reason for this, ranging from fatigue or stress to systems not working properly or impeding what the employee is trying to do. Data and analysis should help to get at the *why* of performance metrics, as well as the *what*.

Tracking computer usage

It is now possible to measure virtually everything an employee does on their computer. Software from Veriato logs web browsing, document use, e-mail use, chat applications and keystrokes, and takes regular screen grabs that are stored for a certain period of time. It also has the potential to alert managers when certain thresholds are met. Personally, I think this is edging very close to the line between what is acceptable for boosting performance and what is infringing on individual privacy. But, speaking to the *Wall Street Journal*, one Veriato client said the system delivered real benefits.[10] Celeste O'Keefe, CEO of Dancel Multimedia, uses the system to measure a team of 16, made up of animators, artists, administrators and salespeople. O'Keefe felt the system allows her team to be more streamlined and focused, and she finds it useful for guiding her people in the right direction. O'Keefe uses the system to skim graphs and screen grabs to spot problems with employee productivity. Often these are the result of someone not being familiar with certain software or systems, thereby identifying opportunities for training and guidance; however, O'Keefe also acknowledged that her using the system had led to at least one firing.[10]

Productivity tools and apps

Other productivity-related tools include Basecamp, which allows staff to add their upcoming tasks for the day, week or month and tick them off as and when they are completed. This allows managers to easily see what people are working on and how much they are able to get done. Similarly, the Asana app allows managers to assign tasks and track their progress in real time. For *sales* teams, Salesforce details how many sales calls and e-mails were made in a day and how much revenue has been generated from that activity. Tools like these can drastically help to cut down the amount of time managers and staff need to spend e-mailing each other with updates on projects or holding team meetings.

AI tools that predict performance

In addition, artificial intelligence (AI) lends a predictive quality to employee performance. AI capabilities mean it is now possible to identify characteristics and activities that are linked to high and low performance, and predict relationships between factors like employee characteristics, training investment, employee engagement and performance. For example, predictive analytics company iNostix provides predictive systems that it claims can lead to faster time to contribution, predict organizational effectiveness, accurately assess employee engagement and predict absenteeism or the risk of work-place accidents.

Intelligently reviewing employee performance

The way in which many companies manage employee performance is through traditional annual reviews that evaluate employees against certain key performance indicators (KPIs). Yet, in today's fast-paced, technology-driven workplaces, annual performance appraisals simply are not working any more. Business moves so much faster these days. It is no surprise then that one study indicated that only 6 per cent of companies thought their performance management processes were working.[11] To me, the traditional performance review model is a perfect example of how *not* to review performance because, by its very nature, the process involves looking backwards far more than looking forwards. Plus, employees dislike annual reviews because they usually have to fill out lengthy questionnaires, and managers dislike them because they are incredibly time-consuming. In fact, an organization's productivity can dip as much as 40 per cent during the annual review period.[12] Now, companies are starting to move away from annual reviews, generating more regular discussions and looking to the future more. Data-driven performance reviewing should be about creating an ongoing dialogue between employees and management, all based on and facilitated by data and evidence. This may include using AI-driven systems, and conducting much more regular (but shorter) reviews, as we will see throughout this section.

A word on linking incentives to performance

Before we get into that, although designing incentive schemes is beyond the scope of this book, I think it is important to note that data-driven employee performance is not about simply hardwiring KPIs and performance reviews to the incentive system. So many companies design narrow metrics that drive all the wrong employee behaviours; when people know they are being evaluated on certain metrics only, those are the activities they focus on, sometimes to the detriment of other value-building activities. Say, for example, I ask my kids to tidy their room and promise a cinema trip in return, but they know I only evaluate how tidy the floor is and never look under the bed or in the cupboard. Which areas do you think they will tidy and which will they ignore? The answer is obvious. And yet employee reviews and incentives are often designed in the same way, which is why, in my mind, it is better to focus on outcomes rather than narrow metrics, ie if the company is performing well and individuals are contributing to that success, then they should be rewarded accordingly.

How big employers are overhauling performance reviews

A number of big companies, such as Accenture and Deloitte, have announced that they are getting rid of the dreaded annual performance reviews and revamping their review processes. This is not unexpected. In a survey Deloitte itself conducted, it found that more than half of the executives surveyed did not believe their employee review systems drove employee performance or engagement.[13]

New approaches to reviewing performance

But what do these companies use in place of old annual reviews, rankings systems and 360-degree feedback models? The new systems generally focus on the employee in their own role, as opposed to ranking employees against one another or comparing performance to other employees. Many review systems in the past were designed to try to simplify employee performance down to a single number: a rating or ranking. This new breed is more about generating a richer, nuanced view of every employee to facilitate better performance. These new systems also provide feedback much more often. Rather than a single review once a year, they tend to conduct more frequent reviews, for example, at the end of each major project or every month. More frequent check-ins and reviews mean that a manager has more opportunities to steer an employee towards their best performance. These more regular reviews typically take far less time to complete. Deloitte, for example, is using only four questions, two of which require 'yes' or 'no' answers.[14] There is also a new focus on looking to the future, instead of past performance. Rather than reviewing an entire year's performance in one go, these shorter, more frequent reviews are designed to help employees move forward with their careers rather than looking back on past accomplishments or failures. This means people are no longer dwelling on what happened in the past, but instead focusing on how to improve in the future.

Making reviews more objective

One major problem with standard performance reviews is that a reviewer's assessment of an employee's skills says more about the reviewer than the employee. But these new ways of reviewing performance help to remove subjectivity from the process. For example, to combat potential bias, Deloitte has changed its questions to ask what a manager would *do* with a person (promote them, incentivise them etc) rather than what they *think* of that person.[14]

The use of AI in performance reviews

So, many companies have undergone a move away from traditional, metrics-based performance assessment in recent years. Sometimes this is because they have been found limiting, but sometimes it was found that employers and managers are too easily inclined to simply ignore them, if their findings do not line up with their personal 'gut feeling' on who they like or dislike.

Reducing biases

Much of the difficulty in assessing performance has been put down to difficulties caused by workplace biases. These are well-documented, conscious or unconscious behaviours that can unfairly influence an assessment of an individual's contribution to an organization. Race and gender are perhaps two of the most obvious sources of individual bias. Fortunately, they are often quite easy to spot; however, others are more ephemeral, and it may not be so immediately obvious when they are taking place. One is known as contrast bias, meaning an assessor is inclined to compare an individual's performance to that of their peers, rather than to defined standards of achievement. Another is recency bias, where actions in the recent past are given more weight, perhaps unfairly, than actions which happened further back in time (but still within the period where performance is being assessed). This is where AI can come in, as bias is a human failing that AI does not have to overcome. Kris Duggan, founder and CEO of BetterWorks, which provides an analytical goal-setting and performance assessment platform, believes the traditional annual performance review is behind the decline in usefulness of performance assessment. He argues that an ongoing feedback process is part of the solution, and intelligent, AI-driven systems can help us to achieve this. As Duggan told me: 'We think that if you can make collecting feedback much more frequent and agile, and more lightweight... and it's open and collaborative... those things really do drive performance'.[15]

Machines will not put off conducting performance reviews

One great thing about AI is that it will not treat the job of performance reviews as something to do 'when I've got time'. Unlike many human managers, it will not put off assessments until the last minute; tell it you want an ongoing, 360-degree view of your workforce's effectiveness and (in theory) that is what you will get. And because AI-driven assessment can happen in real time (with systems monitoring targets, quotas and how these are affected by people's connections), incentives and praise for good performance can be dished out immediately. If targets are not being met or performance standards are slipping, then intervention can take place before the problem grows and becomes unmanageable.

Implementing more regular, or even continual, feedback loops

In Chapter 8 we saw how short, regular 'pulse' surveys from providers like Glint can be used to gather more regular feedback from employees. Technology like this will form a critical part of feedback loops within data-driven HR. But this process works both ways. As well as the company benefitting from regular employee feedback, employees themselves benefit from regular feedback. Regular feedback, be it from a line manager, peers or a mentor, helps employees to understand their performance, feel recognized for their contribution and feel more connected with the company, thereby boosting engagement.

Increasing the frequency of feedback

BetterWorks' AI-driven tool is again leading the charge in increasing the frequency of feedback. BetterWorks' implementation of AI is powered by what it calls its 'work graph'. This is a map of all the connections within a workforce, not just in terms of which employees' jobs are intertwined, but also where goals and targets are shared. The work graphs' AI algorithms can be used to track employee goals and progress, and provide comments, nudges and recognition where needed. The system then prompts feedback from the relevant people, such as a line manager. Importantly, the system also recognizes an individual's preferences for feedback and interactions, such as real-time feedback notifications or batches of notifications. This type of instant or very regular feedback could provide the ideal solution to the problem of annual reviews based on data that are already out of date (like the annual review). Managers can evaluate performance and deliver feedback based on real-time data, and employees can get helpful feedback and recognition also in real time.

Peer reviews in the workplace

Peer feedback is another growing aspect of performance reviews. Start-up company Zugata has developed a software solution that delivers continuous, anonymous peer feedback to employees, alongside mentor recommendations to help them improve their performance.[16] The system figures out who individuals work with and asks for anonymous feedback from those peers every week. Tools like this allow team members to communicate openly and regularly with each other, and help employees identify their strengths and opportunities for growth and improvement. And for managers and HR teams, Zugata's system provides information that helps them to understand wider skills, strengths and areas for improvement, to help them design more effective learning and development programmes. But, as we will see later in the chapter, employee peer review systems need to be approached with caution. When used as part of an employee ranking system, which pits employees against each other, they can be open to abuse and attempts to rig the rankings by delivering negative feedback on peers. But, used carefully, it is easy to see how open, supportive feedback from peers could help individuals to improve their performance, grow as employees and achieve their potential.

Looking at the potential backlash

Of course, there are legitimate privacy concerns about monitoring employee performance. Employees have a right to privacy, and that must be carefully managed alongside the need to better understand their performance. Improper use of data not only can tarnish your employer brand, but also could potentially land you in legal trouble.

Troubling examples

Say, for example, that employees wear badges that track their interactions with customers and other staff. A manager could potentially use this information to identify which member of their team went to HR with a complaint about their conduct. If the manager then fired that employee based only on what the data told them, and with no other grounds, the employee would have an excellent case for unfair dismissal. Or, if employees are wearing fitness tracking devices, for example, there is a danger that health data could be used to discriminate against those who are less physically healthy, regardless of how well they perform in their job. One real-life example of employee monitoring backfiring came from the *Daily Telegraph* in 2016. Journalists reportedly arrived at work one morning to find motion sensors had been installed under their desks, without any warning or explanation whatsoever.[17] The employees' union got involved and the newspaper's management quickly removed the devices. I find it pretty shocking that this measure was not communicated to staff prior to the installation, if it had been handled better, all the uproar could have been avoided.

Output is not the same as performance

It is also important to remember that improved performance and increased output are not necessarily the same things. If all you are doing is trying to increase output, with no consideration of employee wellbeing and engagement, the strategy is likely to backfire. And that is especially true in today's working environment, where 80 per cent of HR directors are worried about losing their best employees to burnout.[18]

Lessons from Amazon: how *not* to handle people monitoring and reviews

In the United Kingdom, working conditions at Amazon's distribution centres have made national news in the past, with stories of workers reportedly walking up to 15 miles during a shift, having their every move monitored by global positioning system (GPS) tracking tags and having just 30 minutes to walk the equivalent of nine football pitches to get to the canteen, eat lunch and get back to the warehouse.[19] The company reportedly had the ability to monitor staff during every minute they were on site, including their precise location in the warehouse, exactly how many items they picked or packed, and even how many bathroom breaks they took and for how long. This delivered huge efficiencies for Amazon, but no doubt harmed their employer brand in the United Kingdom.

Huge workloads and secret feedback

In addition, the retailer's feedback culture came in for significant criticism in a 2015 *New York Times* article, which focused on the company's headquarters in Seattle. The article, which featured interviews with many ex-Amazon employees, describes a 'bruising' feedback culture that encourages employees to criticize colleagues' ideas and send secret feedback to their managers.[20] According to the article, every new employee has to subscribe to 14 leadership principles, ranging from the not so unusual like 'think big' to the slightly ominous sounding 'disagree and commit' and 'frugality'. Amazon clearly wants to push each person as far as possible to get maximum value, and many employees talk positively of how this has helped them to excel. Other interviewees, however, describe a culture where huge workloads and pressure are commonplace, with one saying she did not sleep for four straight days and others reporting working nights, weekends and holidays. According to the article, the harsh performance review culture includes weekly or monthly reviews where individual employees are given lengthy reports (sometimes 50 or 60 pages) on the various metrics that they are being held accountable for. They are then quizzed on various aspects of the report.

Amazon's internal feedback tool perhaps raised the most eyebrows. Called the 'Anytime Feedback Tool', this system allows employees to send positive or negative feedback about their colleagues to management. And while managers would know who sent the feedback, individual employees would not know who had given feedback on them and do not have a chance to see their own feedback for themselves; it is always passed on by a manager. This system is open to abuse. Team members are ranked, and those scoring lowest are reportedly eliminated each year, which means employees are effectively competing against each other for their jobs and everyone feels they have to outperform against everyone else.

Average employee tenure is just one year

It is perhaps no wonder that a PayScale survey ranks Amazon second on a list of companies with high staff turnover.[21] According to the data, Amazon employees stick around on average for just one year – one of the very briefest tenures in the Fortune 500. Amazon founder and CEO Jeff Bezos responded to the article by writing a memo to Amazon staff stating that the article did not reflect the culture he knew, and asking staff to report any unfair practices to HR.[22] But the high staff turnover indicates that the internal feedback system is having a negative effect on employee satisfaction. For me, one of the main problems with the Amazon feedback system is not only that employees feel driven to outperform against each other, but also that their access to feedback filters down only from their managers. To really help employees grow and improve, they should be able to ask for or access feedback when they need it, using systems like the continuous performance reviews discussed earlier in the chapter.

Lessons from UPS: how to drive performance without alienating people

With vehicle sensors and GPS data, it is possible to know exactly where delivery drivers are, which route they are taking or how fast they are driving, and many companies are routinely using these sorts of data to improve driver behaviour and optimize delivery routes. UPS, however, has taken the use of data and analytics to a whole new level. For example, the hand-held computer that drivers have been carrying for years (those electronic boxes that you sign to say you have received your parcel) is actually a sophisticated device that helps drivers make better decisions, such as which order to deliver parcels in for the most efficient route.[23] But it is the delivery trucks themselves that provide a wealth of data about driver performance. UPS trucks are fitted with more than 200 sensors that gather data on everything from whether the driver is wearing a seatbelt, or when the back doors are open, to how long the vehicle spends idling as opposed to in motion and how many times the driver has to reverse or make a U-turn. The company has almost 100,000 vehicles on the roads, delivering nearly 17 million packages to more than 9 million customers every day, with drivers making an average of 120 stops each day.

Big benefits from big data

With this many drivers on the road, improving driver performance so they drive as efficiently as possible means big savings. The company has said that shaving just one minute off the time each driver spends idling as opposed to in motion saves over US $500,000 in fuel across the whole fleet. UPS has also said that same minute adds up to operational savings of US $14.6 million a year. One insight gained from the sensor data was that drivers opening the truck door with a key was slowing them down and eating up valuable time. So the company gave drivers a key fob with a simple push-button to open the doors much more quickly. Tiny time savings like this make a huge difference across a fleet the size of UPS. And the savings are clear. By monitoring their drivers and providing feedback and training where needed, UPS has achieved a reduction of 8.5 million gallons of fuel and 85 million miles per year.[24] Plus, while drivers now make an average of 120 stops a day, that number used to be less than 100, meaning the same drivers with the same trucks are now able to deliver significantly more packages than they used to.

Protecting and rewarding employees

This increased performance has been reflected in increased wages, with UPS drivers now earning around twice what they did in the mid-1990s.[23] The company is widely regarded as the biggest and most efficient parcel shipper in the world – largely thanks to its innovative use of data – and its drivers are among the best paid in the industry. That no doubt helps to support employee buy-in for monitoring so much of what drivers do. But the company has also had to take other steps to ensure it does not face a huge backlash from drivers; for example, under the terms of drivers' contracts, UPS cannot collect data without informing drivers of what it is gathering. And neither can it discipline a driver based only on what the data have told them. Sensible safeguards like this would work for almost any type of performance data in any industry. When implemented and properly followed, such safeguards help to facilitate employee buy-in, ensure transparency and minimize the risk of damage to morale or the employer brand.

Six best-practice tips for your organization

Based on what has been discussed in this chapter, the following are six simple best-practice guidelines to help you walk the fine line between legitimately useful performance measurement and privacy-invading surveillance.

1 Be transparent

Be transparent with your employees about exactly which data you collect and how you intend to use them. Be specific on how this data collection will benefit them and help to improve company performance overall. Make it clear that it is about looking at performance, not watching over every little thing employees do, and that it would never be used to punish individuals.

2 Minimize the data you collect

Practice thoughtful data minimization and only collect the data you need to have a genuine impact on performance. You should always be able to justify exactly why you need certain data. If there is no good business case for collecting certain data, do not collect them.

3 Get consent

You must ask your employees for consent to use their performance data. And, once you have got consent, only use those data for the purpose for which employees have given consent.

4 Work with the union

If your employees are members of a union, like UPS drivers are, you will need to consult with the union and gain agreement on performance measurement practices before you implement any measures.

5 Maintain dialogue

Keep your employees informed when you make any changes as to which data are gathered and how they are used. Just because you got their buy-in once, does not give you carte blanche to monitor anything you like in future.

6 Demonstrate clear benefits from the data

Be vocal about successes and show how data-driven performance measuring and reviewing improves the bottom line and helps the company meet its goals, just as in the UPS example. When improved employee performance delivers better financial performance for the company as a whole, reward your people accordingly.

Key takeaways

Clearly, this is one of the trickier areas of data-driven HR, and a lot of careful thought is needed regarding what is right for your organization and what will best help your employees. The following is a summary of what has been covered in this chapter:

- There is a very fine line between performance improvement and employee surveillance, and companies that have overstepped this line have faced huge backlashes. Done badly, measuring performance can destroy employee motivation.

- You should be looking at metrics such as what motivates employees, what stops them performing at their best, where people are dissatisfied in the organization etc, rather than metrics like how long employees spend in the bathroom.

- The idea is to help individuals and the company as a whole to perform better, not to punish individuals who are not performing well. If someone is not performing a task as well as expected, there may be a very good reason for this, such as fatigue or stress.

- The IoT again has a huge role to play in driving employee performance. Connected workers are generally happier and more productive.

- In today's fast-paced, technology-driven workplaces, annual performance appraisals are simply not working any more. Companies are starting to move away from annual reviews, instead generating regular discussions and looking to the future more.

- Improper use of data not only can tarnish your employer brand, but also potentially could result in legal action, so follow my six best-practice guidelines for using performance data in a fair, ethical way.

We have now reached the end of our journey into the world of data-driven HR. But, before you put this book down and start charting your own way forward, I would like to leave you with a look at where data-driven HR might be going in the future. In Chapter 12, I take a peek at key future trends in data and technology and explore how these might impact on the HR teams of tomorrow.

Endnotes

1 Catapult Sports [accessed 23 October 2017] Integrating Wearable Performance Data into AMS by Catapult [Online] http://www. catapultsports.com/uk/media/catapult-clearsky-wearable-athlete-tracking-applied-indoors

2 Singer, E (2011) [accessed 23 October 2017] Extra Sleep Boosts Basketball Players' Prowess [Online] http://www.technologyreview. com/view/424608/extra-sleep-boosts-basketball-players-prowess

3 Alvarez, E (2017) [accessed 23 October 2017] FIFA Envisions a Future Where Players Wear In-game Fitness Trackers [Online] https://www. engadget.com/2017/08/03/fifa-epts-wearable-technology

4 Wilson, H J (2013) [accessed 23 October 2017] Wearables in the Workplace [Online] https://hbr.org/2013/09/wearables-in-the-workplace

5 Tractica [accessed 23 October 2017] Wearable Devices for Enterprise and Industrial Markets [Online] https://www.tractica.com/research/wearable-devices-for-enterprise-and-industrial-markets

6 Lee, T (2015) [accessed 23 October 2017] Hitachi Creates Wearable Sensor to Measure Employee Happiness [Online] http://www.ubergizmo.com/2015/02/hitachi-creates-wearable-sensor-to-measure-employee-happiness

7 Frankel, S (2016) [accessed 23 October 2017] Employers Are Using Workplace Wearables to Find Out How Happy and Productive We Are [Online] https://qz.com/754989/employers-are-using-workplace-wearables-to-find-out-how-happy-and-productive-we-are

8 Rawlinson, K (2013) [accessed 23 October 2017] Tesco Accused of Using Electronic Armbands to Monitor Its Staff [Online] http://www.independent.co.uk/news/business/news/tesco-accused-of-using-electronic-armbands-to-monitor-its-staff-8493952.html

9 Hobbs, M (2017) [accessed 23 October 2017] The Internet of Things: Aligning Asset and Worker Performance [Online] http://www.telegraph.co.uk/business/digital-leaders/horizons/telegraph-horizons-asset-versus-worker-performance

10 Greenwald, T (2017) [accessed 23 October 2017] How AI Is Transforming the Workplace [Online] https://www.wsj.com/articles/how-ai-is-transforming-the-workplace-1489371060

11 Bernard Marr & Co [accessed 23 October 2017] What Is Performance Management? [Online] http://www.ap-institute.com/what-is-performance-management.aspx

12 Shekhawat, S (2016) [accessed 23 October 2017] Bots and Artificial Intelligence – Next Wave of Disruption in HR [Online] https://yourstory.com/2016/12/bots-artificial-intelligence-hr

13 Barry, L, Garr, S and Liakopoulos, A (2014) [accessed 23 October 2017] Performance Management Is Broken [Online] http://dupress.com/articles/hc-trends-2014-performance-management

14 Buckingham, M and Goodall, A (2015) [accessed 23 October 2017] Reinventing Performance Management [Online] https://hbr.org/2015/04/reinventing-performance-management

15 Marr, B (2017) [accessed 23 October 2017] The Future of Performance Management: How AI and Big Data Combat Workplace Bias [Online] https://www.forbes.com/sites/bernardmarr/2017/01/17/the-future-of-performance-management-how-ai-and-big-data-combat-workplace-bias/2/#427c2c502e58

16 Zugata (2015) [accessed 23 October 2017] Big Data Startup Zugata Re-imagines Performance Reviews, Launches with a New Approach to Empower Employees to Reach Their Fullest Potential and Funding from Silicon Valley VCs and Angel Investors, press release [Online] http://www.marketwired.com/press-release/big-data-startup-zugata-re-imagines-performance-reviews-launches-with-new-approach-empower-2063217.htm

17 Waterson, J (2016) [accessed 23 October 2017] Daily Telegraph Installs Workplace Monitors on Journalists' Desks [Online] https://www.buzzfeed.com/jimwaterson/telegraph-workplace-sensors?utm_term=.xnadY9JN#.rrKVW9lJ

18 Robert Half (2013) [accessed 23 October 2017] Employee Burnout Common in Nearly a Third of UK Companies, Say HR Directors, press release [Online] https://www.roberthalf.co.uk/press/employee-burnout-common-nearly-third-uk-companies-say-hr-directors

19 Ledwith, M (2013) [accessed 23 October 2017] Tagged by Their Bosses, Zero-hour Amazon Workers: Employees Wear Monitoring Devices and Are Not Guaranteed Any Income [Online] http://www.dailymail.co.uk/news/article-2382800/Tagged-bosses-zero-hour-Amazon-workers-Employees-guaranteed-income.html

20 Kantor, J and Streitfeld, D (2015) [accessed 23 October 2017] Inside Amazon: Wrestling Big Ideas in a Bruising Workplace [Online] https://www.nytimes.com/2015/08/16/technology/inside-amazon-wrestling-big-ideas-in-a-bruising-workplace.html

21 PayScale [accessed 23 October 2017] The Least Loyal Employees [Online] http://www.payscale.com/data-packages/employee-loyalty/least-loyal-employees

22 Cook, J (2015) [accessed 23 October 2017] Full Memo: Jeff Bezos Responds to Brutal NYT Story, Says It Doesn't Represent the Amazon He Leads [Online] http://www.geekwire.com/2015/

full-memo-jeff-bezos-responds-to-cutting-nyt-expose-says-tolerance-
for-lack-of-empathy-needs-to-be-zero

23 Goldstein, J (2014) [accessed 23 October 2017] To Increase Productivity,
UPS Monitors Drivers' Every Move [Online] http://www.npr.org/
sections/money/2014/04/17/303770907/to-increase-productivity-
ups-monitors-drivers-every-move

24 UPS Pressroom [accessed 23 October 2017] Big Data Delivers Big
Results at UPS [Online] https://pressroom.ups.com/pressroom/
ContentDetailsViewer.page?ConceptType=Speeches&id=
1426415450350-355

The future of data-driven HR   12

I hope this book has given you a good idea of the current and emerging data and analytics possibilities and how they are beginning to transform people management. I also hope I have sparked your interest and excitement. I certainly believe this is an exciting time for businesses and the people who work in them; however, as you have probably guessed, the technology is changing fast – faster than even I would have anticipated 10 or even 5 years ago – so it is likely that how HR teams function in just a few years' time will be quite different again. Anyone who says they know with absolute certainty where data-driven HR is going is, quite frankly, lying. There are technological advancements coming that we cannot even imagine right now, but it is possible to make some predictions about what might be coming our way in the future based on some emerging trends. Therefore, in this chapter, I set out the potential data-driven HR landscape of the future, including the challenge facing tomorrow's HR teams, how the digital transformation will affect all our workplaces, and the key data and technology trends every HR professional should be aware of. I finish by returning to the importance of a robust data strategy and how this should be your first step on the journey ahead.

The challenge facing the HR teams of the future

The 'datafication' of our world and the proliferation of Internet of Things (IoT)-enabled devices is only going to continue, and this will continue to impact on the way in which HR works, just like every other area of the business.

Finding HR's unique role

The challenge for HR teams is to find a balance between technology (specifically, the increasing automation of work) and the human role in the organizations of the future. I believe the biggest challenge facing HR teams going forward is not keeping up with technology and learning new skills like data analysis; it is finding the uniquely human place in the organization and within the HR team itself. Yes, naturally there will be greater automation in the future, both in HR tasks and across the business, but if absolutely everything is automated and performed by robots, what need is there for HR? Therefore, the HR teams of today need to be thinking about what HR will look like in the future, and this includes what exactly can be automated and what cannot. They need to figure out HR's contribution to the workplace of the future. Personally, I do not believe we will ever reach a point where the HR function is entirely redundant. But the role of HR will undoubtedly shift away from the more administrative tasks concerning people management (which can be easily automated in the future) to activities that help the organization to meet its goals. It is vital that HR delivers real value and unique benefits that cannot be delivered by any other function in the organization.

Should HR be restructured?

This is why, in Chapter 1, I argued for a two-team approach to HR: one team to focus on people analytics and one on people support. The people analytics team looks at people more scientifically and supports the company with insights and analytics, answering questions such as: 'What are our talent gaps?' 'What makes a good employee in our company?' and 'Which employees have got the most potential?' (as we will see later in this chapter, this does not mean HR people need to become data scientists). The people support team then focuses on supporting everyone in the company, from the frontline to the senior leadership team. This includes helping employees with their development, ensuring staff engagement, identifying issues with morale and generally looking after the wellbeing of the people in the business. Anything outside of these two functions, like administrative, bureaucratic tasks, should be either outsourced or, more probably, automated.

How the digital transformation will change all of our workplaces

Across every industry and almost every job role, the nature of work is changing. Politicians like President Trump may vow to bring jobs back to communities, but have they really considered how automation could throw a spanner in the works? Aside from reading the odd attention-grabbing news story about how robots will take everyone's jobs, most people give little thought as to how their workplaces will change in the future. But now, more than ever, it is vital that those charged with ensuring their organization is appropriately skilled to navigate the choppy waters of digital transformation understand how data, artificial intelligence (AI) and automation are going to impact on the workplace.

Essential skills for surviving the fourth industrial revolution

The fourth industrial revolution is here (see Chapter 2), and it is completely transforming the way in which we live and work. Our world is now fuelled by data and Internet-connected devices that are capable of collecting and processing ever-growing amounts of information. It is important for everyone, in every job and every industry, to consider the implications of this new transformation and how it will change their job and employment prospects over the coming years. This does not just apply to HR teams, but to most people in any typical organization. For HR teams, however, it is particularly pertinent because not only are HR professionals finding their own way in this new world, but also they have to equip the people in their organization with the essential skills for helping the business succeed in the future. The following are my top three tips for HR professionals wondering how to navigate these changes on a personal level and boost their own development.

Tip 1: consider the future of your job

Think hard about how much of what you do every day is repetitive and potentially could be done by intelligent robots or computers.

Remember, we already have self-driving cars and trucks, and computers that can recognize faces as well as any human. In an HR sense, as we have seen throughout this book, it is possible to completely or partly automate tasks like assessing job candidates, corresponding with candidates, answering simple employee queries like 'When is the office closed over Christmas?' and even measuring employee satisfaction. But the areas that computers still struggle with include creativity, problem solving and connecting with people on a human level – all of which I would say are, or should be, vital skills in HR. These are the areas where HR can add real value to the organization, so it makes sense to try to develop your skills in those areas and reshape your job to do more of those things that robots cannot do.

Tip 2: become data savvy

I am not saying HR professionals have to become data scientists, far from it. But it is important to have a good understanding of the possibilities of data and how they can help you to solve problems, run a more efficient organization and make your customers (your employees) happier. Demonstrating that you are able to use data in original ways to solve key problems is a certain path to success in the information age. Being comfortable with using data in your job will only become more important.

Tip 3: make friends with your AI colleagues

AI is being adopted at an incredible rate. We can see that in our own private lives with AI assistants such as Apple's Siri, Microsoft's Cortana and Amazon's Alexa becoming increasingly competent at helping us to run our lives. They can manage schedules, proactively let us know about travel delays or breaking news and inform us of forthcoming events that they think will interest us. Increasingly, they can do this without us telling them to do so, all they have to do is monitor our behaviour and they will be able to work out what information is relevant to us. This type of technology is fast becoming commonplace in our workplaces, and that understandably makes people nervous. HR teams need to be leading the way in embracing AI technology and showing how collaborating with AI systems can drive efficiencies and help the business to succeed.

How employees of all kinds will become more data savvy

Throughout this book, we have seen how data and analytics have the potential to create efficiencies, help us better understand business processes and predict problems before they occur. But imagine how much greater the potential for change could be if it could spontaneously emerge anywhere in an organization. This is part of the thinking behind the democratization of data, where everyone across the company has access to whatever data they may need to make improvements (more on this later in the chapter). The idea is that, when everyone has access to the tools, skills and knowhow to harness technology to do their job better, or drive efficiencies, then a workforce looks better equipped to deal with the challenges of the future.

Opening up data and analytics to a wider audience

This thinking is shared by Infor CEO Charles Phillips, and was the driving force behind the software company's decision to establish its Educational Alliance Program.[1] The initiative involves rolling out its training programme into colleges and leveraging its customer and partner networks to supply students with placements and, eventually, jobs. Given the move towards platform infrastructure and software-as-a-service tool sets, it is no longer necessary to have an academic background in computer science or statistics to effectively lead data-driven transformation within an organization. It is just a question of getting that message out there to students or professionals who may be wondering what their next move should be, to ensure they are viably skilled for a place in the workforce of tomorrow. Infor CEO Charles Phillips told me: 'Our assumption is that pretty much every business is going to become a digital business to some degree. So even if you're not a computer science or tech major, you need some exposure to learn how to use and apply technology'.[1] The course gives students hands-on training with Infor's enterprise software as it is used by more than 70,000 of its clients, delivered either online or, increasingly, thanks to a growing number of arrangements with US universities, in a formal educational setting. Pushing the course into colleges and universities has been seen as a priority. Phillips admits that initially there was some scepticism from academia. But it has so far managed to get its course into 27 institutions nationwide – 25 of which are colleges and two of which are high schools – and is working towards its target of gaining 50 more by next year.

Data-savvy employees will be more valuable

It is certainly true that there is a growing need for people capable of understanding both business and technology. Those who become best at analysing a business problem and devising how it could be solved most effectively with automation, AI and data are likely to be able to name their price in the workforce of tomorrow, regardless of what industry they are in. As Phillips puts it: 'Automation can build a car but it can't tell it where to go. You have to know where you want to go'.[1]

How other business functions are being impacted by data and analytics

Big data technology, particularly AI and machine learning, is affecting every area of the business, so I thought it might be helpful to highlight a couple of specific functions outside of HR and the kinds of changes they are facing. This not only demonstrates more of the practical changes coming our way, but also equips HR teams with the knowledge to help colleagues elsewhere in the organization. After all, as HR professionals wonder about how their roles will change in this new data-driven world, those questions are echoed right across the typical organization.

The rise of AI and machine learning in sales

It is safe to say that organizations that transform their sales functions due to machine learning and AI will find themselves rising above the competition. Now that we generate and collect vast amounts of data, we are able to give machines the amount of data that are required for them to learn (by using algorithms) to interpret the data and predict outcomes. Of course, there is a personal side to selling that machines will not (at least for a long time) be able to replace. Humans, and exemplary sales professionals in particular, are uniquely suited to listen, convince, negotiate and empathize, as well as explore and answer the very critical question of: 'Why is this the best product or service for me?'; but the power of machine learning to contribute to successful sales initiatives cannot be emphasized enough and will only continue to grow in importance. The following are just a few of the ways in which machine learning will transform sales.

Interpreting customer data   Machine learning helps us to make sense of the data we collect about our customers. Even though many organizations have systems or resources in place to gather and store customer data, machine learning will help to make more effective use of those data in ways that relying on humans alone could not.

Improving sales forecasting   Sales colleagues gather all kinds of data on a prospect (company size, stakeholders, solutions they want etc) and machine learning provides the ability to compare those data to historical sales efforts. This means sales teams can connect the dots and better predict what solutions would be effective, the likelihood of the deal closing and how long it will take. This insight helps sales management to better allocate resources and predict sales projections.

Predicting customer needs   Business success relies on how well we provide what our customers need. Machine learning can improve how responsive and proactive we are to anticipate the needs of our customers. The better sales teams are at addressing clients' needs before they get escalated, and at suggesting a solution that could help to make their lives better and easier, the stronger the company's relationship with customers will be. Machines will not forget to follow up or be too busy to proactively share solutions.

Handling transactional sales   According to *Harvard Business Review*, by 2020, customers will manage 85 per cent of their interactions with an organization without interacting with a human.[2] Having machines step in to handle certain sales efforts quickly and effectively will free up the human salesforce to focus on the relationship.

Improving sales communication   There probably will be dramatic changes to sales communications as a result of machine learning. If business communication mimics the transformation of consumer communication, the business equivalent of short-form communication such as tweets and text messages will be AI responses. Machines can quickly and easily answer queries about pricing, product features or contract terms. Within the next decade, virtual reality (VR) could allow prospects to tour a factory, 'join' in to conferences and meetings with the entire team and see products being manufactured, all without leaving their own office.

Fine-tuning sales processes   We get a glimpse into the way in which sales functions will change by looking at the promises of Einstein, the AI solution from the customer relationship management (CRM) company Salesforce. Einstein aids sales personnel by reminding them who to follow up with, suggesting what opportunity should be prioritized because of a high probability of conversion and helping to predict the best product or service for each prospect.

Taking care of the more mundane tasks   Machines can take care of transactional sales to free up the human salesforce to build relationships and nurture their leads in ways only humans can. By taking care of mundane tasks for sales staff, machines clear the way for the sales process to be better and more effective. This mimics the way in which HR may change in the future, to move away from more administration-type tasks to focus more on identifying questions and insights and better supporting people throughout the organization.

The rise of AI and machine learning in accounting

Okay, robots are not going to replace your beloved accounting colleagues (not anytime soon, at least). But it is true that white-collar workers who are part of the knowledge economy are beginning to experience what manual labourers have in the past when new technology made their jobs obsolete. Given the improvements we have recently seen in computing, many accounting professionals fear for their future as machines threaten to overtake them. But, rather than fearing the changes that machine learning will make in accounting tasks, it is an opportunity for accounting professionals to be excited. The profession is going to become more interesting as repetitive tasks shift to machines. There will be changes, but those changes will not completely eliminate the need for human accountants; they will just alter their contributions. The following are just a few of the ways in which machine learning will transform accounting.

Handling repeatable accounting tasks   Currently, there is no machine replacement for the emotional intelligence requirements of accounting work, but machines can learn to perform redundant, repeatable and often extremely time-consuming tasks, a few of which are included in this list.

Auditing expense submissions   Machines could learn a company's expense policy, read receipts and audit expense claims to ensure compliance and only identify and forward questionable claims to humans for approval; otherwise, machines could handle the bulk of this task.

Clearing invoice payments   Today, when customers submit payments that might combine multiple invoices or that do not match any invoices in the accounting system, it is time-consuming for accounts-receivable staff to apply payment correctly without making a call to the client or trying to determine the right combination of invoices. Smart machines could analyse the possible invoices and match the paid amount to the right combination of invoices, clear out short payments or automatically generate an invoice to reflect the short payment without any human intervention.

Handling bank reconciliation   Machines can learn how to completely automate bank reconciliations.

Undertaking risk assessments   Machine learning could facilitate risk assessment mapping by pulling data from every project a company has ever completed to compare them to a proposed project. This very comprehensive assessment would be impossible for humans to do on this scale and within a similar timeline.

Providing analytics calculations   The accounting department is contin-uously barraged with questions along the lines of 'What was our revenue for this product in the third quarter last year?' or 'How has this division grown over the last 10 years?' Given the data, machines can learn to answer these questions very quickly.

Automating invoice categorization   Accounting software firm Xero is deploying a machine learning automation system that will be able to learn over time how to categorize invoices, something that currently requires accountants to do manually. As accounting departments begin to rely increasingly more on machines to do the heavy lifting of calculations, reconciliations and responding to enquiries from other team members and clients about balances and verifying information, accountants will be able to deliver more value to the organization than ever before. This will allow them to focus less on the tasks that can be automated and more on those inherently human aspects of their jobs.

The key data and technology trends every HR team should recognize

For the rest of this chapter, I want to focus on my top 11 (I just could not whittle it down to 10!) predictions for the next few years (see Figure 12.1). HR teams wanting to stay ahead of the curve will want to ensure they are exploring all of the opportunities indicated by these trends, and fully consider how these developments may impact on their data strategy (see Chapter 3).

Trend 1: smart devices will become well and truly smart

Thanks to machine learning, smart devices such as watches, home appliances and entertainment, and even infrastructure like lighting and wiring, will finally live up to their names. After all, although we have called phones 'smartphones' for a decade or so now, it would probably be more accurate (although less catchy) to have called them 'multi-tasking phones'. Embedding AI such as Siri into the operating system was the first step towards making them truly 'smart'. And we can certainly expect to see more of this in the next few years. Expect

Figure 12.1   Key HR data and technology trends

1	Smart devices will become truly smart
2	Companies will spend more on data software but less on hardware
3	More time will be spent in the virtual world than the real one
4	More organizations will discover their 'digital twin'
5	Technology will allow us to be 'present' in two places at the same time
6	Companies will make greater use of external data
7	HR teams will move from reporting to predicting
8	Quantum computing revolution
9	Greater democratization of HR data
10	HR data will be more valuable to the business
11	Intelligent HR teams will become more people-focused rather than data-focused

automated personal assistant features to become more proactive and predictive, and IoT devices such as smart lighting, security and air conditioning to become better at adapting to how we want them to behave. From an HR data point of view, all this means that the volume of data we have the potential to gather and extract insights from is going to increase even further.

Trend 2: companies will spend more on data software but less on hardware

Corporate infrastructure spending is increasingly being put into software, as much more functionality becomes available 'as a service' through cloud providers. At the same time, hardware spending is falling, partly due to the increase in the number of services carried out off site, and partly due to a preference for cheap, commodity hardware such as servers and storage space over expensive, bespoke, hardware solutions. This is a trend which will continue in the coming years. For HR teams, this boom in software as a service opens up a whole new world of analytics possibilities, without having to invest in costly on-site hardware or an army of in-house data scientists.

Trend 3: we will be spending less time in the real world and more time in virtual ones

Technologically advanced mass-market VR headsets are now readily available as consumer devices from several manufacturers. While VR has been growing in popularity in the technology industry for a few years now, its use mostly has been limited to large companies with budgets to build bespoke systems and software. With mass-market devices becoming available, and a growing amount of open-source software enabling users to design their own worlds and realities, expect its reach (and that of augmented reality (AR)) to extend significantly in the next few years. As we have already seen in this book, VR and AR can provide real benefits to organizations in the areas of employee learning and development, and in boosting your employer brand to recruit the best talent.

Trend 4: more organizations will discover their 'digital twin'

I talked a bit about digital twin technology in Chapter 10, and I think 'digital twin' is a phrase companies can expect to hear more of in the future. Essentially, the thinking behind this technology is that, due to increases in computing power and the affordability and accuracy of sensor technology, most things can be simulated on a computer these days with a high degree of precision. The obvious application for this in an HR sense is in learning and development, but it could go much further. A digital twin could even be built of a whole company, along with data-driven simulations of all its processes, effectively providing a 'sandpit' for experimenting with driving change. The data used to build the twin also could serve as the input for advanced predictive analytics, allowing the likely outcomes of changes to procedures and processes to be examined in a safely simulated environment.

Trend 5: we will get used to the idea of being in two places at the same time

No, I have not gone mad or taken a detour into science-fiction writing. Telepresence combines ideas from VR/AR and the digital twin concept to effectively enable a human to be in two places at the same time. Drones and remote-control devices increasingly will be used to extend our immediate field of influence outside the range of our own hands and arms. Surgery can be performed remotely by a surgeon controlling a robot, or remote-controlled surgical equipment, and unmanned vehicles and equipment increasingly will be used to access places that are hazardous to our health, or which they are able to reach more quickly than we can. The simplest applications are remote meetings, which take place in a virtual environment (eg Skype) but use technology to give the impression or effect of everyone being present – like the Harvard virtual classroom we saw in Chapter 10. More advanced applications are unlimited, ranging from exploring deep space to the bottom of the oceans in a fully safe but immersive fashion. For businesses, this technology is likely to centre on making operations more effective and efficient by having people complete tasks remotely where it is beneficial.

Trend 6: companies will make greater use of external data

There is no doubt that internal data provide a fantastic competitive advantage because they are so uniquely tied to your business, your industry, your challenges, your customers and your employees; however, companies are increasingly supplementing their internal data with external data. This has been happening in marketing and sales teams for a number of years (eg think of your marketing colleagues making use of Facebook data to target advertising appropriately). Over the next couple of years, HR teams will also increasingly supplement their internal people-related data with external data from the government, data brokers, sites like Glassdoor etc, to look at things like trends in the employment market and general trends in terms of how engaged people are. Just focusing on internal data is a bit like putting blinkers on, so it is important to bring in additional data to put your own data into context. This means HR teams in the future will need to strike more of a balance between their own valuable internal data and the wealth of data that are available outside the company.

Trend 7: HR teams will move from reporting to predicting

Traditionally, HR teams have produced reports that tell us about what happened over the last year, using data that may be just a month or two old or a full 12 months old. Increasingly, we will see HR departments, and other functions within the business, move away from these legacy data to real-time analytics. Much more analysis needs to happen in real time for a company to be truly competitive in this data-driven world, which means understanding exactly what is happening right now and taking action where needed to remedy problems before they take root. A great example of this is the regular pulse employee surveys that are starting to replace the annual employee survey (see Chapters 7, 8 and 9). Over the next couple of years, we will see many more companies move to this approach. And, as we have seen throughout this book, the more data you gather (eg through regular surveys), the greater your predictive capabilities become. Machine learning and AI capabilities mean companies will be able to spot indicators that employee satisfaction may be about to drop, or that a key employee could be about to leave the company, for example.

Trend 8: quantum computing revolution

Today's smartphones have the computing power of a military computer from 50 years ago that was the size of an entire room; however, even with the phenomenal strides we have made in technology, there remain problems that standard computing just cannot solve. This is where quantum computing may come in: solving complex problems beyond the capabilities of a traditional computer.

How does quantum computing work?

When you enter the world of atomic and subatomic particles, things begin to behave in unexpected ways. In fact, these particles can exist in more than one state at a time and it is this ability that quantum computers take advantage of. Instead of bits, which conventional computers use, a quantum computer uses quantum bits (known as qubits). To illustrate the difference, imagine a sphere. A bit can be at either of the two poles of the sphere, but a qubit can exist at any point on the sphere. So, this means that a computer using qubits can store an enormous amount of information and uses less energy doing so than a classical computer. By entering into this quantum area of computing where the traditional laws of physics no longer apply, we will be able to create processors that are significantly faster (a million or more times) than the ones we use today.

Perhaps Eric Ladizinsky, co-founder of quantum computing company D-Wave, explained the differences between a regular computer and a quantum computer best when he spoke at the WIRED 2014 conference.[3] He said to imagine that you only have five minutes to find an X written on a page of a book among the 50 million books in the Library of Congress. In this scenario, you would be a regular computer and you would never find the X. But, if you had 50 million parallel realities and you could look at a different book in each of those realities (just like a quantum computer), you would find the X. A quantum computer splits you into 50 million versions of yourself to make the work quick and easy. We are venturing into an entirely new realm of physics and there will be solutions and uses we have never even thought of yet. But when you consider how much classical computers revolutionized our world with a relatively simple use of bits and two options of 0 or 1, you can imagine the extraordinary possibilities when you have the processing power of qubits that can perform millions of calculations at the same moment. We do not actually know all the possibilities of quantum computing yet, but what we do know is that it will be game-changing for every industry. It is no coincidence that some of the world's most influential companies, such as IBM and Google, and the world's governments are investing in quantum computing technology. They are expecting quantum computing to change our world because it will allow us to solve problems and experience efficiencies that are not possible today.

What are the applications of quantum computing?

One area that will be greatly impacted by quantum computing is AI. The information processing that is critical to improving machine learning is ideally suited to quantum computing. Quantum computers can analyse large quantities of data to provide AI machines with the feedback required to improve performance. Quantum computers are able to analyse the data to provide feedback much more efficiently than traditional computers and therefore the learning curve for AI machines is shortened. Just like humans, AI machines powered by the insights from quantum computers can learn from experience and self-correct. Quantum computers will help AI to expand to more industries and help technology become much more intuitive very quickly.

There are many other anticipated uses for quantum computing, ranging from improving online security to making better weather and climate-change predictions. But, for me, what is most exciting about quantum computing is, instead of troubleshooting issues bit by bit as we do now with classical computers, quantum computers tackle the entire problem at once. This opens the door for amazing developments in every field from financial services to our national security. By the very nature of this cutting-edge field, there will be discoveries, innovations and solutions we have never dreamed of yet, but it is clear that quantum computers give us the ability to solve complex problems that are beyond the capabilities of classical computers.

Trend 9: greater democratization of HR data

We have seen a new wave of data democracy in recent years and there is every indication this will only continue. For the bulk of the last five decades, data were 'owned' by IT departments and used by business analysts and executives to drive business decisions. As organizations became inundated with data and bottlenecks increased due to volume, it became apparent that more business users needed to have access to those data to explore them on their own without IT being a gatekeeper. Now, organizations are allowing more business users access to data to expedite decision making, influence sales and customer service, and uncover opportunities. This increased access is what is known as data democratization (sometimes referred to as data socialization).

Why data democratization matters

Expanding the pool of people who can analyse and develop meaningful business actions from data is critical to gaining a competitive edge for a business, seeing the big picture and, in some cases, could ensure its survival. Ultimately, the goal of data democratization is for the people in your organization to be able to quickly and easily get to the business insights they need without help, essentially so the right people have the right data at the right time. It has become apparent that embedding data and analytics throughout an organization, and ensuring their effects can be measured on every process, is often a more productive approach than attempting to impose data directives in a top-down, centralized manner. The applications of this range from giving shop-floor sales staff instant access to personalized (but not necessarily personal – the analytics might be done using anonymized data sets) insights about customers, to allowing engineers to know when an essential machine is likely to fail.

What this means for HR teams

The 'datafication' of our world and the increase in the number of IoT devices mean that HR teams will have more data available to them to enhance their decisions and operations. But these data also have relevance and use outside of the HR team. Line managers, for instance, need information on how their people are performing and how satisfied they are. Data democratization means HR teams should ensure their data are increasingly relevant, useful and *available* to those who need them, whenever they need them, regardless of whether those people are inside or outside the HR team. This does not mean that everyone in the organization needs to become data scientists. In the future, as technology progresses, data democratization will be less about analysing data to extract critical insights and more about asking the right questions of the data. Rather than HR professionals and managers throughout the company reading and interpreting data, advancements like natural language processing and chatbots mean it will be possible to have a conversation with your data analytics tools and ask questions like: 'Who in my team may be about to leave the company?'

Trend 10: HR data will be more valuable to the business

I wrote an article a little while ago arguing that HR data are now becoming more valuable to businesses than their financial data.[4] My reasoning was that, if a business's people are its most valuable asset, surely it stands to reason that information on people comprise the most valuable data for a business. I believe this is becoming increasingly true in the information age. At many tech-driven companies and start-ups, the humans that make up the company – and the intellectual property that they produce – may literally be its only assets, beyond the commodity hardware and software they need to do their jobs. So, it is no wonder that, across many sectors of industry, employers are increasingly investing in technology capable of measuring and analysing the behaviour and performance of their personnel – at all levels from the shop floor to the boardroom. After all, a company that understands its employees is without doubt better placed to keep them motivated, happy and productive. As increasingly more aspects of business become managed through smart IoT-enabled technology, it is inevitable that management of HR will go the same way. In this way, human information will be just as critical as financial data when it comes to informing business strategies and setting goals. But the most value is likely to be unlocked by organizations that use these data sources together – combining HR data with financial, operational and customer data – for example, matching customers to the representative most likely to get on with them, based on personality profiling. This again shows how the democratization of data will be increasingly important. For HR data to provide maximum value, however, they need to be clearly linked to the wider business context and overarching key performance indicators (KPIs) of the business. Now, more than ever, HR data need to link to business objectives in terms of revenue, profit, customer services, talent acquisition etc, which is the best way to ensure that HR data, and the HR team itself, deliver real value to the business.

Trend 11: intelligent HR teams will become more people-focused rather than data-focused

I have worked with so many different HR teams over the years and, in my experience, the world of data and numbers is not exactly what gets the average HR professional's heart racing. Most HR professionals go into the job because they are intrinsically people-focused, ie they are interested in human interaction, not analysing data sets. So, if you have read this book and feel like you need to become a data scientist to keep your job, you can relax. In fact, the opposite is true. The great news is that a lot of the data analysis tools coming onto the market will allow us to produce automated analysis and insight generation through AI and machine learning capabilities. Quantum computing will transform computing capabilities, enabling us to perform way more advanced AI algorithms in no time and with little effort.

Is this the end for data scientists?

Based on a survey by online employment analyst Glassdoor, 'data scientist' was voted the best job in America in 2016.[5] But that may have been a little premature as the role of data scientist could be at risk, as machine learning, AI and big data could make the job obsolete. New machine learning algorithms can autonomously analyse data and identify patterns, even interpret the data and produce reports and data visualizations. In addition, natural language processing technologies can help to break down the barriers to widespread use of data analytics by making complex analytics possible for just about anyone, regardless of their technical ability. IBM, for example, believes that it can offer a solution to the skills shortage in big data by cutting out the data scientists entirely and replacing (or supplementing) them with its Watson natural language analytics platform. IBM's Vice President for Watson Analytics and business intelligence, Marc Altshuller, explains: 'With a cognitive system like Watson you just bring your question – or if you don't have a question you just upload your data and Watson can look at it and infer what you might want to know'.[6] In addition, new technologies are emerging that will allow lay people in any field to create detailed infographics and other story-telling devices to help interpret the data such technologies will return. Visualizations are usually used as a layer on the top of data, designed to make those data more digestible. In big data analytics, reporting the insights we have gleaned from analysing large amounts of messy data sets is the crucial 'last step' of the process, and it is often a step which causes us to stumble. We may have crunched terabytes of data in real time to come up with our world-changing revelations, but unless we can communicate them convincingly to those who need to take action, they are useless and, worse than that, a waste of valuable time and money.

Programs that can visualize data start with the graphing functions available in Excel and get progressively more complex. But one program, called Quill, takes the trend a step further, producing text-based reports that explain the data clearly and concisely. Think of it as an executive summary created by a computer to explain a set of data – at the click of a button. Combined, these types of technologies mean that the data scientist simply may not be needed in the big data landscape where lay persons can conduct their own analytics at will.

What this means for HR

With this in mind, it is completely reasonable to imagine that in the not-too-distant future an HR manager could sit in front of their computer and ask its analytics software a question about employee engagement, for example, and get an accurate response, report or visualization based on real-time data. In this landscape, data analysis skills for HR teams will become less relevant, not more, which is not to say you do not need to know anything about data and analytics. Of course you need to stay abreast of developments and possibilities to be able to deliver maximum value for your organization. But, rather than retraining to become a data analyst, it is actually much more important that you are able to ask the right questions of your data so that you can get the right insights. Once you understand exactly what it is you need to know, and you have the right data and algorithms in place to answer those questions, you will be able to get at the answers you need without performing any fancy analytics yourself. And this is combined with the fact that many simple administrative tasks will be automated and this will free up the HR teams of the future to focus on the people aspect, which is exactly what they went into the job to do. Right now, I admit that we are in a tricky transition phase, where it feels like data analysis is on top of other work, and systems are not yet in place to automate a lot of tasks. But, looking to the future, with advances in computing and analytics, the HR teams of tomorrow ideally will spend their time focusing on helping the business to deliver its objectives and supporting people throughout the organization as they grow and contribute in their own way to the business's success.

Remember, it all starts with strategy

Now is the time that every HR team needs to create a robust data strategy. If you are just embarking on the data-driven HR journey, your data strategy will help you to get started and identify the best path for you. And if you are already some way into your data-driven HR journey, now is a good time to review your strategy to ensure it ties in with the business's wider objectives and that you are taking account of the full range of possibilities open to you. Circle back to Chapter 3 for advice on creating or revising your data strategy, or, if you want more detailed guidance, my book entitled *Data Strategy: How to Profit from a World of Big Data, Analytics and the Internet of Things* will help.[7] Finally, I cannot stress enough how vital it is that your HR data strategy and activities are firmly rooted in the wider business context and what your organization is trying to achieve. In this way, your data strategy should demonstrate exactly how HR will add value by contributing to the business's objectives and helping to drive the business forward. That, for me, is the mark of truly intelligent HR.

Key takeaways

The following is a reminder of the key learning points from this final chapter:

- The 'datafication' of our world and the proliferation of IoT-enabled devices is only going to continue.

- The technology is changing fast and developments like quantum computing and VR will bring advancements and possibilities that we cannot even imagine yet.

- HR teams need to embrace automation where relevant and figure out their uniquely human role in their organization. What value do they deliver that cannot be delivered by technology or other areas of the organization?

- Across every industry and almost every job role, the nature of work is changing and employees of all kinds will need to become more data savvy; however, this does not mean that everyone needs to become data scientists.

- As technology progresses, we will be able to produce more automated analysis and insight generation through AI and machine learning capabilities. Human value will become more about *asking the right questions* of data.

- Combine this with the fact that many simple administrative tasks will be automated and this will free up HR teams to focus on people, not the data themselves.

- Now is the time to create or review your HR data strategy, ensuring it is firmly rooted in the context of your organization's wider business objectives.

I hope this book and this glimpse into the future have inspired and motivated you to implement your own intelligent, data-driven HR systems and processes. It is clear to me (and you, hopefully) that we are on the edge of a dramatic change in how we do business. You and your HR colleagues will be pivotal in helping companies to navigate this changing workplace.

Endnotes

1 Marr, B (2017) [accessed 23 October 2017] Digital Transformation and Data Will Change All of Our Workplaces – Are You Prepared? [Online] https://www.forbes.com/sites/bernardmarr/2017/03/24/how-digital-transformation-and-data-will-change-all-of-our-workplaces/#3761d4985e04

2 Baumgartner, T, Hatami, H and Valdivieso, M (2016) [accessed 23 October 2017] Why Salespeople Need to Develop 'Machine Intelligence' [Online] https://hbr.org/2016/06/why-salespeople-need-to-develop-machine-intelligence

3 Marr, B (2017) [accessed 23 October 2017] 6 Practical Examples of How Quantum Computing Will Change Our World [Online] https://www.forbes.com/sites/bernardmarr/2017/07/10/6-practical-examples-of-how-quantum-computing-will-change-our-world/2/#42a2f9a11c20

4 Marr, B (2017) [accessed 23 October 2017] Is HR Data Even More Valuable to a Business Than Its Financial Data? [Online] https://www.forbes.com/sites/bernardmarr/2017/03/30/is-hr-data-even-more-valuable-to-a-business-than-its-financial-data/#740396c93789

5 Glassdoor [accessed 23 October 2017] 50 Best Jobs in America [Online] https://www.glassdoor.com/List/Best-Jobs-in-America-LST_KQ0,20.htm

6 Marr, B (2016) [accessed 23 October 2017] Big Data: Will We Soon No Longer Need Data Scientists? [Online] https://www.forbes.com/sites/bernardmarr/2016/04/27/will-we-soon-no-longer-need-data-scientists/#4e840aee6897

7 Marr, B ( ) *Data Strategy: How to Profit from a World of Big Data, Analytics and the Internet of Things*

INDEX

Page numbers in *italics* and bold refer to figures and key takeaways respectively.

CPSIA information can be obtained
at www.ICGtesting.com
Printed in the USA
BVHW02s0414120418
513163BV00006B/17/P

9 780749 482466